CRIME CONTROL
BY THE
NATIONAL GOVERNMENT

Da Capo Press Reprints in

AMERICAN CONSTITUTIONAL AND LEGAL HISTORY

GENERAL EDITOR: LEONARD W. LEVY

Claremont Graduate School

CRIME CONTROL
BY THE
NATIONAL GOVERNMENT

By Arthur C. Millspaugh

DA CAPO PRESS • NEW YORK • 1972

Library of Congress Cataloging in Publication Data

Millspaugh, Arthur Chester, 1883-1955.
    Crime control by the national government.
    (Da Capo Press reprints in American constitutional
and legal history)
    Original ed. issued as no. 34 of the Studies in admin-
istration of the Institute for Government Research,
Brookings Institution.
    Includes bibliographical references.
    1. Law enforcement — U.S. 2. Crime and criminals —
U.S. I. Title. II. Series: Brookings Institution,
Washington, D.C. Institute for Government Research.
Studies in administration, no. 34.
HV8141.M5   1972   353.007   70-168678
ISBN 0-306-70418-8

This Da Capo Press edition of *Crime Control by the National
Government* is an unabridged republication of the first edition
published in Washington, D.C., in 1937 as No. 34 in the Studies
in Administration series of the Institute for Government Research
of the Brookings Institution. It is reprinted by permission from a
copy of the original edition in the collection of the Bryn Mawr
College Library.

Published by Da Capo Press, Inc.
A Subsidiary of Plenum Publishing Corporation
227 West 17th Street, New York, New York 10011

CRIME CONTROL
BY THE
NATIONAL GOVERNMENT

BY

ARTHUR C. MILLSPAUGH

WASHINGTON, D.C.

THE BROOKINGS INSTITUTION

1937

Printed in the United States of America
George Banta Publishing Company
Menasha, Wisconsin

DIRECTOR'S PREFACE

If we are to judge by the amount of currently published material, crime and crime control are popular subjects. Detective and mystery fiction has reached flood tide and pours through all the available channels of communication—books, magazines, "pulp," comic-strips, motion-pictures, and the radio. So far as the material purports to deal with facts, it ranges from the cautious authoritativeness of detached criminological research, at one extreme, to the absurd exaggerations of mere sensationalism, at the other. Aside from its entertainment value, much of this current literature probably serves a beneficial social purpose. The same may be said even of that portion which is patent propaganda.

Nevertheless, the recent tendency seems to have been to throw public thinking out of perspective. Undue emphasis seems to have been given to certain spectacular types of crime, with the result that the entire range of anti-social behavior is not seen in proper proportion. The fascinating aspects of criminal apprehension appear to have obscured the problems of deterrence, protection, and prevention. Federal activity tends to divert attention from urgent situations in state and local governments; and the current interest in federal activity seems to be largely concentrated on one or two well-advertised agencies. The present study is based on the belief, therefore, that contemporary public opinion and recent governmental trends make it desirable that the essentials of the national problem of crime control should be presented from a detached point of view, in comprehensive and brief form, and in readable style.

To fulfill these purposes, the first need seemed to be to understand clearly what the federal government is doing in this field, how it functions, and how it is organized for its work. Seven of the twelve chapters of the book are concerned directly with those federal crime-control agencies that appear most significant with reference both to policy and administration. Their historical background is sketched, their present activities are set forth, and their jurisdictional and operating relationships with each other and with state and local agencies are made clear. In these and other chapters, various possibilities of reorganizing these agencies are explored. Some of these possibilities are accepted; others are rejected.

But the book is not restricted to a description and discussion of federal agencies. It views law-enforcement as only one of several subdivisions of a crime-reduction program and as only one of several steps in the process of criminal justice. The study gives attention, therefore, to fundamental questions of emphasis and of philosophy, and to the need of keeping thought and action on an even keel. Related to all these questions is the basic problem of the division of powers and overlapping of functions between the federal government and the states. With respect to this problem, an examination is made of present facts and future needs. Out of this analysis, some evidence emerges of a trend toward centralized policing; but the trend does not appear to rest on a thoroughly deliberated and generally accepted policy. Indeed, the necessary elements of intelligent policy-making are lacking, since we do not have at hand adequate statistical means to check what we are doing or what we are talking about. So, in the end, the author feels that he is able to point out with some definiteness the next step which, as a nation, we must take if we wish to place policy and organization on a sound basis. To the extent that the book deals with federal agencies, it has grown out of a study of federal law-enforcement activities made in 1936 for the Senate Committee on Investigation of Executive Agencies of the Government, headed by Senator Harry F. Byrd of Virginia. In that study, which was a part of a comprehensive survey conducted by the Brookings Institution of the entire executive organization, the heads of the various federal agencies cordially assisted by supplying information; and for their helpful co-operation acknowledgment is here made.

The advisory committee for this study consisted of Lewis Meriam and Laurence F. Schmeckebier.

Fred W. Powell

Acting Director

Institute for Government Research
September 1937

CONTENTS

CONTENTS xiii

CONTENTS

CHAPTER I

SOME ELEMENTS OF THE PROBLEM

One of the recollections of my youth concerns a paper-bound volume entitled *The Detective with the Iron Arm*, which, I suspect, was smuggled into the house by my older brother. I was an omnivorous reader; and previously had never failed to scan every word of any book that "swam into my ken." This time, however, I was to meet with abrupt disappointment. When I was barely half through the book, it suddenly and mysteriously disappeared. I made no verbal protest; for, as a matter of fact, I had been acting stealthily and knew quite well why my prize had been spirited away; although where it had gone and what family discussion had preceded its going I had not the faintest idea. Many other inquisitive contemporaries of mine must have launched similar hopeful enterprises and met with similar frustrations. According to the peculiar morality of the class and community in which I lived, "dime novels" and detective stories were fatal to adolescents. They were thought to be habit forming, and any youth who sank to the depths of reading them was as good as doomed.

In that age, the prolific Nick Carter was in the ascendancy; and he could hardly be blamed for his lack of uplifting influence when Edgar Allan Poe had failed to make the mystery yarn permanently respectable. But times were changing, owing largely to the entrance into the field of Sherlock Holmes. Today mystery and detective stories constitute a voluminous literature, to which renowned scholars condescend to contribute and which is read by everybody from presidents and Supreme Court justices down. Indeed, according to modern ideas, these stories not merely do no harm to the morals but actually exert a positive therapeutic effect on the mind. It may be surmised that the rapid growth of this fictional literature is a phenomenon of considerable significance. Its peculiar fascination may lie in the fact that crime, like war, is a challenge to group solidarity, and the reader of a crime story finds in the activities of the sleuth a vicarious means of restoring a sense of social security.

It is significant that for many years the detectives most familiar to us were purely fictitious characters. Nor was it an accident that in detective fiction the police officer was usually pictured as burly, dull, ignorant, brutal, and inefficient, an obstacle rather than a help to the solution of the crime. Unfortunately, that is what the police officer appeared to be in the estimation of the public. More unfortunately, that is what in too many cases he actually was; and, in real life, there was no amateur detective with an iron arm or a sixth sense to save us from the mistakes of our own public servants. But certain significant changes have occurred or are occurring. The facts themselves have changed; and we have grown in understanding of the facts.

THE POLICE AND THE PUBLIC

Administration is a reflection of public policy; and public policy, in a democracy, is a crude compound of the demands and assumed needs either of the population as a whole or of particular self-conscious and articulate groups. Each group—the largest embracing the whole of society—has its own ideas of what should be done to promote its material and cultural interests. The history of American democracy has revealed an increasing disposition to look to the government for the satisfaction of group needs. Sometimes the demand is for subsidies or services directly to members of the group; but not infrequently it is for the regulation or suppression of another and competing group. Consequently, administrative organization is a reflection of the social structure, a somewhat impressionistic and distorted reflection because the political power of a group in a democracy is not always an accurate measure of its social significance or a fair means of determining the priority of its claims.

Administrative organization, however, is more than a reflection; it is a functioning integral part of the social structure. Administration, like the floor-space of an exposition building, is apportioned among those who are fortunate enough to have political purchasing power. Here are the potent economic groups, agriculture, labor, and manufacturers; here are the railroads, aviation, motor vehicles, and radio; here are the bankers, brokers, and exchanges; here are the professions—medicine, psychiatry, education, engineering, and social work; and here, in a dark but rather ample corner, is the underworld.

Certain interests are difficult to departmentalize; for example, the interests of the consumers and the taxpayers. One would think that the consumer and taxpayer points of view would be strongest of all, since from time immemorial everybody has consumed and nearly everybody has paid taxes. Nevertheless, these all-inclusive groups are conspicuously ineffective, probably for the reason that they are all inclusive. What is everybody's business is nobody's business.

The crime-ridden public is in much the same situation as the consuming and taxpaying public. J. Edgar

Hoover estimates that the criminal population of the
United States numbers 4,300,000 persons, who commit
1,333,526 felonies annually.[1] The Wickersham Commission issued in 1931 a bulky report on "The Cost of
Crime."[2] The Commission found that the "aggregate
amount of losses to private individuals due to criminal
acts is quite impossible of exact determination," but was
convinced that "crime imposes a tremendous economic
burden on the community."[3] In monetary terms, the total cost has been roughly estimated by other authorities
at from 3 to 15 billion dollars. This financial loss, together with the degradation of character and menace to
human life which accompany it, represents the most pernicious form of social parasitism. Frontier settlements
were quick to organize against it. Even now, an especially shocking crime or series of crimes may arouse a
community to spasmodic mobilization. On the whole,
however, the active awareness of public opinion to the
crime menace is sporadic, temporary, and unorganized.

Perhaps this is so because crime, like lightning, does
not appear usually to strike twice in the same place.
Perhaps it is because few of us are ever actually eye-
witnesses of crime in its more terrifying aspects. Perhaps
it is because all of us are, either on a small scale or in
occasional mass movements, potential or actual law-
breakers. Perhaps it is because we love liberty and ad-
mire individuals who have nerve enough to defy authority. Perhaps it is because legal rules do not always coin-
cide with moral standards. Perhaps it is because the
modern view of crime causation tends to explain, rather

---

[1] Address before the American Newspaper Publishers' Association, at
New York City, Apr. 22, 1937.
[2] National Commission on Law Observance and Enforcement, *Report
on the Cost of Crime*, No. 12, June 24, 1931.
[3] The same, p. 3.

than condemn, the criminal. Be these things as they may, the organizer and administrator in the field of crime control must take into account the fact that public functions and public agencies concerned with crime control customarily lack the support of an electoral group which knows what it wants and how to get it.

In an international war, acts which in other circumstances are considered dangerously anti-social become in the public mind legal and legitimate, even praiseworthy. Crimes such as murder, robbery, and arson are then no longer crimes. In our domestic life, we have at times in the relations between capital and labor something in the nature of a diluted state of war. The strike is a veiled combat in which government seeks to lay down the rules and to act as referee. But a serious strike inevitably tends to rioting and other acts of violence. At such times, the immediate effect of efficient policing is to put labor at a disadvantage. Labor, however, has more votes than capital; and the influence of labor opinion has accordingly been strongly exerted in some important phases of law enforcement. Organized labor has generally felt that locally controlled police are less likely to be used repressively in industrial disputes than is a centralized and remote police force. As a result it has frequently defeated proposals for the establishment of state police departments; and, where such departments have been established, it is often stipulated that the state police shall not be used in industrial disputes.

In other directions, efficiency in law enforcement depends in exceptional degree on the temper of public opinion. The experience of the country under prohibition illustrates this truism. In some communities the shooting of a revenue officer has long been considered a meritorious deed. A really effective harnessing of public opinion to enforcement can not be quickly accomplished. Nevertheless, progress is being made.

Recently, in the popular literature of crime detection, the real detective, who is not represented as a bungler, has been gradually coming into his own. Books and syndicated articles are narrating his exploits. Apparently, truth is found to be as interesting as fiction; and some of our law-enforcement officers, living and dead, have become almost popular heroes.

In 1906, the American Bar Association meeting at St. Paul listened to an epochal address by Roscoe Pound on "The Causes of Popular Dissatisfaction with the Administration of Justice." From this date, the Association has demonstrated with steadily increasing force its aliveness to the peculiar responsibilities of the Bar.[4] The American Institute of Criminal Law and Criminology was founded in 1909; and since then, through its *Journal of Criminal Law and Criminology*, it has not only represented and helped to develop criminal science but has also provided intellectual leadership. The American Law Institute's *Code of Criminal Procedure* has been a constructive influence. Substantial contributions to leadership have been made by universities, such as Harvard, Columbia, Northwestern, and California; by local organizations, such as the Cleveland Foundation, the Missouri Association for Criminal Justice, the Illinois Association for Criminal Justice, municipal research bureaus, and other unofficial associations; by official judicial councils and crime commissions; and by individuals, usually members of universities, such as Roscoe

---

[4] For this address and the circumstances under which it was delivered, see *Journal of the American Judicature Society*, Vol. 20, No. 5, February 1937, pp. 176-87.

SOME ELEMENTS OF THE PROBLEM 7

Pound, Felix Frankfurter, Raymond Moley, Sheldon
Glueck, Bruce Smith, and August Vollmer.

JUSTICE AND TRADITION

The age of an interest, an idea, or a public function is
no guaranty of its present popularity or power. The
police is one of the most ancient of present-day institutions. We are told that the term is derived from a Greek
genitive which means "of or pertaining to an organized
community." The sheriff, constable, coroner, and jury
are relics handed down from Anglo-Saxon England.
Many, if not most, of our prosecuting and judicial institutions and procedures have their roots in the distant
and rural past when men knew their neighbors and
feared government, and when both crime and criminal-law administration were amateurish.

The present organization of law enforcement in the
United States can not be understood without reference
to the unique characteristics of our national growth and
expansion. Fundamentally, American forms of government were fixed when the future nation was in embryo,
represented by thirteen separate and sparsely settled
colonies, each jealous of the others. The westward movement of population was marked by the establishment of
self-sufficient and isolated pioneer communities. In these
communities, which in course of time coalesced into
states, ideas of local self-government naturally prevailed. Law enforcement, the primary symbol of government, was universally localized in villages, towns, townships, counties, and cities.

Thus, our system of criminal justice long ago passed
into the lengthening shadow of precedents and was inextricably caught in a "cake of custom." It became identi-

fied with some of our most precious and durable political ideas: liberty, individualism, local self-government, democracy, distrust of centralized authority. As a result, we find in the United States the ultimate of decentralization in criminal-law administration. No one knows the exact number of separate governmental agencies that are functioning in this field. Of sheriffs, constables, marshals, police departments, coroners, prosecutors, attorney generals, courts, and prison and parole administrations, there must be somewhere around 85,000, each functioning more or less independently. Of agencies engaged in the detection and apprehension of law-breakers, there are probably around 40,000; and of these, about 20,000 are of real importance. Most of them are county and municipal agencies; state and federal forces are a mere sprinkling. As a rule each of these agencies has a limited territorial jurisdiction; within its jurisdiction, it overlaps and in part duplicates other agencies; and many of these agencies, including practically all of the rural sheriffs' forces, are hopelessly deficient in numbers, skill, and equipment. Throughout a large part of our rural territory, our method of apprehending "big-time" crooks is much like sending out a flock of kindergarten pupils with beanshooters to capture a tiger.

Generally speaking, the size of an administrative organization should be commensurate with the problem that it faces. Crime in the present age shows conspicuously six characteristics that are practically new, so far as the nation as a whole is concerned: (1) it is gang activity, loosely but effectively organized; (2) it holds human life cheap; (3) it boldly and ruthlessly plays for large stakes; (4) it is in many cases better equipped with instruments of attack and defense than are law-enforcement officers; (5) it is swift to strike and equally swift in making its get-away; and, (6) its operations are usually interstate, frequently national, and sometimes international in scope.[5] Of the many different conditions that have conspired to produce the American gangster, as distinguished from his frontier prototype, the following stand out as obviously important: the great city; accumulated wealth; modern transportation; corrupt politics; and decentralized criminal-law administration. Of these conditions, the last named would seem most easily modified; and a slow process of modification has begun. It is being realized that society can not fight a big war with a multitude of unco-ordinated detachments and no commanding general. A number of commonwealths maintain central bureaus of identification; several have established state police forces; and the federal government participates substantially in the suppression of crime. On the whole, a good deal of co-ordination has been brought about, but relatively little unification.

Change and progress mark also the methods of detecting crime. Emphasis in crime detection has shifted from physical force to intelligence. It is now recognized that criminal investigators and police officers must be qualified, educated, trained, and adequately equipped. Crime and law-enforcement situations are now carefully surveyed; crime and accident occurrence is mapped; and a system of criminal statistics is in process of development. The specific job of catching criminals has been objectively studied, experience carefully appraised, and various scientific aids devised. The detective must still have physical stamina, courage, determination, patience, and imagination; but he also has the uncanny as-

[5] Frontier lawlessness displayed essentially the same characteristics. The significance of these characteristics in "modern" crime lies in the fact that they are no longer sectional or transitional.

sistance of many specialized procedures and scientific aids
—teletyping, the radio, fingerprinting, photography,
moulage, ballistics, the lie detector, *modus operandi*
files, handwriting comparisons, the microscope, toxi-
cology, chemistry, x-rays, soil-analysis, etc. Thus factual
analysis, scientific research, and technical invention have
come to disturb the wayside slumbers of the ancient
constable.

STAGES IN LAW ENFORCEMENT

The police organization is only one link in a ponder-
ous chain of enforcement. A prior link is legislation; for
crime-control agencies are concerned only with those
activities which are legally defined as crimes or misdemeanors. Offenses having been defined, the police can
then move only to the threshold of the temple of justice.
Beyond are the legal profession, the prosecutors, the
courts, the correctional institutions, and those who have
power to parole and pardon. Each of these sets of authorities or institutions is, as a rule, practically independent
of the others. Between the police and the correctional
institution stretches an area where the law and the legal
profession hold almost undisputed sway, where problems
are numerous, technical, complicated, little known, and
well-nigh incomprehensible to the average layman, and
where change is very slow.

The existence of several distinct steps and independent
authorities in the law-enforcement process renders difficult if not impossible the locating of responsibility for
failures. It also accentuates fundamental conflicts of policies and philosophies. The prime duty of the police officer is to catch criminals. He knows quite well, if he does
his duty, with what hatred he is regarded by the underworld. Naturally, he reciprocates; he has little interest
in those points of view which regard the criminal as an

unfortunate victim of circumstances who should, if such a course is humanly possible, be sympathetically rehabilitated and returned to society. Those who are in close contact with the criminal element know that few adult "repeaters" can be rehabilitated or safely returned to society. To the typical honest police officer, the hardened criminal is a "rat"; and, from this police point of view, those who are too narrowly devoted to the explanation of criminality and the rehabilitation of criminals are merely "sob sisters."

To these generalizations there are, of course, many individual exceptions. At one extreme are police officers who find political safety and personal profit in an alliance with the underworld. At the other are members of the police who participate in programs of prevention and rehabilitation.

Prosecutors, criminal-court judges, and criminal lawyers in general differ from police officers in their education and professional associations; but their attitude toward crime and criminals, is, by and large, not essentially different from that of the police. As a general rule, they perform their public duties in accordance with antiquated ideas. The theory which they ordinarily apply is one of social vengeance. It has been long since society could exact a tooth for a tooth or an eye for an eye, but it still does the next most convenient thing: it attempts to fit the punishment to the crime. It names and defines offenses; and attaches to each specified offense a fine or a term of imprisonment, regardless of the fact that a particular offense or alleged offense gives as a rule little indication of the defendant's criminal character, of what crimes he is likely to commit in the future, or of his real danger to society.

Legislative bodies, of course, are primarily responsible

for anachronisms and inconsistencies in the criminal law; for judges are expected merely to apply the law. Nevertheless, the legislative changes can usually be brought about when strongly urged by bench and bar; and accordingly, lawyers must bear a goodly share of the blame for what the law is and how it is applied.

Much progress is being made. Juvenile courts, probation systems, the indeterminate sentence, and various procedural improvements bear witness to it. Judicial councils and integrated bar organizations are promising developments. But thus far in no jurisdiction have the principles been unreservedly accepted that all persons who commit serious crimes require diagnosis and treatment; that a proper diagnosis can only be made by experts; that treatment must be adjusted to the character of the offender; and that, regardless of the nature of their crimes, those dangerous individuals who do not respond to treatment must be confined for life.

After the offender has been convicted and sentenced, he passes into the final stages of the punitive-protective process, represented by the jail, prison, or reformatory, the noose, gas chamber, or electric chair, and sometimes parole or pardon. In this phase of his involvement, the offender is likely to be confronted by traditional conceptions similar to those which in all probability he met in his apprehension, prosecution, and trial; but he has, on the whole, a somewhat better chance of encountering newer and more flexible attitudes. Today, lip service at least is generally given to the principle that each prisoner should be individually studied and classified for treatment; first offenders should be segregated from recidivists, misdemeanants from criminals, the insane, feebleminded, and degenerate from the mentally normal, and the sick from the well; all should engage in work suited to their capabilities; each should learn to be honestly self-supporting; and none should either be pampered or degraded. In theory and to an increasing extent in practice, it is generally held that, since practically all prisoners are to be eventually released, the essential function of a correctional program is to readjust the prisoner to life in a law-abiding society. From this it logically follows that the date of a prisoner's release should be determined by his own personality make-up and by an expert evaluation of the prospects of his readjustment; that all releases should be conditional; and that during the period in which the released convict is making his readjustment, he should remain under close supervision.

Advanced penological thinking still falls far short of its goal. Most jails and prisons are structurally obsolete. Diagnosis, classification, and segregation are in many institutions little more than distant and unattainable ideals. Pardons and paroles are, in too many cases, merely acts of executive caprice, or worse. Parolees are generally unsupervised. The parole system is at present in many jurisdictions neither wisely nor thoroughly administered. In fact, though law-enforcement officers are sometimes called upon to supervise parolees, parole administration marks the point where police and correctional philosophies definitely part company.

Unless a prisoner is to be executed or is really destined to serve a life term, he is one of about 400,000 persons who are annually graduated from our penal institutions. An average prisoner remains in custody only from two to three years, a period considerably shorter than that devoted to the training of high-school students. If the criminal's period of retraining were positively remedial, it would still be absurdly short; but, when he receives his parting handshake and suit of clothes, he is, as a rule, more thoroughly educated in crime, more embittered, and more dangerous to society than he was on the date of his conviction. His depredations may have been temporarily halted by his incarceration; but only temporarily. In short, if the supposedly remedial stage of criminal-law administration were appraised by what it does to the men who go through it or by the protection that it gives society, it could hardly be put at more than 25 per cent efficient.

Proposals have been made looking to the elimination of at least some of the overlappings, duplications, conflicts, and confusion which appear among the several levels of criminal-law administration. The Attorney General of the United States (the legal counselor and prosecuting officer of the federal government) has under him in the Department of Justice a bureau for investigation and apprehension, and one for administration of the federal penal institutions, probation and parole; he also has the duty of supervising the federal courts, the United States attorneys, and the United States marshals. In the states, movements are under way for the merger of prosecution and policing; but perhaps quite as logical would be the incorporation of the prosecutor within the organization of the court. Judges usually have charge of probation; and they are occasionally involved in parole administration. The prosecutor's office is sometimes tied in with the parole system. Prison administration is occasionally connected with detection and apprehension, and frequently with parole. In spite of these various proposals, experiments, expedients, and accidents, it is obvious that the gaps between different stages of criminal justice can not all be bridged. The several separate agencies can not be administratively consolidated. Nor can they even be closely co-ordinated. Professional differentiation and conflicts of philosophies are inherent in the system and in the problem which the system is designed to solve.

CRIME PREVENTION

If the machinery of criminal-law administration were 100 per cent efficient, crime might be appreciably reduced but some of the most potent causes of crime would still be in full operation. In recent years, therefore, criminology, like medicine, has tended more and more to emphasize prevention.

Society has long gained a measure of security through various deterrent and protective devices. Deterrence works on the fear of getting caught. Common means of deterrence are the police patrol, traffic officers, guards, night watchmen, street lighting, and burglar alarms. Quick and certain apprehension and conviction are obvious deterrents. Protective measures are illustrated by locks and bars, safes and vaults, armored cars, systems of licensing and registration, witnessing of signatures, and the thousand and one other devices which recognize the prevalence of criminal tendencies and are intended to make the commission of crime difficult.[6]

Prevention—a better name for it would be prophylaxis—aims to go much deeper than deterrence or pro-

[6] With reference to the recently completed bullion depository at Fort Knox, Ky., designed to hold several billions in gold, Mrs. Nellie Tayloe Ross, director of the Mint, stated during the congressional hearings in January 1937, that only twenty-four guards were to be employed, working in three eight-hour shifts. It was suggested that "the chief protection is the remoteness of the depository. Robbers would not have any way to transport the gold even if they could get their hands on it." On this, Mrs. Ross commented: "I think the mechanical devices are such that nobody could get to the gold, but at the same time we must have an adequate guard system to get a report if anybody makes an attempt to do so." 75 Cong. 1 sess., *Treasury Department Appropriation Bill for 1938*, Hearings before H. Committee on Appropriations, p. 336.

tection. Up to about thirty years ago, it was hoped to find in criminals some common and identifiable characteristic, such as a physical peculiarity or a mental deficiency or defect. It is now realized that there is no single cause or determinant of crime. The personality distortion which manifests itself in anti-social behavior appears at an early age; and such behavior, like what we are pleased to call "normal" conduct, results from the interplay of mental and emotional qualities and environmental influences. The general environmental factors which influence an individual during his formative years are principally those identified with the home and the neighborhood. The methods and skills which are available for the social readjustment of children include psychology, psychiatry, medicine, education, and social work. Of considerable efficacy are such measures as parent education, the juvenile court, probation, better housing, slum clearance, boys' clubs, and supervised recreation. Crime prevention through personality adjustment overlaps at least four fields of public administration: education, public welfare, public health, and judicial administration. It draws in at least four professions: education, social work, medicine, and law.

But if crime prevention is to reach the roots of the problem, it must go still farther and deeper. It must deal with the environment. Fundamental to environmental reconstruction are stabilized employment and the elevation and equalization of standards of living; and, of all the sciences, economics, when heavily tinctured with social ethics, may make the most relevant and salutary contributions to an approximate solution of the crime problem. Prevention is thus another step—really the initial step—in the crime-control process. A preventive program can not eliminate all law-breaking; but it can probably do more to reduce crime than all of the deterrent measures, protective devices, and enforcement agencies put together.

Active recognition of this larger and deeper aspect of crime control has to some extent complicated and confused the problem of crime-control organization. Here and there, it is seriously proposed that the police should be made responsible for crime prevention, or at least should play a conspicuous rôle in preventive activities; and, in a few police departments, "crime-prevention bureaus" have been established. It would seem, however, that crime prevention can not under present circumstances be viewed as a logical or practicable police function, probably not even an incidental one. The police may make highly beneficial contributions to deterrence and protection; but preventive work is inconsistent with the major purpose of police personnel, their temperamental outlook, their basic philosophy, and their specialized skills. Nothing could be more foreign to their essential duties than such a task as the readjustment of personalities or the reconstruction of environments. Police work, to be efficient, should be limited in scope. It must be sharply focussed on the detection and apprehension of law-breakers. Other specialized activities should be left to other and more appropriate agencies.[7]

SUMMARY AND CONCLUSIONS

In the field of law enforcement, more perhaps than in any other area of social action, we meet the formidable obstacles which are presented by the instincts, emotions, and prejudices of the individual and by the complexities, traditions, and inertia of organized society. Public ad-

[7] For a fuller discussion of the various subjects which are briefly touched upon in this chapter, see Sheldon Glueck, *Crime and Justice* (1936).

ministrative organization is an indispensable approach to the solution of the crime problem; but organization involves the clarifying and refocussing of public opinion, as well as the recognition of different and conflicting attitudes and philosophies. When divergent ideas can not be reconciled, they should be segregated and each harnessed to an appropriate function. The problem has many ramifications; its solution must take place in fairly definite sequences; and each step calls for a different set of attitudes and skills. On the extensive crime-reduction front, detection and apprehension occupy a strategic position, but not the only position. Society's total effort against crime can never be authoritatively centralized. It is inherently heterogeneous.

CHAPTER II

ASPECTS AND INSTRUMENTS OF CONTROL

When I drive downtown in the morning, I pass one intersection where a policeman directs traffic. I am stopped at several other intersections by red lights which have been installed by the police. When I prepare to park, I am barred or restricted by signs which also have been put up by the Police Department. My freedom to drive at all, or at least my peace of mind while driving, is dependent on my driver's license, which is issued by that same department. When I read my evening paper, I notice a fairly long list of my fellow-citizens who have been arrested and punished for traffic violations. Occasionally, I see in the list the name of someone who I am quite certain is a reputable person. Once or twice, I have been arrested for a traffic violation, but have not felt that either my violation or my arrest stamped me as a criminal. When driving my car on the streets, I might, if more than usually negligent, inadvertently commit a crime such as manslaughter; but such crimes, born of traffic, are not relatively numerous.

Familiarity has obscured the fact that traffic regulation is not an orthodox or theoretically essential police function. Logically, it is not a necessary part of the crime-control job. When regulating traffic, police officers are primarily engaged in the protection of their fellow-citizens from hazards and accidents. In other words, they are promoting public safety. To any city resident, however, this extension of the scope of policing which came with the multiplication of automobiles seems, as it is, an entirely appropriate administrative arrangement. That

logic or theory should be permitted to dictate a different
set-up would be a ridiculous idea.

In most of the states where a state police force has
been created, highway patrolling is done by that force;
but Pennsylvania and Texas maintain separate forces,
one for state policing and the other for highway patrolling; and a number of states maintain more or less specialized highway patrols, but no state police, properly
speaking. Where there is no state police, highway or
traffic patrols, even though they may possess general
police powers, are usually under the highway or motor-
vehicle department; and it is known that in some states
such a set-up seems not only logical but also eminently
practical. Traffic control by the federal government, outside the District of Columbia, is not extensively developed; but, such as it is, the work is scattered among various agencies. Traffic control, or something analogous to
it, enters into the work of such agencies as the Bureau of
Air Commerce, the Bureau of Marine Inspection and
Navigation, the Corps of Army Engineers, the Coast
Guard, the Interstate Commerce Commission, the National Park Service, and the Bureau of Indian Affairs.
The Department of Justice has nothing directly to do
with it.

VARIABILITY IN POLICE FUNCTIONS

Traffic control has been offered as a striking illustration of the fact that a somewhat different distribution of
functions and a different location of emphasis may be
found in a municipal police force, a county sheriff's office, a state police department, and a federal crime-control agency. Additional illustrations are not hard to find.

In a city, the crowding of buildings, the frequent occurrence of fires, the danger of conflagrations, the need

of instant concentration on every outbreak, and the application of technical equipment and special training to the job of fire fighting justify the maintenance of a department solely concerned with this special protective function. No one seriously proposes to consolidate municipal police and fire departments, though they are both engaged in the protection of life and property and the promotion of the public safety. It is considered sufficient that the two departments, when occasion requires, should co-operate with each other. On the other hand, a state government, though it may aid in suppressing forest fires, ordinarily has no important fire-fighting duties; but many states have assumed fire-prevention functions and investigatory and enforcement work in connection with fires of suspicious origin. For these purposes, the state may establish a fire marshal who, with the help of some assistants, receives reports from local sheriffs and fire chiefs and looks into the causes of fire. One of the principal, frequently the primary, duty of the state fire marshal is to detect arson and apprehend those who commit that particular crime. He is engaged, therefore, not only in fire prevention but also in a narrow and specialized form of crime control or criminal-law enforcement. In Massachusetts, the State Fire Marshal is placed in the Department of Public Safety, the state police agency; and the laws of several other states designate the state police as fire wardens. In Pennsylvania, the state police have especially important functions with respect to fire protection. The law provides that they shall receive reports of all fires and investigate every fire, and, upon complaint or when deemed necessary, shall inspect buildings and premises with regard to their fire hazards. In the federal government, however, fire fighting is chiefly a matter of national forest administration and is handled by the Forest Service. It is, for good reasons, looked upon as an inseparable function of that agency.

Many cities have fish-ponds and zoos; but enforcement of fish and game laws is, for obvious reasons, not a municipal function. On the other hand, it is a state function of considerable importance. A highly essential part of administration in this field is the detection and apprehension of those who violate the fish and game laws. In most states, the game wardens are under the fish and game or conservation department; but it has not gone unnoticed that these officials operate in much the same way as the police. In Michigan, which has an efficient state police department, the fish and game wardens remain under the Conservation Commission; but in New York they are a part of the state police force, and in other states, including Michigan, the state police are designated as fish and game wardens and in that capacity may make arrests for violations of the fish and game laws. In the federal government, the protection of wild life is divided between the Bureau of Biological Survey in the Department of Agriculture and the Bureau of Fisheries in the Department of Commerce. Patrolling, detection, and apprehension are not major functions of either bureau, though each has officials who operate in much the same way as the state game and fish wardens. No one, so far as is known, has suggested that these officials should be incorporated in a national police force or be transferred to the Department of Justice.

States and municipalities are called upon to enforce numerous laws and ordinances relating to morals. The enforcement of such legislation presents peculiar difficulties. Four well-known practices may be selected for illustrative purposes: drinking of alcoholic beverages, use of narcotic drugs, prostitution, and gambling. To set forth in detail how public policy vacillates in its attitude toward these practices and how administration has been organized and reorganized to reflect changing public attitudes would require several separate volumes. It will be sufficient to point out here that the federal, state, and local governments are all more or less concerned with these so-called evils, but in different ways. The suppression of prostitution and illegal gambling is, as a rule, handled in federal, state, and local jurisdictions, as a recognized and routine police function. On the other hand, alcohol and narcotics enforcement involves regulation and taxation, as well as detection and apprehension. Neither of these two branches of enforcement is left wholly to police or investigative agencies. For example, in the federal government, both are assigned in effect to the Treasury Department; alcohol to the Alcohol Tax Unit of the Bureau of Internal Revenue and the Federal Alcohol Administration, and narcotics to the Bureau of Narcotics.

All police agencies are expected, in emergencies, to render first-aid and save lives. Such activities are not necessarily involved in crime control. In municipalities, they are performed by fire departments and emergency hospitals perhaps as often as they are by the police. In the federal government, the Coast Guard under the Treasury Department combines life saving with its law-enforcement, regulatory, and miscellaneous work.

Regulatory work is usually performed by specialized administrative agencies, such as public health services, labor departments, or industrial commissions, and public utility commissions. Yet, because of the fact that a police force has a large personnel, much of which is mobile, and maintains a wide acquaintance and contact with persons and places, police departments are often required to perform a variety of miscellaneous services. These are more numerous in the cities than anywhere else. Municipal police are thus called upon to issue licenses, inspect weights and measures, enforce sanitary and health regulations, make building and plumbing inspections, impose censorships, suppress nuisances, regulate parades, locate missing persons, and supervise pawnshops, dance halls, and amusement places. A state government, dealing less directly with the intimate affairs of its people and possessing a more broadly developed administrative organization, is less tempted to burden its police force, if it has one, with miscellaneous regulatory and service functions. Nevertheless, in Massachusetts the Department of Public Safety, which has charge of the state police, has a division for the inspection of buildings and boilers, regulates boxing, controls Lord's Day entertainments, supervises the sale and carrying of firearms, licenses private detectives, and inspects oil plants, oil tankers, and motor boats. In some other commonwealths, the state police examine applicants for drivers' licenses; inspect motion pictures, pawnshops, and amusement parks; regulate outdoor advertising and weights and measures; transfer prisoners from one place of detention to another; and act as health officers. Administrative regulatory work is in general technical; and the enforcement job is usually only a part of the regulatory process. Thus, in the federal government, where most administrative work is highly specialized, enforcement of regulatory laws is in large part scattered among the various regulatory agencies, rather than centralized in the agencies which are primarily concerned with the detection and apprehension of law-breakers in general.

Investigations in civil cases, the execution of court

orders, service of subpoenas, and keeping order in court rooms represent still another type of work, large in volume, which lies squarely in the field of judicial administration or law enforcement, but which may or may not be assigned to police agencies. In the state and local governments, civil cases to which the commonwealth is a party are usually investigated by the attorney general or a local prosecuting attorney. In the federal government, many such investigations are conducted for the Attorney General by the Bureau of Investigation, which is primarily a criminal-law enforcement agency. In the counties, the serving of court processes and the maintenance of order in the court are usually important duties of the sheriff, who is the county police officer. In the federal government, they are duties of the United States marshals. These officials are supervised by the Department of Justice and they still have some slight responsibility for the detection and apprehension of criminals; but they do not form a part of the Bureau of Investigation.

In the cities, counties, and states, the crime-control agency, whatever name it may bear, is not used as a matter of course for personnel investigations outside its own organization. In other words, it would only in exceptional cases be called upon to investigate the past records of applicants for positions in another department of the government. In federal crime-control agencies, on the contrary, the technique of investigation is generally emphasized, while the techniques of pursuit, apprehension, and repression are something in the nature of afterthoughts. It is significant that not one of the federal agencies concerned with crime has the word "crime" or "police" in its official title. Because of their emphasis on investigative technique and for other reasons, they are frequently called upon to look into the records of applicants for positions in other federal bureaus.

If law-enforcement situations in the city, county, state, and nation warrant different distributions of work, it follows that one level of government is never justified in blindly imitating another. It is by no means contended that crime-control organization is now at each level of government exactly what it ought to be. Reorganization is more or less urgently needed at all levels. It is especially needed in state governments and in the rural subdivisions of the states. To facilitate co-ordination and co-operation, uniformity in certain respects is desirable in set-up, functions, and procedures. Federal agencies can not be wisely reorganized without reference to the states and their subdivisions. But the federal problem is different from the problems of other jurisdictions; and we must, in the main, faithfully follow the outlines of our problem in sketching the pattern of administrative organization.

GENERAL CRIMES AND CENTRAL FUNCTIONS

Some years ago students of public administration, seeking a short-cut to the goal of efficient organization, adopted quite generally what may be called the unifunctional or major purpose theory. Proponents of this theory believed that they had found in governmental administration a few primary objectives, such as finance, education, health, welfare, conservation of natural resources, and justice or law enforcement. It was held that functions having the same objective were administratively related and should therefore be consolidated, other and unrelated functions being assigned to other groups. Thus, it was thought, a relatively few clear-cut fields of administration would emerge, overlapping would be reduced, duplications and conflicts eliminated, departmentalization made possible, and responsible executive control realized.

The basic difficulty in the application of the unifunctional theory is to determine what are the few major purposes or primary objectives of public administration. One who is disposed to synthesize may see in government one ultimate goal, the promotion of the general welfare. The Preamble of the federal Constitution states six objectives: a more perfect union, justice, domestic tranquility, common defense, general welfare, and liberty. Only two of these objectives—justice and defense—have had any substantial concrete embodiment in the federal administrative organization. Only one—justice—has given its name to a federal department. One who is analytically inclined might now go much further than could the founding fathers. He might find in modern governmental administration a score or a hundred, rather than a half-dozen or a dozen, different purposes. To be sure, some objectives are probably more important than others; but a major or principal purpose from one point of view may seem minor or incidental from another.

For example, the federal government has for several years made promotion of labor interests a distinct and a major administrative objective. One can guess, however, that most industrialists and many economists would view the interests of labor as only one of several important factors in a vast and diversified problem and as strictly subordinate to the major economic objective of government. Likewise, the promotion of agriculture is often conceived as a primary and distinct governmental purpose, but it is now well known that agriculture can not be promoted in isolation from other governmental purposes. It is a part of the larger problem of land use and of the still larger problems of economic stability and social welfare. Any administrative field inevitably overlaps other fields. Each objective blurs into other objectives.

In the field of crime control, attempts have been made to find a name which will include everything that belongs in the field and exclude all unrelated functions. The term "police" is generally used; but it has lost its descriptive quality. "Public safety" describes an objective; but it is an objective of many administrative agencies. "Protection of life and property" is used by the Census Bureau to cover policing and fire protection. "Law enforcement" is commonly used; but, in a sense, all administrative agencies are engaged in law enforcement, since they execute laws. In general, names are of little significance in a scientific appraisal of administrative organization, though, to the unthinking, they have much emotional content and value. In the present study, we shall use the terms crime control, policing, and law enforcement interchangeably. By doing so, we shall avoid the danger of drawing too precise boundaries around our field; and thus we may be in a better position to avoid generalizations until we have examined particulars.

When we examine particulars, we find that certain administrative functions are clearly differentiated from others. The tracking down of kidnapers and robbers has little or nothing in common with the collection of labor statistics, the maneuvering of battleships, the organizing of 4-H clubs, topographic mapping, or the reporting of the weather. Accordingly, if we set up a hypothetical field of crime control, certain functions automatically gravitate to it, while others refuse to enter it. To such a field would go without doubt the duty of suppressing all those violations of the law which are customarily as well as legally criminal, which are in essence and by common consent anti-social. Of this nature would be most offenses against the person, such as assault, blackmail, extortion, kidnaping, murder, and rape; most offenses against property such as arson, breaking and entering, embezzlement, and larceny; probably counterfeiting and forgery; many offenses against chastity and morality, such as bigamy, indecent assault, and obscenity; and various other transgressions, when committed under ordinary circumstances, such as disturbing the peace, bribery, contempt of court, and impersonating, obstructing, or resisting an officer.

Uniform Crime Reports, issued by the Federal Bureau of Investigation, gives statistics of offenses known to the police for about 1,700 cities with a total population of over 60 million. According to these statistics the total number of crimes in each of eight categories during the year 1936 was as follows:[1]

Criminal homicide:
    Murder, non-negligent manslaughter 3,736
    Manslaughter by negligence 3,136
Rape 4,758
Robbery 33,603
Aggravated assault 27,830
Burglary—breaking or entering 165,795
Larceny—theft 381,398
Auto theft 113,733
                                    _____
    Total 733,989

Crimes against the person, that is, murder, non-negligent manslaughter, manslaughter by negligence, rape, and aggravated assault, totaled during this period

[1] *Uniform Crime Reports,* Vol. VII, No. 4. Some of the figures are based on reports from a lesser number of cities with a smaller aggregate population. These are only the Class I, or "serious" crimes.

39,460, or about 5.4 per cent of the offenses reported. Criminal homicides alone totaled only 6,872, or less than one per cent of all offenses. There were 5 robberies, 24 burglaries, and 55 larcenies to one homicide. Crimes in general against property outnumbered criminal homicides more than a hundred to one. Murder is the most shocking and the most fascinating of crimes; but the detection and apprehension of murderers is by no means the most important function of a law-enforcement agency. Indeed, murders would be automatically reduced if society were adequately protected with respect to crimes against property.

AUXILIARY LAW ENFORCEMENT

Near the end of the "Instructions" on my income tax returns I find these alarming paragraphs:

For willful failure to make and file a return on time.—Not more than $10,000 or imprisonment for not more than one year, or both, together with the costs of prosecution, and, in addition, 5 per cent to 25 per cent of the amount of the tax.

For willfully making a false or fraudulent return.—Not more than $10,000 or imprisonment for not more than five years, or both, together with the costs of prosecution.

Only in exceptional cases is a taxable person bitten by these statutory teeth; but they are in the law to be used when necessary. A few years ago, penalty clauses in the income-tax law put Al Capone into prison. This Public Enemy No. 1 had avoided successful prosecution for the general crimes which he is alleged to have committed. He is now in Alcatraz largely because of the skillful work of the Intelligence Unit of the Bureau of Internal Revenue, a bureau whose primary function is not the suppression of crime but the collection of taxes. In the Bureau of Internal Revenue, crime control is ordinarily an incidental activity, performed to facilitate the accomplishment of the Bureau's essential task, which is revenue collection.

Likewise, in many other governmental agencies, crime control is a facilitating, subsidiary, or auxiliary function. Smuggling is a crime; but it is such only because we have decided to collect customs revenues. If one is an alien, it may be a crime to enter the country. The reason why this is so is that we have chosen to restrict immigration. A public health officer or a factory inspector may, in an extreme case, arrest or cause the arrest of a person violating the law. In taking such action he is concerned, not with the suppression of general criminality, but with the promotion of the public health or of industrial safety.

Incidental law enforcement is not confined to public agencies. Banks have their armed guards; hotels, department stores, railroads, and some industrial corporations employ detectives. Private concerns engage in crime-control work primarily for their own protection, in order that they may operate with a minimum of loss and disorder.

Students of administration are familiar with the fact that a function, under certain circumstances, may be practically an end in itself, while, under other circumstances, it may be only a means to an end. Take, for example, engineering and construction activities, library management, collection of statistics, research, laboratory work, legal counselling, filing, stenography and typewriting, accounting and auditing, and custody of funds. Complete centralization of the administration of such functions is rarely, if ever, attainable or desirable. The fact that legal counselling is one of the distinctive functions of the United States Department of Justice does not obviate the necessity of attaching law officers to other federal departments. Certain files may be appropriately centralized in the National Archives, but others can not be. The existence of the vast Library of Congress does not render unnecessary the maintenance of departmental and bureau libraries. Stenography and typewriting are often partially centralized within a department or bureau; but a stenographic "pool" for an entire government would be ridiculous. Certain types of construction work or engineering service may be centralized, as they now are in certain agencies of the federal government, and further centralization may or may not be advisable; but it would be unsound and impracticable to bring into any scheme of consolidation all types of construction or engineering operations.

It is easy to find in any state government, as we have previously indicated, more than one agency engaged in the detection and apprehension of law-breakers. In the federal administrative organization, it is possible to find a score or more of separate agencies specializing in different aspects of crime control or law enforcement. It is natural to infer at first glance that there must be something seriously wrong in this "scattering" of functions which appear essentially the same. We have been taught to believe that "diffusion of responsibility" is the root of all administrative evil and that "consolidation" or "centralization" is a tested cure-all. We have been slow to realize that functions are different, not only in their nature and purposes but also in their working relationships with other functions. Any administrative field or department, which is created by the assembling of subsidiary, facilitating, or auxiliary functions, cuts straight across those other fields which are delimited by more fundamental and vital factors. Administrative organization can not be treated as if it were a plane, to be divided and subdivided into neat rectangles. On the contrary, administrative organization is a three-dimensional affair. We have to cut our functional material both vertically and horizontally; and one pattern is often inconsistent with the other. We cannot follow either pattern to the end; and at many points we must compromise between them.

Accordingly, if we are to understand the problem of crime control by the federal government, we must determine as precisely as possible the nature of the numerous specific activities which contribute to crime control and the relationship of each activity to other aspects and purposes of federal administration.

In certain cases, difficulties will arise when an attempt is made to differentiate auxiliary from general law enforcement. Detection of tax-dodgers, the Capone case notwithstanding, is rarely for any purpose other than revenue collection. Suppression of smuggling of commodities is clearly auxiliary enforcement, for, with respect to most commodities, its sole objective is the protection of the customs revenues. When we come to a crime such as counterfeiting, however, a reasonable difference of opinion may exist whether enforcement work is general or auxiliary. The suppression of burglary and robbery is assuredly to be classified as general crime control; but what if the crime is a post-office burglary or a mail robbery? In that case, is crime control subsidiary or auxiliary to the operation of the postal service?

In general, public opinion condemns as reprehensible any compromise with law-breakers. Yet, we know that bargaining with criminals is a daily occurrence. Every policeman is constantly called upon to exercise discretionary authority. Honest officers wink at minor violations because they know or have been told that it is impossible to do anything about them. Other officers, not so honest, disregard crime and vice for a pecuniary or political consideration. Prosecutors bargain with criminals in order to get pleas of guilty. Public agencies, for obvious reasons, act half heartedly, if at all, against mobs and sit-down strikers. In still other cases, we temper justice with mercy, or with expediency. Nevertheless, in basic law-enforcement work the public conscience is opposed in principle to compromise.

In auxiliary law enforcement the situation is somewhat different. Here, the offender does not as a rule wear the brand of criminality. Crime control is a means rather than an end; and, in many cases, the operations of the auxiliary enforcement arm of an administrative agency are controlled in significant measure by a policy which has much to do with the principal work of the agency but little if anything with criminality in general.

With regard to smuggling, there apparently can be but one basic policy, a policy of suppression. Nevertheless, the degree to which suppression can be carried and its application to individual cases are to some extent necessarily dependent on the discretion or policy of the collecting authorities. In many cases, a vigorous running down of offenders and a rigorous application of penalties may not be required by law and as a practical matter may be meddlesome and unfair as well as ineffective. Better enforcement results may often and legitimately be obtained by other methods, such as propaganda, conference, and the seeking of co-operation. In some cases, therefore, law-enforcement work is dependent to such an extent on a larger bureau or departmental policy that to separate the enforcement function from the other functions of the bureau or department would be a manifest absurdity.

ADMINISTRATIVE INSPECTIONS

We have already mentioned the fact that in the federal government investigative agencies are used for internal personnel control. In the Treasury and Post Office Departments, for example, thousands of employees handle money or other evidences of value. Naturally, thefts and embezzlements occasionally occur, though probably less frequently than in private employments. In these and other agencies of the government, it is the duty of officials to award contracts, approve claims, grant rights, make purchases, and act as custodians of public property. In such classes of work, opportunities exist for negligence, irregularities, collusion, and bribery. Unscrupulous employees in key positions may cause enormous losses to the government; and on occasion, as in the Teapot Dome affair, create a national scandal.

The first line of defense is the selection of honest employees. It is essential, therefore, that applicants for fiduciary positions should be carefully investigated. The second line of defense is the maintenance of procedures, precautions, protective devices, checks, and reviews, calculated to make wrongdoing difficult. The third line of defense is a system of inspections. Auditing, so far as it concerns the fidelity of employees, is a familiar form of administrative inspection. The fourth and final line of defense is the detection and apprehension of the guilty, followed by trial and punishment, which may be either judicial or administrative or both. Another type of inspection work is concerned with efficiency rather than honesty. It has to do with organization, management, methods, procedures, and equipment. Both types of administrative inspection work are particularly necessary in an organization which functions largely through a field force or which makes grants or loans of money to public and private agencies which are not under its direct control. Only by carefully devised systems of accounting and reporting and frequent inspections can the central agency feel assured that its field offices or its public and private beneficiaries are observing the conditions, instructions, and standards laid down for their guidance.

On September 30, 1936, the civil officers and employees of the executive branch of the federal government numbered 835,704. Of these, no less than 721,093 were outside the District of Columbia. Of the Treasury Department's 72,910 employees, 51,545 were in the field. Of the 268,556 employees of the Post Office Department, 264,543 were scattered near and far throughout the country. Agriculture had 11,704 in Washington and 56,795 outside. Interior had 9,814 at the Capital and 35,239 in other more or less distant places.

To control the personnel, properties, and performance of its vast and far-flung organization, the federal government, through numerous specialized units, exercises a function that we may call internal enforcement. Regulations are enforced more often than laws; and the detection of crime is a minor feature of internal enforcement. As a rule, each department or establishment, if it is to be held responsible for administrative results, must have charge of its own internal enforcement activities. The Secretary of the Treasury, for example, could hardly be held responsible for customs collections if the collectors' offices were inspected solely by some agency outside the Treasury Department. Moreover, an inspector can be efficient only when he is informed and experienced; and the best inspector is likely to be a man who is a veteran of the service which he inspects. Consequently, internal enforcement work is and must be scattered. Its consolidation or centralization is out of the question.

Internal enforcement as such is not of primary interest in a study of federal crime-control agencies. Yet, internal enforcement is interwoven with auxiliary and general crime control. In certain branches of the federal organization a belief based on long experience exists that the investigative qualifications and techniques required for the detection of crime are also appropriate for administrative inspection work. It has also been found economical for the same body of men to conduct internal and external enforcement operations. Moreover, an administrative inspection sometimes uncovers a crime which has been committed from the outside. Even burglaries are occasionally engineered through collusion between inside employees and professional criminals. Finally, the detection of a crime, whether committed against government property or not, frequently requires an examination or use of the internal machinery of a government agency. Mail tracings furnish a good illustration.

Accordingly, we shall find in the federal government that in many cases the same agencies and persons who are responsible for external enforcement, either general or auxiliary, are also charged with duties relating to the internal operations of a department or establishment. Probably the best example of intertwined activities is provided by the Chief Inspector's Office in the Post Office Department. The Bureau of Investigation of the Department of Justice likewise shows a mixture of activities different in character and much less complex.

THE HEART OF THE PROBLEM

As we have previously noted, all federal agencies are engaged, in a sense, in law enforcement. Numerous agencies enter into the crime-control problem, most of them indirectly and incidentally.

The Department of State, with reference to extradition proceedings and through its Foreign Service, Passport Bureau, and other units, co-operates with other federal agencies in the detection and apprehension of law-breakers. The function that it performs in the organization and administration of narcotics control will be mentioned in a later chapter. Nevertheless, it is safe to say that the Department of State is on the outer fringe of our problem.

One may speedily reach the same conclusions with respect to the Public Health Service in the Treasury Department, which is charged by law with preventing the introduction of epidemic diseases and with making physical examinations of aliens. To perform these duties, Public Health officers are stationed at all seaports and at certain ports of entry on the land borders. The War and Navy Departments maintain Intelligence Divisions. These Divisions co-operate in crime control; but they primarily serve military and naval ends.

The Division of Investigations of the Department of the Interior was established by the Secretary of the Interior on April 27, 1933. The Director of Investigations was charged with investigating all irregularities, official misconduct, and alleged violations of law affecting the Department of the Interior, and the offices, bureaus, and territories within its administrative jurisdiction. There were on August 7, 1936, five field divisions with headquarters at San Francisco, California, Billings, Montana, Salt Lake City, Utah, Albuquerque, New Mexico, and Washington, D.C. The Division had eighty-seven field agents. It was charged with co-operating with the Bureau of Investigation of the Department of Justice; and agents of the Division were instructed, when they found that an investigation fell within the jurisdiction of some other agency, to cease their own work on the case and to call it to the attention of the agency having jurisdiction. The enforcement work of this Division is thus mainly internal. Its outside and inside operations seem to be inseparable. While the law-enforcement work of the Interior Department is worthy of study, it is not a significant factor in the general crime-control problem.

In the Department of Agriculture, the Bureau of Plant Industry and the Bureau of Animal Industry maintain a limited inspection force along both the Canadian and Mexican borders; and the Bureau of Entomology and Plant Quarantine has men stationed on the highways to protect certain areas from plant pests. The Bureau of Biological Survey (Agriculture) and the Bureau of Fisheries (Commerce) have a few wardens. The Solicitor of the Veterans' Administration had in 1936 over ninety Field Examiners; but their work was almost purely administrative. In the fiscal year 1936, less than 2 per cent of the cases investigated by them were based on complaints involving criminality. The Civil Service Commission employed[2] fifty-eight persons in its Investigations Division. While this Division investigates frauds and may initiate criminal prosecutions, its work seems to be strictly auxiliary to, and an integral part of, the examining function of the Commission.

The National Park Service of the Interior Department polices the parks. It is the duty of the superintendents of national parks to see that all federal laws and rules and regulations issued thereunder are enforced within the park boundaries. This is done through the ranger forces in the majority of national parks and by

[2] Oct. 12, 1936.

the park policemen in the Hot Springs National Park. There were in the fall of 1936 about 180 permanent and 344 seasonal park rangers outside of the District of Columbia and its environs. The National Park Service also has jurisdiction over the guards in federal buildings and the park police in the District of Columbia and its environs. Here, to be sure, is police work; but it is restricted to special areas and places and is conducted for special purposes.

Much the same may be said of the Office of Indian Affairs. In October 1936, there were 189 Indian police stationed on Indian reservations. There were also 33 special officers or deputy special officers, most of whom were whites. Indian police paid by and responsible to the federal government are appointed by the superintendent in charge of the reservation, in many cases on the recommendation of the Indian Tribal Council. It is stated by the Office of Indian Affairs that the law-enforcement officers on Indian reservations co-operate with state and local officers and with federal agencies, such as the Bureau of Investigation, the Alcohol Tax Unit, the Bureau of Narcotics, the Bureau of Customs, and the Immigration and Naturalization Service. Police forces are supervised by other federal agencies, such as the Division of Territories and Island Possessions in the Department of the Interior, the Bureau of Insular Affairs in the War Department, the Office of Island Governments in the Navy Department, and the Panama Canal.

Many other federal agencies are authorized to investigate and may cause the prosecution of more or less flagrant offenses; for example, the Food and Drug Administration, the Bureau of Air Commerce, the Bureau of Marine Inspection and Navigation, the Federal Trade Commission, the Securities and Exchange Commission, the Federal Alcohol Administration, the Federal Communications Commission, the Federal Power Commission, the Interstate Commerce Commission, and the United States Maritime Commission. But the objective of such agencies is not the solution of the crime problem. Detection of law-breaking is subsidiary to and inseparable from their main task.

The agencies which we find at the heart of the federal crime-control problem and which we must study intensively are nine in number:

The Bureau of Investigation of the Department of Justice

The Secret Service Division of the Treasury Department

The Intelligence Unit of the Bureau of Internal Revenue, Treasury Department

The Enforcement Division of the Alcohol Tax Unit of the Bureau of Internal Revenue, Treasury Department

The Customs Agency Service of the Bureau of Customs, Treasury Department

The Bureau of Narcotics of the Treasury Department

The Coast Guard, Treasury Department

The Immigration Border Patrol of the Immigration and Naturalization Service, Labor Department

The Office of the Chief Inspector of the Post Office Department

SUMMARY AND CONCLUSIONS

Neither experience nor research has yet supplied us with a rule or principle by which to determine exactly what a law-enforcement agency should or should not do. A county sheriff's office may properly discharge one assortment of functions; a municipal police department, another; and a state police force, yet another; while, in a federal crime-control agency, one may find additional and equally justifiable variations. To understand the problems of crime control by the national government, we must give attention to three broad classes of law enforcement: general, auxiliary, and internal. Auxiliary enforcement and internal enforcement are incidental and subordinate departmental tools. The former tool might conceivably be wielded for the whole federal government by a single agency, though the presumption is against centralization. Internal enforcement activities, except perhaps in rare instances and under unusual circumstances, must be retained by and scattered among numerous departments, bureaus, and establishments. On the basis of this functional analysis, various federal agencies which maintain enforcement or investigative officials require no detailed examination. The problem of federal crime-control organization boils down to nine agencies, located in four different departments; six in the Treasury Department, one in the Department of Justice, one in the Post Office Department, and one in the Department of Labor.

CHAPTER III

FEDERALISM

In a unitary government, the establishment of a single national police force is a simple question of legislative policy. The law-making body may decide on centralization or decentralization; and it may at any time change from a centralized system to a decentralized one or vice versa. Theoretically, any plan of organization may be promptly adopted which seems administratively most desirable. Great Britain has a unitary government, in which, to all intents and purposes, a single Parliament possesses supreme and exclusive power; but the British maintain a considerable measure of decentralization in law enforcement. Continental governments of the unitary type favor as a rule a highly centralized system of policing.

For reasons which at that time were compelling, the men who framed the Constitution of the United States adopted a federal system. In such a system, powers are divided between the central government on the one hand and the governments of the several states on the other. In our Constitution, the powers of the central government are enumerated; and the Tenth Amendment provides that "the powers not delegated to the United States by the Constitution, nor prohibited by it to the states, are reserved to the states respectively or to the people."

EXPRESS POWERS OF THE FEDERAL GOVERNMENT

The enumerated powers of the federal government are surprisingly few. It may impose taxes, borrow and

appropriate money, make treaties, regulate interstate and
foreign commerce, establish uniformity with respect to
naturalizations and bankruptcies, coin money, stand-
ardize weights and measures, establish post offices and
post roads, provide for patents and copyrights, set up
courts inferior to the Supreme Court, declare war, raise
and support armies, provide and maintain a navy, call
forth the militia to execute the laws of the Union, suppress insurrections and repel invasions, exercise exclusive jurisdiction over areas and places owned by the
federal government, and suppress counterfeiting, piracies, maritime offenses, and treason.

It will be noted that few of these enumerated powers
relate specifically to criminal-law enforcement. Congress, to be sure, is given power to provide for the punishment of counterfeiting, as well as to define and punish
piracies and felonies committed on the high seas and
offenses against the law of nations. It also has power to
declare the punishment of treason. The Constitution
provides that the "President, Vice-President, and all
civil officers of the United States shall be removed from
office on impeachment for and conviction of treason,
bribery, or other high crimes and misdemeanors." The
federal courts are given by the Constitution criminal as
well as civil jurisdiction; and provision is made for the
extradition of fugitive criminals from one state to another.

These provisions lie on the surface of the document.
Their general meaning is that the federal government
has no definitely granted and comprehensive criminal
jurisdiction throughout the nation, though it has such
jurisdiction in the District of Columbia and various
other areas, and may prosecute and try various criminal
cases when the crimes are committed under specified cir-

cumstances. Moreover, five of the early amendments
to the Constitution were designed to safeguard in various
particulars the rights of those accused of crime, thus re-
stricting in certain respects the law-enforcement powers
of both the federal and the state governments.

It is difficult at first glance to see how the voluminous
federal *Criminal Code* could have been erected on such
a meager constitutional framework. But, in addition to
its specific powers, Congress is authorized "to make all
laws which shall be necessary and proper for carrying
into execution the foregoing powers, and all other powers vested by this Constitution in the government of the
United States, or in any department or officer thereof."
This provision is the constitutional foundation of most
of the auxiliary and internal law-enforcement activities
performed by the federal government. If Congress has
power to lay and collect taxes, it becomes necessary and
proper to prescribe penalties for the non-payment of
taxes; and it is likewise in order to maintain a force of
men to prevent and detect tax evasions. If Congress has
authority to establish post offices, it may also protect
these institutions from robbers, and, in order to do so,
may maintain a force for inspection, investigation, and
policing. So, too, it becomes appropriate for Congress
to define as criminal the impersonation or assault of a
federal officer, though the Constitution itself says nothing of assaults or impersonations. The authority of Congress to regulate interstate and foreign commerce has
been used to penalize various acts for different purposes.

RESERVED POWERS OF THE STATES

General criminal-law enforcement is reserved by the
Constitution to the states. In practice, as we have already
noted, state law-enforcement work is for the most part

delegated to the political subdivisions of the state and is thus scattered among a multitude of relatively small units—counties, cities, towns, villages, and townships. The results of this minute subdivision of jurisdiction and its lack of correlation with certain characteristics of modern criminality have already been pointed out. It should be emphasized, however, that there is nothing in the fundamental law or in any basic geographical, economic, or social condition which requires that each community, however small it may be, should do its own policing within its own tight little jurisdiction. Extreme decentralization is required neither by our federal system of government nor by the facts of a realistic democracy; the states themselves are responsible for general law enforcement; and, here and there, with hesitating steps, they have been slowly actualizing their fundamental responsibility.

Nevertheless, if criminal-law enforcement were completely centralized in each state, the national crime problem would be only partly solved. The states themselves are too small and too numerous to satisfy all requirements of effective crime control. The automobile makes it possible to enter, leave, or cross a state in a matter of hours or even minutes, where it was formerly a question of weary days. It is the customary tactics of modern gangdom to plan a crime in one state, execute it in another, and then return to the first state or hurtle into some other remote locality for the hiding-out and cooling-off period. The territorial range of detection activities, to be effective, must be commensurate with the territorial range of crime. Pursuit can not stop at state lines. A clue found in one jurisdiction must be followed up in another. Evidence in a major offense may be scattered all over the map. A robber caught in Missouri may have his fingerprints on file in Maryland. The court or prison record of a single suspect may have to be compiled from the separate records of two or a dozen different commonwealths.

The federal Constitution did not, of course, overlook the need of interstate co-operation. The provision regarding extradition has already been mentioned. It is further prescribed: "Full faith and credit shall be given in each state to the public acts, records, and judicial proceedings of every other state. And the Congress may by general laws prescribe the manner in which such acts, records, and proceedings shall be proved, and the effect thereof." Moreover, the citizens of each state are, according to the Constitution, "entitled to all privileges and immunities of citizens in the several states." Particularly interesting is the constitutional provision which permits a state, with the consent of Congress, to enter into an agreement or compact with another state. Up to 1934, only eight compacts had been approved by Congress in the field of criminal-law enforcement; and all of them related to the service of criminal process on, or to jurisdiction over, boundary waters.[1] In 1934, Congress enacted a law which apparently gives advance consent to any agreement or compact between two or more states, "for co-operative effort and mutual assistance in the prevention of crime and in the enforcement of their respective criminal laws and policies, and to establish such agencies, joint or otherwise, as they may deem desirable for making effective such agreements and compacts." Such a compact may, for example, authorize the officers of one state to pursue and arrest a criminal in

[1] Gordon Dean, "The Interstate Compact—A Device for Crime Repression" in *Law and Contemporary Problems*, October 1934, Vol. I, No. 4, p. 461.

another state. The compact idea might also be used to simplify the rendition of fugitives, the serving of criminal process, and the compelling of the attendance of witnesses. Interstate compacts for crime control will probably increase in number during the next few years, with some beneficial results; but, if sole reliance is placed upon this device, it is likely to be disappointing. It would be difficult if not impossible to establish by this means an actual unity of command covering the areas of two or more states; and, without unity of command, the shortcomings inherent in a territorial apportionment of law enforcement responsibility can be only partially overcome. As a matter of fact, police departments in different states, without the formality of an interstate compact, have long been in the habit of co-operating. They have, for example, made investigations and arrests for one another; exchanged fingerprints, photographs, records, and other information; and in other ways practiced reciprocity.

FEDERAL ASSISTANCE TO THE STATES

McLaughlin in his *Constitutional History of the United States* says that one of the salient features of the federal system formulated in 1787 was that neither national nor state government "was to be inferior to the other or in ordinary operation to come into contact with the other."[2] While the American people still maintain in their federal and state constitutions the principle, implicit in federalism, of a division of powers and functions, this principle has tended, under the pressure of nationalizing forces, to become more and more a legal fiction. In most of the major fields of governmental

[2] P. 194.

service and regulation, public administration is a federal-state co-operative undertaking. Federal and state administrative organizations are intermeshed. "In ordinary operation," they are in constant contact with each other. In some fields, for example highway and public works construction, agriculture, education, and social security, federal administrative authorities not only co-operate with, but also in a measure control, state agencies. In some cases, the federal authority dictates the general form of the state administrative set-up. Assistance, co-operation, or control is exercised in different ways. The federal agency may administer financial grants-in-aid; it may conduct research, collect statistics, and disseminate information; it may perform technical services; it may lend personnel and equipment; or it may in one way or another promote improvements in state legislation and state administration. Most of these federal "invasions" of state jurisdiction rest on the powers of Congress "to lay and collect taxes, duties, imposts, and excises, to pay the debts and provide for the common defense and general welfare of the United States."

In the field of criminal-law enforcement, the scope of federal activities might be enlarged by amending the federal Constitution. This was in fact done by the Thirteenth Amendment which prohibited slavery. It was also done by the Eighteenth Amendment, now repealed, which prohibited traffic in intoxicating liquors. There seems to be, however, no prospect in the immediate future of another amendment which will specifically and directly add to the crime-control functions of the national government.

The federal government has not yet made use of financial grants-in-aid to assist the states in their criminal-law enforcement work;[3] but it has sought by other means to strengthen, co-ordinate, and supplement state effort. Thus, it maintains an identification file for the use of all detection and apprehension agencies. |It provides a central clearing-house of information regarding criminals| It compiles and publishes crime statistics, which are voluntarily contributed by state, county, and municipal police officers. It conducts research in methods of crime detection and does laboratory work for state and local agencies. It assists in training members of police forces from all parts of the country. These various co-operative and co-ordinative activities will be described more fully in subsequent chapters. In addition, federal law-enforcement agencies frequently work in close association with local officers in the detection and pursuit of criminals. Important also are the promotive activities of the federal government. President Hoover's Commission on Law Observance and Enforcement, commonly called the Wickersham Commission, is to be credited with the most exhaustive survey yet made of the national crime problem. Attorney General Cummings' Conference on Crime in December 1934 was a noteworthy effort to focus thinking and consolidate national leadership.

These activities, striking as they are, are less significant than recent extensions of federal jurisdiction over general criminal offenses. These have come in part from the expansion of auxiliary law enforcement accompanying an increase of federal regulatory functions, and in part from a recognition of the limited effectiveness of state and local forces. The federal government now

[3] See Paul H. Sanders, "Federal Aid for State Law Enforcement" in *Law and Contemporary Problems*, October 1934, Vol. I, No. 4, pp. 472-83.

exercises law-enforcement functions which are in no way auxiliary to other federal services. The new functions are aimed directly at crime as such; and are designed to supplement, if not to supplant, state and local activities. The new policy makes use, for the most part, of the power of Congress to regulate interstate and foreign commerce; and, to some extent, it utilizes the postal and taxing powers. One of the early examples of federal legislation dictated by this policy was the White Slave Traffic Act, usually referred to as the Mann Act, enacted in 1910. This was followed a few years later by a federal law prohibiting the interstate transportation of prize-fight films. Another illustration is found in the national Motor Vehicle Theft Act, known as the Dyer Act, passed in 1919. Under this act, persons who transport a stolen motor vehicle from one state to another, knowing it to have been stolen, may be prosecuted in the federal courts for the transportation of the stolen vehicle. Furthermore, persons who receive, conceal, store, barter, sell, or dispose of any motor vehicle which moves as, or which is a part of, or which constitutes, interstate or foreign commerce, knowing the same to have been stolen, may be prosecuted in the federal courts. The national Stolen Property Act, approved May 22, 1934, extended the provisions of the Motor Vehicle Theft Act to all other stolen property having a value of $5,000 or more.

Other examples are furnished by the federal laws against kidnaping. The first of these, the so-called Lindbergh Law enacted in June 1932, provided for the punishment of any person guilty of transporting a kidnaped victim across state lines. A companion act, also passed in 1932, penalized the sending of threats through the mails. Under the provisions of an act approved May 18,

1934, whoever transports or aids in transporting in inter-state or foreign commerce any person who has been un-lawfully seized, confined, inveigled, decoyed, kidnaped, abducted, or carried away by any means whatsoever and held for ransom or reward or otherwise, is guilty of vio-lating a federal law. Also, if two or more persons enter into an agreement, confederation, or conspiracy to violate the provisions of this act and do any overt act toward carrying out such unlawful agreement, confederation, or conspiracy, such person or persons are guilty of violat-ing the federal kidnaping law. Further, on January 24, 1936, the President approved an act making it a viola-tion to receive, possess, or dispose of any money know-ing the same to have been delivered as ransom or re-ward. Moreover, the federal statute relative to extortion provides that whoever, with intent to extort from any person money or other things of value, mails or causes to be mailed any communication containing any threat to injure the person or property of any person, or to kidnap any person, or any demand or request for ransom or reward for the release of a kidnaped per-son, is chargeable with a federal violation. If the mes-sage is transmitted interstate by means of telephone, telegraph, radio, or oral message, there is likewise a vio-lation of the extortion statute.

A further illustration is supplied by the federal Fugi-tive Act, approved May 18, 1934, which makes it a federal offense for any person to move or travel in inter-state or foreign commerce with intent to avoid prosecu-tion for any of the following offenses, committed or attempted: murder, kidnaping, burglary, robbery, mayhem, rape, assault with a dangerous weapon, and ex-tortion accompanied by threats of violence. This act also makes it a federal offense for any person to travel in interstate or foreign commerce to avoid giving testimony in any criminal proceedings in a place where the commission of a felony is charged.

A federal law aimed at racketeering, enacted June 18, 1934, makes it a felony to obtain compensation by the use of, or the threat to use, force, violence, or coercion when such conduct has relation to an act affecting interstate commerce.

The national Firearms Act of June 26, 1934 provides for: the collection of a federal tax on machine guns, sawed-off shotguns and rifles, and firearm silencers; the licensing of dealers; the registration of weapons; and the restriction of importations.[4]

The amendment of the federal bank-robbery statute, effective August 23, 1935, extended federal investigative jurisdiction to robberies of any banks insured in the Federal Deposit Insurance Corporation. This amendment more than doubled the number of banks afforded federal protection, increasing the number so protected to 14,182.

While these do not exhaust the examples of federal participation in a type of law enforcement which in the past was left to the states, they make it evident that the federal government has now assumed large and increasing responsibilities in the field of general law enforcement. The recent federal policy, therefore, represents one possible answer to the challenge of modern criminality, with its regional, national, and international organizations, and its activities which frequently transcend state boundaries.

FEDERAL-STATE OVERLAPPING

The defunct Eighteenth Amendment carried this extraordinary enforcement clause: "The Congress and the

---

[4] John Brabner-Smith, "Firearm Regulation" in *Law and Contemporary Problems*, October 1934, Vol. I, No. 4, pp. 400-14.

several states shall have concurrent power to enforce this article by appropriate legislation." For the first time, it is believed, the states were requested by the federal Constitution to enforce one of its provisions; for the first time overlapping and duplication in administration were given express constitutional endorsement; and, also for the first time, the national and state governments were invited by the highest authority to "pass the buck." The results are still fresh in our memories. An error in policy produced an impossible administrative situation. Certain of the states failed to assume their share of the task and shifted the distasteful burden to the broad but slightly stooping shoulders of Uncle Sam. Prohibition leaders, misled by unwarranted faith in the omnipotence of federal enforcement, abandoned the localized methods which had gradually created a substantial temperance sentiment.

First, we tried control of the liquor traffic by municipalities and counties. Then we applied extensively the principles of local option and state prohibition, enforced in the main by municipal and county authorities. Then we experimented with nationally enforced prohibition. Now we are in a régime, ostensibly of state control, but really of federal-state-local control. The Twenty-first Amendment, repealing the Eighteenth, makes it the duty of the federal government to protect the dry states by preventing the transportation or importation for delivery or use therein of intoxicating liquors. The federal government, furthermore, taxes alcoholic beverages and to a certain extent regulates the liquor business. The gist of the matter has been stated as follows: "In a very real sense the whole administrative task of liquor control is one of law enforcement. It consists in keeping unauthorized persons from manufacturing or selling liquor and in seeing that those who are given the privileges abide by all of the restrictions contained in statute and regulation."[5]

But the keeping of unauthorized persons from manufacturing or selling liquor, that is, the suppression of bootlegging, is still mainly a federal function. A recent study finds that "the states, for the most part, have been only mildly interested in liquor-law enforcement, and they have disliked dipping into revenues from the legal business to provide the means for driving out the bootlegger and for revoking the permits of his licensed customers."[6] The same study finds that two and one-half years after repeal the bootlegger retains a half or more of the business he had during prohibition. Accordingly, it is recommended that the Federal Alcohol Tax Unit should have at least a thousand additional men and that the federal government should subsidize state prohibition enforcement activities.[7] The liquor problem, therefore, has by no means been "returned to the states." In this perplexing field of law enforcement, the federal government and the states still overlap. They still exercise what is essentially concurrent jurisdiction.

It may well be that, in the handling of the liquor problem, federal-state overlapping is unavoidable. It is quite possible, too, that the fiscal and social importance of this problem justifies, not only the expansion of a federal law-enforcement agency, but also a measure of support and control of state and local police forces. On the merits of this particular question, we are not competent to pass judgment. It is treated here at some length because it provides an apt illustration of a condition and

[5] Leonard V. Harrison and Elizabeth Laine, *After Repeal* (1936), p. 228.
[6] The same, p. 211.
[7] The same, pp. 211, 227.

a trend, a condition of disequilibrium in the federal system, and a trend toward centralization.

Much the same situation exists with reference to the narcotics problem. Both the federal government and the states have enforcement powers. The federal government, for reasons which will appear more clearly later on, can not divest itself of its responsibilities. On the contrary, it may be expected that in this area of enforcement, as in others, the tendency will be toward further centralization.

When the Lindbergh baby was kidnaped, an intense emotional revulsion swept over a shocked country. It was instantly demanded that the federal government "do something." President Hoover responded by instructing all federal agencies to assist in bringing the perpetrator to justice; and Congress responded, as we have seen, by making certain features of kidnaping federal offenses. Apprehension of kidnapers is now, in effect, a function of both the federal government and the states. In this area of crime, overlapping activities and concurrent jurisdiction have been substituted for a division of powers.

Other acts, in one or another of their manifestations, are crimes under both federal and state laws. Overlapping is, or may be, involved in cases of counterfeiting, forgery, bank robbery, extortion, impersonation, assaults, larcenies, motor-vehicle thefts, arson, illegal cohabitation, blackmail, lotteries, and obscenity.

Federal and state activities also overlap in the person of the criminal pursued. Criminal jurisdiction is generally defined by offenses; but the criminals themselves can not be distributed for enforcement purposes according to their technical statutory violations. In the past certain types of law-breaking were specialized pursuits. A safecracker, becoming expert in his peculiar craft, devoted his extra-mural career to that branch of criminality. Picking pockets, counterfeiting, forgery, porch climbing, highway robbery, and working confidence games were more or less distinct specialties. At present, persistent violators of the law do not ordinarily restrict themselves to one class of offense. As a rule, they start their anti-social careers early with mild delinquencies and then rapidly progress by fairly predictable steps to acts of definitely dangerous criminality. Of the 461,589 criminal fingerprint records examined by the Federal Bureau of Investigation in 1936, about one-third were of persons who had previously been convicted of one or more offenses. Of 4,838 persons arrested for robbery, whose fingerprints showed they had previously been convicted one or more times, 86 per cent had been convicted of crimes other than robbery. Of 26,698 repeaters arrested for burglary and larceny, about two-thirds had previously been convicted of a different crime. More than 70 per cent of the repeaters arrested for counterfeiting and forgery had dabbled in other illegal occupations. Of those committing criminal homicide, more than 90 per cent had been previously found guilty of some other infraction.

These figures are by no means conclusive; but they seem to indicate that the majority of hardened criminals today have committed or are in the habit of committing different sorts of crimes. Some crimes are often merely incidental to others; for example, automobile thefts and murder may be perpetrated to facilitate some other crime or to escape from it. On the whole, the modern criminal is likely to be many sided. He is, in a sense, resourceful. When opportunity knocks on his door, he opens it— with a sawed-off shotgun in his hand. He is a composite of portents.

Of course, certain criminal pursuits may be at times

more profitable and therefore more popular than others. New crimes and variations of old crimes reflect changes in the social, economic, and legal situation. Bootlegging and racketeering were stimulated by prohibition. The separation of law-enforcement activities according to the statutory definition of offenses means one sort of enforcement for one group of crimes and a different sort of enforcement for the other group. If one sort of enforcement is nation-wide, concentrated, and comparatively effective while the other sort is scattered and lax, the result may be merely to drive criminals from a precarious field of law-breaking into a relatively safe one. Maximum efficiency demands that any law-enforcement agency should be able to deal with crime in general and the criminal in all of his aspects, not merely with a few selected manifestations of criminal activity.

Because of this fact, the natural tendency has been for the federal government to extend its law-enforcement activities administratively as well as legislatively. In prosecuting Al Capone, federal agencies were well within their legal powers; but, nevertheless, they were doing something administratively which long before should have been done by the State of Illinois. When the federal government apprehends a counterfeiter, like "Count" Lustig, or a bandit, like Alvin Karpis, it is catching some one who has violated state as well as federal laws. Smugglers, narcotic peddlers, automobile thieves, and white slavers are frequently, perhaps usually, wanted for violations of state laws. The federal crime is often incidental, or accidental; the serious criminality is a state affair. Under the circumstances, it becomes difficult if not impossible for federal agencies to stay within their jurisdiction, even though it liberally overlaps the jurisdiction of the states. The natural temptation is to "get in" at the start on any serious or widely publicized crime, whether or not it is technically a federal case. This temptation is especially strong in kidnaping cases. In such cases, prompt supervision of law-enforcement activities is imperative; and, as soon as ransom is paid or the victim's body discovered, the kidnaper may be presumed, though not known, to have put himself within federal jurisdiction by an interstate flight.

Administratively, much of the significance of federal-state overlapping lies in the fact that it divides both effort and responsibility. It creates an opportunity, on the one hand for conflicts and jealousies, and on the other for duplications and waste. Where unity in a common purpose is impossible, co-operation and co-ordination become indispensable.

SUMMARY AND CONCLUSIONS

In the United States, criminal-law enforcement is divided between the federal government and the states; and, in the states, it is infinitely subdivided. It is not a function that can be completely and effectively exercised by the states acting independently. Consequently, the federal government, aiming not only to co-ordinate but also to supplement state and local effort, tends to expand its jurisdiction at the price of overlapping and at the risk of duplication and conflict. For this trend toward nationalization of criminal-law enforcement much can be said; but the sound planning of a nation-wide law-enforcement policy should direct attention to the disadvantages as well as the advantages of centralization. The problem of law-enforcement reorganization, therefore, divides itself into three parts: (1) reorganization within the state; (2) reorganization within the federal government; and (3) reorganization of federal-state relations.

CHAPTER IV

HOW THE AGENCIES GREW

Topsy was an ebon character whose precise rôle in *Uncle Tom's Cabin* has long passed out of memory; but she is still a lively figure, or at least a lively figure of speech, in the literature of public administration. Topsy confessed that she had "just growed." During the last third of a century, it has been said with monotonous frequency of American administrative organization that it has grown "like Topsy," that is, without plan or design. It is rarely, if ever, mentioned that Abraham Lincoln and Thomas A. Edison grew in much the same way as Topsy. Whether the negro lass was adapted to the duties she had to perform and to the environment in which she lived has apparently not been considered. Ignoring her possible virtues, we administrative theorists dwell on what we deem to be her one unpardonable defect, namely that she had not been planned in the beginning and had never been subsequently reorganized.

We are inclined to think that the planning or organizing of administration is something that takes place all at once and once for all, that there is just one correct way to do it, and that the one correct way has been discovered only in recent years. As a matter of fact, whenever a new service, function, or activity is born in the legislative mind and wrapped in the swaddling clothes of law, the task of organizing or reorganizing starts afresh. It is a task that we can not avoid if we would. As soon as we have decided that the government shall do something that it has not previously done, unless our decision is to be merely a pious wish, we must allocate the doing of the job to some official, department, bureau, board, or whatnot.

In the hurly-burly of a legislative session, this problem of organization is, in many cases no doubt, handled unwisely. Where the new function will go is sometimes answered by a careless afterthought or an accidental circumstance, sometimes by considerations of pure expediency or of partisan advantage, often by illegitimate pressures from the outside, and in not a few cases by the personal ambitions of a chief executive. In cases where the public service to be allocated is a quite novel one and is still in the experimental stage, the natural tendency is to establish a new, often an independent, agency for its exercise. Sometimes this is done because it is the easiest thing to do; but more often because, in the light of the facts then available, it seems to be the best thing to do. In the majority of cases, the national Congress or a state legislature answers the question of allocation in a surprisingly sensible manner; and it does so numberless times every legislative session.

In those cases where mistakes have been made, we may come after a time to a consciousness of error. In other cases, functions take on, after their original establishment, changed meanings and unforeseen ramifications and relationships, which may make a reallocation appear desirable. In still other cases, changes occur in the social and economic environment to which the administrative organization must adapt itself; society itself develops new conceptions of its needs; objectives, once remote, draw near and become apparently attainable; and, thus, an administrative function, once considered incidental, may leap to the forefront of critical public interest. In such cases, a regrouping of functions throughout a fairly large administrative area may become necessary. Such regrouping is what we ordinarily call administrative "planning" or "reorganization"; but it is usually a manifestation of hindsight rather than foresight, and it is only one of the phenomena of an organizing process which is carried on continuously with little noise, and, on the whole, satisfactorily.

Thus, with the creation, metamorphosis, and readjustment of functions and agencies, administrative organization constantly evolves. It grows, presumably as Topsy grew, and as any other living thing must grow. Accordingly, each of the federal crime-control agencies has its individual historical background; and, in order to understand the agency, one must understand, at least in outline, the manner of its evolution. For this purpose, we shall take up the agencies somewhat in the order of their development.

PROTECTION OF THE MAILS

It was natural that the arts of investigation and detection should first be used to facilitate the performance of the traditional governmental services which were included within the specific powers assigned by the Constitution to the federal government. The inspection service of the Post Office Department originated as a means of supervising the internal administration of the postal system. As such, the service dates back to colonial times, originating, perhaps, in the inquiring mind of Benjamin Franklin. During the early years of the United States Post Office, postmasters general, without specific statutory authority, appointed special agents to make inspections. On July 2, 1836, Congress specifically authorized the Postmaster General to pay the expenses of agents employed to investigate mail depredations, examine post routes and post offices, and perform similar services. The Inspection Service, as a definite branch of the postal organization, seems to have had its inception in 1840, although the inspectors were then called "special agents."

In his report for the year 1853, the Postmaster General made the following comments on the work of the special agents, who then numbered 18:

To these special agents the Department must look for much of the local information necessary to enable it to determine what service is required in the different states, and how the service is performed. It is an important part also of their duties to see that the postmasters properly perform their duties, and report a want of ability, attention, or fidelity on their part, or on that of contractors, promptly to the Department.

. . . A most important part of their duty is that connected with depredations. A citizen who entrusts his moneys in the mails should have every assurance given him that his property will be properly cared for and that if it be abstracted or stolen every exertion will be made by the government to restore it to him and bring the offender to justice. To perform these duties in a satisfactory manner more agents are necessary, and they should be divided into two classes. To one class should be assigned the supervision of the transportation of the mails and business connected with the appointment and contract offices, and to the other class all matters connected with mail depredations.

The number of special agents increased to 33 in 1865; to 48 in 1869; and to 59 in 1872. In 1875, the Postmaster General announced that appointments of special agents "have been made, and will continue to be made, almost exclusively from the employees already in some other branch of the service. . . ." The appropriation act of June 11, 1880 changed the name "special agents" to "Post Office inspectors," the Postmaster General having pointed out in his report for the fiscal year 1879 that

. . . the duties of these officers are by no means confined to the detection and arrest of offenders against the postal laws. On the contrary, most of their time is occupied in the inspection of the postal service, the examination of postmasters' accounts, the investigation of the solvency of their bonds, the collection of debts due the Department by postmasters, and the general supervision of all officers and employees of the postal service.

In 1891, the Post Office inspectors were placed in the Bureau of the Fourth Assistant Postmaster General but in 1905 they were transferred to the office of the Postmaster General, where they have since remained.

The following general justification of the inspection service is quoted from the House appropriations hearings in 1936:

The Postmaster General and his assistants are entrusted with the disbursement of appropriations totaling $728,000,000 for 1936, and with the rendition of varied services affecting the daily life of every citizen.

The proper administration of such an enterprise obviously requires the services of a mobile force of highly trained postal experts responsible directly to the Postmaster General, upon whom he and the Assistant Postmasters General may rely with confidence for dependable information and sound technical advice concerning the condition and needs of the service.

The growing complexity of postal operations, arising out of the developing needs and desires of the people and the changes in legislation to meet those needs and desires, have gradually but inexorably increased the needs of the Department for the services of inspectors. In 1915 the postal revenues were $287,000,000; in 1935 the revenues amounted to $630,000,000; an increase of 119 per cent. During the same period the number of inspectors increased from 420 to 540, an increase of 28.5 per cent.[1]

CONTROL OF SMUGGLING

The American colonists were familiar with the fact that customs and navigation laws required enforcement.

[1] 74 Cong. 2 sess., *Post Office Department Appropriation Bill for 1937*, Hearings before H. Committee on Appropriations, p. 121.

Indeed, smuggling of one kind or another was a rather common colonial pastime. Rum-running by colonial ships was by no means unknown. The Revolution, however, transferred the enforcement shoe to the other foot; and it became incumbent upon the government of the United States, if it were to be financially independent of the states, to prevent the various and devious modes of smuggling and evasion.

In order to do so, a careful and suspicious eye had to be kept on the coastal waters. The need for a floating police force as a part of the national fiscal organization was recognized by Congress in an act approved July 31, 1789.[2] It set up a surveyor at each port, whose duties were to include "the employment of the boats which may be provided for securing the collection of the revenue"; but no provision was made for the boats themselves. In the following year, an act was passed authorizing the construction and equipment of revenue cutters. There was no navy at that time; and the Treasury Department was the logical, indeed the only, place for the Revenue Cutter Service.

In 1797, when a war with France was threatening, Congress authorized the use of the revenue cutters for defensive purposes; and, in 1799, when a United States navy was in creation, it was provided that the cutters "shall, whenever the President of the United States shall so direct, co-operate with the Navy of the United States, during which time, they shall be under the direction of the Secretary of the Navy. . . ."[3] In the several wars since that date, including the World War, the Revenue Cutter Service, now called the Coast Guard, has functioned as a part of the Navy.

[2] Darrell Hevenor Smith and Fred Wilbur Powell, *The Coast Guard*, pp. 1-2.

[3] The same, pp. 5-6.

It was early seen that it would be convenient and economical for this maritime police force to exercise other
functions on the seas. Its aid was enlisted in 1799 for the
administration of quarantine laws; in 1800, for the suppression of the slave trade; in 1818, for the enforcement
of neutrality laws; in 1819, for the protection of American ships from pirates; and in 1837, for a rendering of
aid to vessels in distress and the removal of obstructions
to navigation. Since then, various other duties, to be performed on the high seas and coastal waters, have been
imposed upon this maritime agency.

Shore life saving in this country was at first done by
volunteers, much as fire fighting was. Although Congress had previously provided for giving aid to the shipwrecked from the shore, it was not until 1848 that
money was appropriated for lifeboats and other life-
saving apparatus and spent by the government itself
through the Secretary of the Treasury who at that time
had charge of lighthouses.

The Life-Saving Service was set up in 1871 as a
branch of the Revenue Marine Service, which controlled the peace-time operations of the cutters; but in
1878 the Life-Saving Service became a unit of the
Treasury Department with full bureau status. Nevertheless, this Service continued in close relations with the
Revenue Marine or Revenue Cutter Service. It was
proposed by the Commission on Economy and Efficiency
in 1911 that the Life-Saving Service be consolidated
with the Bureau of Lighthouses, which had been placed
in the Department of Commerce and Labor, and also
that the Revenue Cutter Service be dismembered and
its parts distributed among other bureaus which required
the use of marine craft. These recommendations were

endorsed by President Taft. Neither course of action was approved by Congress; instead, the Life-Saving Service and the Revenue Cutter Service were consolidated in 1915 to make what is now called the Coast Guard. It may have seemed to the experts in 1911 that the old-fashioned smuggler, who in his black-hulled craft slithered along an unfrequented shore at dead of night, had long ceased to be a serious threat. But only a decade later, swift bootlegging craft were hovering on our coasts, confirming in a way the prescience of Congress in leaving the Coast Guard intact, contrary to expert and executive advice.

From day to day, however, smuggling and other more subtle forms of fraud and evasion are attempted, for the most part at and through the ports. To protect the customs revenues, as well as to maintain respect for laws generally, attempts to cheat the government must be investigated, violators apprehended, goods seized, fines and penalties collected, and criminal cases prepared for prosecution. Moreover, up to the World War, one-half of our national revenues was collected in customs offices. The Customs Service resembles the Post Office Department, in that both are great fiscal and technical organizations, maintaining many field stations and requiring carefully devised protective procedures. In both, criminal acts or collusion in such acts may occur inside the organization. Accordingly, in both, the personnel must be under rigorous inspection and the procedure subject to continual and expert scrutiny. An act of 1799 authorized the Secretary of the Treasury to have examinations made of the books of customs collectors. Prior to 1846, such examinations were made by clerks who were designated as special agents only for the duration of their assignments. In 1846, independent special agents were appointed by the Secretary for the specific purpose of making such examinations; and in 1870 special agents were authorized by statute. Later, a Special Agency Service under the Director of Special Agents was created; and in 1927 this Service was placed by statute in the Bureau of Customs. The name of the Service was changed in 1929 to the Customs Agency Service.

Smuggling of dutiable or prohibited goods across the land borders has always been a problem, though not usually a major one. The first land patrol officers employed in the Customs Service were mounted inspectors on the Mexican border. In the estimates submitted by the Secretary of the Treasury on January 13, 1886, provision was made for the employment of several mounted inspectors in that area. "Mounted inspectors" or, as their title later became, "Customs Patrol inspectors," were continuously employed on the Mexican border. In 1925 and 1926, the Customs Patrol as an organized body was established on the northern border, and consisted of employees paid from funds of the Prohibition Bureau who were detailed for patrol work under the Collectors of Customs. On July 1, 1928, these employees were placed on the customs rolls, paid from customs funds, and given their present designation "Customs Patrol inspectors." The expansion of the Patrol began in 1925. Numbering 111 in that year, it grew to 723 in 1930.

Prior to September 1, 1936, the Customs Patrol inspectors were responsible to the collectors of customs, to whose districts they were assigned. On that date, they were transferred from the collectors and their control was centralized in the Enforcement Unit of the Customs Agency Service.

INTERNAL REVENUE AND ALCOHOL

The first internal revenue law, that of March 3, 1791, imposed a tax on distilled spirits; and the resulting "Whiskey Rebellion" gave the new national government an opportunity to demonstrate its enforcement power. From that time until 1913, when the Constitution was amended and an income-tax law passed, alcoholic beverages and tobacco were the main sources of internal revenue.[4]

The Bureau of Internal Revenue came into existence in 1862; and, from the start, it had to cope with frauds and evasions, large and small. An act of March 3, 1863 assigned to the Solicitor of the Treasury general supervision over the prevention, detection, and prosecution of violations of the revenue laws. The Commissioner of Internal Revenue was authorized in 1868 to employ not more than twenty-five detectives, or agents, as they were later called, to act under the supervisors of internal revenue or to engage in special duty directly under the Commissioner. Nevertheless, frauds continued; and a well-organized "Whiskey Ring," which for some years had escaped prosecution, was uncovered in 1865. It is significant that "a shameful feature in the conspiracy" was that "it seems to have originated, not with distillers and rectifiers, but with the revenue agents of the government."[5]

The situation indicated the need of a detective force entirely independent of the operating units of the Bureau. This need was met by the creation in 1919 of the

---

[4] No internal taxes of any kind were levied between 1817 and 1861. For the history of the Bureau of Internal Revenue, see Laurence F. Schmeckebier and Francis X. A. Eble, *The Bureau of Internal Revenue*, pp. 1-64.

[5] Quoted from charge to the jury in U.S. *v.* McKee. See Schmeckebier and Eble, cited above.

Intelligence Unit. In the order creating the Intelligence Unit, the Commissioner of Internal Revenue said:

The purpose of this Unit is to concentrate the supervision and direction of investigations of such importance as, in the judgment of the Commissioner or the heads of the administrative units, demand more exhaustive inquiry than could be made advantageously by officers assigned to work of a general nature. Generally speaking, such investigations will relate to (1) serious infractions of disciplinary rules and regulations with respect to which the facts have not been conclusively established by the executive officer who makes the primary report and recommendation, or with respect to which the original complaint or initial investigation indicates probable criminality; and (2) charges indicating serious violations of internal revenue laws, and particularly income tax laws through collusion, conspiracy, extortion, bribery or manipulation of any kind designed to defraud the government, with respect to which the development of the evidence and its orderly presentation to the prosecuting officers can be handled more successfully by the corps of trained investigators who will constitute the field force of the Intelligence Unit, and who will be designated Special Agents.

The Unit consisted at first of a chief and six investigators. Within four years, the personnel had grown to 40 and in 1936 it numbered 196 men.

Regulation of liquor production, established as a war measure in 1917, was first assigned to the Food Administration but soon transferred to the Bureau of Internal Revenue. When the national Prohibition Law was passed in 1919, following the ratification of the Eighteenth Amendment, the Bureau was made the enforcement agency. Federal functions in relation to alcoholic beverages now involved a vastly increased amount of pure police work—patrolling, detection, searches and seizures, pursuit and arrest—for the Constitution and the law had again enlarged the federal *Criminal Code*, thus creating a situation which recognized and bred new and formidable types of lawlessness. Moreover, a part of the liquor trade was legal and required regulation; and taxes were still to be collected on the alcoholic beverages which were authorized to be manufactured and sold.

As the Wickersham Commission remarked:

> The Eighteenth Amendment represents the first attempt in our history to extend directly by constitutional provision the police control of the federal government to the personal habits and conduct of the individual. It was an experiment, the extent and difficulty of which was probably not appreciated. The government was without organization for or experience in the enforcement of a law of this character. In creating an organization for this purpose, it was necessary to proceed by the process of trial and error. The effort was subject to those limitations which are inseparable from all human and especially governmental activities.[6]

Experience showed that the enforcement of prohibition involved the Customs Service and the Coast Guard quite as much as the Bureau of Internal Revenue. To check smuggling of liquors into the country, the Coast Guard and the Customs Border Patrol were expanded; and in 1927 a law was enacted creating in the Treasury Department a Bureau of Prohibition co-ordinate with Customs and Internal Revenue. In 1930, the Bureau of Prohibition enrolled 4,386 employees, of whom 2,836 were enforcement agents. In that year, enforcement functions were transferred to the Department of Justice, where a Bureau of Prohibition was established. Thereupon, the name of the Bureau in the Treasury Department was changed to Bureau of Industrial Alcohol. When the Eighteenth Amendment was repealed, this Bureau was abolished, and an Alcohol Tax Unit was

---

[6] National Commission on Law Observance and Enforcement, *Report on the Enforcement of the Prohibition Laws of the United States*, Jan. 7, 1931, p. 20.

created in the Bureau of Internal Revenue. This action was taken by Treasury decision on May 10, 1934. The Enforcement Division of the Alcohol Tax Unit on June 30, 1936 employed 1,687 agents.

But this is not the only federal agency dealing with alcoholic beverages. The Alcohol Tax Unit is concerned primarily with tax collection; the Federal Alcohol Administration, with the social and industrial aspects of the liquor traffic. This Administration was established in 1935 as a division of the Treasury Department; but in 1936 a law was passed making it an independent establishment under a board of three members. It still maintains its former status, however, since the members of the board have not been appointed.

THE SECRET SERVICE

The annals of the Secret Service Division of the Treasury are comparatively simple, so far as organization is concerned. Its core functions rest on a specific provision of the Constitution: "The Congress shall have power . . . to provide for the punishment of counterfeiting the securities and current coin of the United States." Congress made such provision at an early date; but it was was not until 1861 that an appropriation was voted ($10,000) to "detect, arrest, and prosecute counterfeiters of the coins of the United States." The Treasury Department had charge of the minting of coins and of the engraving of bills, notes, and bonds. There was not even a Department of Justice at that time, much less a Bureau of Investigation; and it seemed logical to give to the Treasury the duty of preserving the integrity of the currency.

A Secret Service Division was organized in that Department and a chief appointed on July 1, 1865. The

Division was first supervised by the Solicitor of the Treasury and later by an assistant secretary; but, in 1933, it was instructed to report directly to the Secretary of the Treasury.

From time to time, various crimes involved in or associated with counterfeiting have been particularly stated and penalized in the law and jurisdiction over them assigned to the Secret Service. The forgery of names on government checks and other valuable documents has likewise been placed by law within the jurisdiction of this agency. The assassination of President McKinley in 1901 called attention to the need of more protection for our chief executives; and, in the appropriation act for the fiscal year 1902, funds were made available to the Secret Service for this purpose. An act of September 14, 1922 created a permanent police force to be known as the White House Police; and on May 14, 1930 this force was placed under the immediate direction of the Chief of the Secret Service.

In the absence of any other federal agency with comparable training and experience, the Secret Service was frequently requested to do detective work for other departments of the government, especially the Department of Justice. Congress put an end to these extra-legal services in 1908. From that time, the Secret Service Division has been restricted to the performance of those duties and only those which are specifically assigned to it by law; but, as we shall see later, some of these duties still involve service to federal establishments other than the Treasury.

THE "G-MEN"

The congressional wing clipping suffered by the Secret Service in 1908 is also a part of the story of the Bureau of Investigation of the Department of Justice;

and, accordingly, we shall have to enter a little more fully into the incidents just referred to.

When the Department of Justice was formally established in 1870, the United States district attorneys were playing the rôle of investigators and collectors of evidence. The United States marshals, who are federal counterparts of the county sheriffs, were engaged, not only in serving the orders of the federal courts, but also in keeping the peace and apprehending law-breakers. Both the district attorneys and the marshals were political appointees, served for short terms, and as a rule were strictly amateurs in law enforcement. To make matters worse, marshals and their deputies were killed with "appalling frequency"; and there was no federal law against assaulting or murdering a federal officer.[7] Moreover, the Department of Justice had no specially trained men in Washington for the investigation of cases which had technical or national aspects.

On March 3, 1871, Congress appropriated $50,000 to be expended under the direction of the Attorney General "in the detection and prosecution of crime against the United States." It was provided in 1878 that the appropriation for the above-mentioned purpose might be used for the investigation of officials, acts, records, and accounts; and in 1882 the words were added: "and the investigation of the accounts of marshals, attorneys, clerks of the United States courts, the United States commissioners." In the appropriation act of June 6, 1900, this further language was appended: ". . . and to include salaries of all necessary agents in Washington, D.C."

The Department of Justice used these appropriations

[7] See Homer Cummings and Carl McFarland, *Federal Justice*, pp. 366-83.

for the temporary employment of individuals from the outside, and borrowed the services of customs inspectors, agents of the Interior Department, bank examiners, and particularly Secret Service operatives. Since 1878, according to Cummings and McFarland, the Department had included in its own personnel "examiners" to go over the records and accounts of clerks of court, marshals, commissioners, and district attorneys. The "examiners" and a special agent for Indian matters worked under the direction of a "General Agent" who soon became a budget and accounting officer.[8] The examiners were reorganized in 1905; and the borrowed operatives from the Secret Service were placed under the supervision of the General Agent.

Attorney General Bonaparte stated in 1907:

. . . the Department of Justice has no executive force and more particularly no permanent detective force under its immediate control. . . . When emergencies arise requiring prompt and effective executive action, the Department is now obliged to rely upon the several United States marshals; if it had a small carefully selected and experienced force under its immediate orders, the necessity of having these officers suddenly appoint special deputies, possibly in considerable numbers, might be sometimes avoided with greater likelihood of economy and a better assurance of satisfactory results. I venture to recommend, therefore, that provision be made for a force of this character; its number and the form of its organization must be determined by the scope of the duties which the Congress may see fit to intrust to it. . . .[9]

Investigations by Secret Service agents, working for the Justice and Interior Departments, had been instrumental in bringing about the indictment and conviction of numerous persons, including certain federal legisla-

[8] The same, p. 375.
[9] *Annual Report of the Attorney General*, 1907.

tors, for land frauds; and it was suspected in Congress that others of its membership were being investigated by the Secret Service. To terminate such unwelcome zeal on the part of an executive agency, an amendment was incorporated in the Sundry Civil Appropriation Act of 1908 which, as we have previously noted, confined the Secret Service to the activities which were specifically given to it by statute. Theodore Roosevelt, then President, vigorously protested this action, declaring that it could be "of benefit only to the criminal class." "Such a body as the Secret Service," he continued, "such a body of trained investigating agents, occupying a permanent position in the government service, and separate from local investigating forces in different departments, is an absolute necessity if the best work is to be done against criminals. It is by far the most efficient instrument possible to use against crime." In conclusion, he urged that the Secret Service "be placed where it properly belongs, and made a bureau in the Department of Justice, as the Chief of the Secret Service has repeatedly requested."[10]

In any event, he urged, the restrictions placed upon the operations of the Secret Service should be removed. He insisted on a generalized investigative agency somewhere. While preferring the Department of Justice for its location, he was willing that Congress should choose between Justice and Treasury. He did not mention the possibility of establishing a generalized agency in Justice, while retaining the Secret Service in the Treasury. But this, in effect, was what Congress in 1908 decided to do. It made a significant change in the wording of the appropriation acts; and, for the first time, voted specific appropriations for the salaries of Department of Justice agents in Washington. In the meantime, identification

[10] *Messages and Papers of the President*, Vol. XVII, pp. 7632-33.

material had been filed on a small scale at Leavenworth Prison; and, in response to a growing demand, Congress inserted in the appropriation act of that year a clause providing for the "collection, classification, and preservation of criminal identification records and their exchange with the officials of state and other institutions."

By an order issued on July 26, 1908, Attorney General Bonaparte placed all investigative functions under the Chief Examiner; and, in his annual report for that year, he included the following statement:

In my last annual report I called attention to the fact that this Department was obliged to call upon the Treasury Department for detective service and had, in fact, no permanent executive force directly under its orders. Through the prohibition of its further use of the Secret Service force contained in the Sundry Civil Appropriation Act, approved May 27, 1908, it became necessary for the Department to organize a small force of special agents of its own. Although such action was involuntary on the part of this Department, the consequences of the innovation have been on the whole, moderately satisfactory. The special agents, placed as they are under the direct orders of the Chief Examiner, who receives from them daily reports and summarizes these for submission each day to the Attorney General are directly controlled by this Department, and the Attorney General knows, or ought to know, at all times what they are doing and at what cost. Under these circumstances he may be justly held responsible for the efficiency and economy of the service rendered. The experience of the past six months has shown clearly that such a force is, under modern conditions, absolutely indispensable to the proper discharge of the duties of this Department, and it is hoped that its merits will be augmented and its attendant expense reduced by further experience.

Attorney General Wickersham issued an order on March 16, 1909, confirming the action taken by his predecessor and naming the new unit the "Bureau of Investigation." The offenses which were within the juris-

diction of the new Bureau included violations of the
anti-trust, national bank, bankruptcy, copyright, and
neutrality laws; burglaries from interstate shipments in
railroad cars; train robberies; bribery; smuggling of
Chinese aliens; libel; lotteries; murder and other crimes
on government reservations; peonage; perjury; and
crimes on the high seas. The Bureau also participated at
times in the investigation of certain counterfeiting, forgery, customs, internal revenue, and postal fraud cases.
Agents of the Bureau occasionally served subpoenas and
looked into applications for executive clemency. It was
still their duty to examine the official acts, records, and
accounts of the marshals, attorneys, and clerks of United
States courts; and, like the Secret Service, the Bureau
was charged by Congress with protecting the person of
the President.

The Bureau's work steadily increased, owing in part to
the expansion of its jurisdiction, in part to increases in
certain classes of crimes, and in part to changes in the
enforcement policies of attorney generals. The White
Slave Traffic Act was passed on June 23, 1910; and by
1912 the Bureau had on its rolls 53 special white-slave
officers. Anti-trust cases multiplied in 1911 and 1912.
Interstate transportation of prize-fight films was prohibited in 1913; and, in the same year, the Bureau was
given jurisdiction when seals were broken from freight
cars moving in interstate commerce. During the War, the
Bureau was busy with neutrality, selective service, enemy
alien, and espionage matters. The close of the War
brought numerous cases under the War Risk Insurance
Act. Other matters were dumped into the Bureau's lap—
passports and visas, agitators and radicals, insurgent activities in Mexico, and frauds in government contracts.
The national Motor Vehicle Theft Act was passed on

October 28, 1919. In 1922, the Bureau started the issuance of identification orders for the apprehension of badly wanted fugitives. Two years later the identification records at Leavenworth Prison and those maintained by the International Association of Chiefs of Police were taken over and consolidated in the Bureau's division of investigation. A fugitive division was created in 1927. The collection and compilation of uniform crime statistics was begun in 1931; and, in the following year, the technical laboratory and the single fingerprint file were set up. The first of the federal kidnaping laws was passed in 1932; and, in 1934 and 1935, a number of laws already described further expanded the Bureau's jurisdiction.

In the meantime, the function of examining judicial officers had been taken from the Bureau of Investigation; but it was restored in 1934. Finally, in 1936, this work was transferred to the Office of the General Agent in the administrative branch of the Department of Justice. This office in 1937 had a force of twelve lawyer-accountants. Thus, the metamorphosis of the Bureau of Investigation was complete. It had sloughed off its chrysalis. Its agents, the "G-men," no longer "examiners," were now armed, trained, mobile, active in the pursuit of criminals, rapidly developing a legend of invincibility, and kept in the spot-light, sometimes to their embarrassment, by a remarkable propaganda policy.

NARCOTICS

When Congress revised the revenue laws in 1890, it levied import taxes of varying kinds and amounts on morphine and its salts, smoking opium, medicinal opium, and preparations of opium, and an internal revenue tax of $10 per pound on opium manufactured in the United

States for smoking purposes. It also prohibited any person, not a citizen of the United States, from manufacturing opium for smoking purposes. It was found in 1909 that the United States was importing 200,000 pounds of opium a year, while our legitimate medical requirements were only 50,000. Thereupon, Congress prohibited the importation of opium and its preparations and derivatives except for medicinal use.

At about the same time, a meeting of the International Opium Commission at Shanghai inaugurated a series of international conferences and agreements, each of which has had a significant relationship to the development of our domestic legislation and administration. The Hague Opium Conference of 1912 formulated a Convention for the Suppression of the Abuse of Opium and Other Drugs, whereby each power promised to "enact efficacious laws or regulations for the control of the production and distribution of raw opium." The Convention did not, however, state to what extent production should be controlled. The powers also undertook the definite obligation to prevent the export of raw opium to countries which prohibited its entry, and agreed "to take measures for the gradual and effective suppression of the manufacture of, internal trade in, and use of, prepared opium, with due regard to the varying circumstances of each country concerned." The powers further agreed to enact laws "to limit exclusively to medical and legitimate purposes the manufacture, sale, and use of morphine, cocaine, and their respective salts."

To carry out the provisions of this Convention, Congress enacted two laws in 1914. One regulated the importation of opium, prohibited the exportation of smoking opium, and permitted the export of opium and cocaine and their derivatives only to countries regulating

their entry. The second law repealed those portions of
the act of 1890 which related to smoking opium produced in the United States, increased the internal revenue tax to $300, and laid down certain requirements for
obtaining a license to manufacture, including the posting
of a penal bond of not less than $100,000. In order to
execute the agreement "to limit exclusively to medical
and legitimate purposes the manufacture, sale, and use
of morphine, cocaine, and their respective salts," under
the Hague Convention, Congress on December 17, 1914
passed what is familiarly known as the "Harrison Narcotic Law," which provided for the registration of dealers in narcotic drugs and aimed to restrict the business to
persons so registered. This law has been amended from
time to time, generally with regard to the amount of
occupational tax to be paid by persons engaged in the
narcotic drug business. The act of January 17, 1914 has
also been amended. It was provided, for example, in
1924, that no crude opium might be imported for the
purpose of manufacturing heroin.

The United States Senate, on March 31, 1932, advised and consented to the ratification of the Convention
for Limiting the Manufacture and Regulating the Distribution of Narcotic Drugs (known as the Narcotic
Limitation Convention of 1931), and the formal instrument of ratification was transmitted, under the terms of
the Convention, on April 10, 1932. This Convention
came into force July 9, 1933, and considerably tight-
ened both international supervision and domestic control, the intention being to limit manufacture in all
manufacturing countries to the medicinal requirements
of the world. Administratively, this control involves (1)
determination of medicinal requirements, (2) control of
imports, (3) internal revenue collections, (4) licensing

and registration of manufacturers and dealers, and (5) detection, apprehension, and punishment of illicit importers, manufacturers, and dealers.

From other angles, Congress has attacked the drug evil. An act of January 19, 1929 provided for the establishment of two federal institutions for the confinement and treatment of persons addicted to the use of habit-forming narcotic drugs; and on May 11, 1930, a law was passed prohibiting and severely penalizing the introduction of any narcotic drug into or upon the grounds of any federal penal or correctional institution. On February 18, 1931, Congress enacted legislation directing the deportation of aliens who should be convicted and sentenced for violation of or conspiracy to violate any federal narcotic drug law; and on March 2, 1931, legislation was enacted providing that, where a federal prisoner is an alien and subject to deportation, the Board of Parole may authorize the release of such prisoner after he has become eligible for parole on condition that he be deported and remain outside of the United States and all places subject to its jurisdiction.

The problem of organizing narcotics control has not been a simple one. At first, in March 1915, a Narcotic Section was created in the Miscellaneous Division of the Bureau of Internal Revenue to enforce the Harrison Narcotic Law, the necessary field investigative work being performed by internal revenue agents as a part of their duty in enforcing general internal revenue laws. Narcotic-law enforcement was transferred in January 1920 to a Narcotic Division organized in the newly created Prohibition Unit of the Bureau of Internal Revenue. Field investigative work was then performed by narcotic agents and inspectors under the supervision of prohibition agents. In July 1921, however, narcotic field-enforcement districts were established under the supervision of narcotic agents who reported directly to the Prohibition Unit, thus constituting a field enforcement organization, separate from that established for prohibition. After the passage of the act of May 26, 1922, known as the Narcotic Drugs Import and Export Act, the permissive features of this statute were administered by the Narcotic Division of the Prohibition Unit, under authority of a federal Narcotics Control Board, which was composed of the Secretaries of the Treasury, State, and Commerce. On April 1, 1927, the Bureau of Prohibition was created in the Treasury Department, under which narcotic-law enforcement was delegated to the Narcotic Unit in charge of a Deputy Commissioner of Prohibition. The special force of narcotic agents and inspectors remained in the field and reported to the Prohibition Bureau (Narcotic Unit). Under the act of June 14, 1930, the federal Narcotics Control Board was abolished and the present Bureau of Narcotics established in the Treasury Department. The Narcotics Limitation Convention of 1931 requires each of the contracting powers to "create a special administration" for the purpose of carrying out the provisions of the Convention. While "special administration" does not mean "independent agency," the United States is obligated to assign narcotics enforcement to some special bureau, section, or unit devoted exclusively to that function.

IMMIGRATION

Functions pertaining to immigration were first assigned to the Department of State (1819-68). Immigrant inspection was made a duty of the Treasury Department in 1882; and in 1891 a Bureau of Immigration was set up in that Department. In 1903, this Bureau with its functions was transferred to the Department of Commerce and Labor; and in 1906 the Bureau became the Bureau of Immigration and Naturalization. When the Department of Labor was established in 1913, the new department took over the functions relating to immigration and naturalization and divided them between two bureaus: the Bureau of Immigration and the Bureau of Naturalization.

Prior to 1924, except for a few mounted customs and immigration guards on the Mexican border, there was no land-border patrol on either the Mexican or Canadian border. Soon after the enactment of the first restrictive immigration law in 1921

... it became apparent that it was useless to close our seaports to the entry of aliens and leave our land borders open and unprotected, for the reason that aliens who could not come in regularly at our seaports under the quota could proceed to foreign contiguous territory and enter by walking across our unprotected land boundaries.[11]

During the period between 1921 and 1924, numerous aliens entered the United States illegally in this manner. Consequently, in the appropriation bill for 1925, Congress appropriated $1,000,000 for the establishment of an immigration land-border patrol, of which $100,000 was made immediately available. Under this authority, the present Immigration Border Patrol was organized. It was made a part of the Bureau of Immigration; and it has since continued in the same administrative set-up, except during the calendar year 1932 and the early months of 1933 when the Border Patrol was made more or less independent of the Immigration Service. At the

[11] Statement of Assistant Secretary of Labor Robe Carl White, 71 Cong. 2 sess., *Border Patrol*, Hearing before H. Committee on Interstate and Foreign Commerce, p. 28.

present time, the Patrol is an integral part of the Immigration and Naturalization Service.

In the act of February 27, 1925 (43 Stat. L. 1049) expenditure from appropriated funds was authorized for coast, as well as for land, border patrol; and any employee of the Bureau of Immigration was empowered (1) to arrest without warrant any alien who, "in his presence or view," attempts illegal entry "and to take such alien immediately for examination before an immigrant inspector or other official having authority to examine aliens as to their right to admission to the United States" and (2) to search for aliens any vehicle, or conveyance, or any vessel within the territorial waters of the United States.

In 1933, the Bureau of Immigration and the Bureau of Naturalization were consolidated; and this consolidation covered also the district and field personnel, including the Patrol.

SUMMARY

With the authorization by Congress of new or expanded activities and the adoption of new policies to meet new or changed conditions, new agencies have been created and, in some instances, functions and agencies have been transferred from one department to another. The evolution of these various forces has been subjected, broadly speaking, to four influences. The influence of the requirements of auxiliary law enforcement is seen in such agencies as the Intelligence Unit of the Bureau of Internal Revenue, the Customs Agency Service of the Bureau of Customs, the Immigration Border Patrol, the Post Office Inspection Service, and, in the beginning, the Bureau of Investigation. Special social objectives, as well as the demands of auxiliary enforcement, largely account for the policing activities of the Bureau of Narcotics. In the Alcohol Tax Unit and its predecessors, the Coast Guard, and the Customs Patrol, one can see, not only the development of auxiliary enforcement, but also the administrative effects of changing public attitudes toward alcoholic beverages.

In addition to these influences, the tendency in recent years has been for the federal government to enter more and more into the field of general criminal-law administration, which formerly lay entirely within the jurisdiction of the states. Here we find the fertile soil in which the Bureau of Investigation is growing. It is interesting to note, however, that the enforcement work of the Department of Justice was, at first, mainly internal; and the early development of the Bureau of Investigation was along the lines of auxiliary enforcement. Nevertheless, for more than a decade, the Bureau has enjoyed a distinctive position and character. Its location in the Department of Justice, the government's general law office, has enabled it with apparent logic to assume a miscellany of functions, including special services to other departments and co-operation with the states in the suppression of crime generally.

The ten law-enforcement agencies which have been sketched in this chapter had a total personnel in 1936 of about 17,000. More than 50 per cent of this manpower belonged to the Coast Guard. Of the agencies operating on land, the Bureau of Investigation of the Department of Justice is, without doubt, the most significant; but the Enforcement Division of the Alcohol Tax Unit is the largest of all, measured by number of employees; and the various land enforcement agencies located in the Treasury Department had in 1936 a total personnel of about 3,500, more than twice the force possessed by the Department of Justice.

CHAPTER V

THE FEDERAL BUREAU OF INVESTIGATION

In the problem of federal law-enforcement organization, the "G-men" seem to be the key men. The fact that they are popularly called "G-men" indicates that the underworld first and the overworld afterward recognized the Bureau of Investigation as the spear point of the federal attack on crime. When the Bureau had its real beginning in 1908 it was clearly the intention of Congress that general crime control and the rendering of investigative service to other federal agencies should be centered to the greatest possible extent in the Department of Justice, and that the other national law-enforcement agencies should be kept so far as practicable within the jurisdictional boundaries of their respective departments. As further evidence of this intention, Congress has named the Bureau the *Federal* Bureau of Investigation.

The development of the Bureau as a generalized law-enforcement organization is due only in part to its position in the Department of Justice and only in part to the need, forcefully presented by Theodore Roosevelt, for a central service unit in the federal government. The strongest influence in the expansion and perfecting of the Bureau during the last ten or twelve years has been the demand for a national agency to assist, co-ordinate, and supplement the state, county, and municipal forces. The bulk of crime is still essentially local; and responsibility for crime control continues to rest largely on the states, which have delegated their responsibility to agencies infinitely more numerous than those of the federal government. Accordingly, federal services in the law-enforcement field are primarily designed for and used by state and local agencies. Their application to and use by federal agencies may be considered, at present, secondary or incidental. Though the services on the federal level are less significant and differ somewhat in kind from those extended to the states and their subdivisions, the two classes of service have much in common, their combination in one agency is obviously economical, their development has been correlative, and they are inevitably characterized by a vital mutuality. In short, the federal agency, if there is to be one, which nationalizes state and local crime-control functions, must likewise provide the nucleus of a federal consolidation, if, as, and when consolidation takes place.

INTER-AGENCY SERVICE

Inter-agency service is no rarity in other areas of federal administration. Without it, the costs of administration would be much greater than they are. Its necessity and desirability spring from certain conditions which develop in any elaborate organization. Generally speaking, each federal agency employs experts in some particular line, or possesses equipment that can not economically be duplicated, or operates in emergencies, in seasons or in cycles, or exclusively occupies a peculiar geographical location. Certain services, moreover, are of such a nature as to require some measure of centralization for the sake of convenience, economy, or uniformity.

Thus, the experts of the Public Health Service give assistance in the medical field to the Bureau of Prisons, the Office of Indian Affairs, the Immigration and Naturalization Service, and the Coast Guard; and the Corps of Engineers of the Army is engaged in various non-military engineering activities. Moreover, the Army performs its essential mission only in emergencies; and, during peace time, its personnel is available for peace-time services. Because of its specialized personnel, its expensive equipment, and the cyclical character of its basic work, the Census Bureau collects statistics which are used by all other governmental agencies, as well as by the public. Because of the strategic geographical location of its field force and the nature of its primary function, the Bureau of Customs collects the statistics of imports and exports, not alone for its own use but principally as a service to other agencies, the business community, and the public generally. Since the Department of State has diplomatic and consular officers stationed all over the world, it obtains and transmits information for other federal agencies. Purchasing and legal counselling provide examples of functions which intrinsically are of such nature as to justify substantial centralization.

The wide prevalence and admitted justification of inter-agency service and the obvious savings that may accrue from it suggest that law-enforcement agencies should be carefully examined from this angle. To do so will require a more detailed description than we have thus far presented of the functions and operations of each agency, the qualifications, training, and skills of its personnel, the kind of special equipment that it uses, and the time flow of its work, whether steady, emergency, seasonal, or cyclical.

IDENTIFICATION

Some systematic means of identifying the perpetrator of a crime is frequently essential to his detection and successful prosecution. Where fingerprints are left by a criminal at the scene of his crime, a comparison of them with those of suspects is a practically infallible method of eliminating the innocent. No two persons—not even identical twins—have the same arrangement of digital lines. If everybody were fingerprinted, the chances of identification would be the best possible. Since universal fingerprinting is not yet considered feasible, the next best thing, from the standpoint of catching law-breakers, is to preserve in one central place, filed and indexed for instant reference, all the fingerprints of living persons who have been arrested at any time in any part of the country for the commission of felonies. This is the kind of file that is maintained in Washington by the Bureau of Investigation; and on it is based a number of services performed by the Bureau for law-enforcement agencies generally.

On July 1, 1936 the Bureau had on file 6,094,916 fingerprint records, consisting of 5,571,995 criminal records and 522,921 personal identification, Civil Service, and miscellaneous non-criminal records. On that date, 9,904 law-enforcement officials and agencies throughout the United States and foreign countries were contributing 4,700 fingerprint cards daily. Six months later, that is, on December 31, 1936, the number of fingerprint records had increased to 6,682,609; and the number of contributing agencies, to 10,229.

Each card in this file bears ten prints, one of each finger and thumb. At the scene of a crime, however, it is usually a single finger or thumb smudge that is found. So in February 1933, a single fingerprint file was started; and it contained, on December 31, 1936, the prints of 13,528 known kidnapers, bank robbers, gangsters, and racketeers. Multiply this figure by ten, and you have the number of cards in the file—135,280, each card representing one finger or thumb. A murder occurs in Oklahoma, let us say; an abandoned automobile is found; and on the steering wheel there is a latent fingerprint. This is dusted with a chemical, transferred to a special paper, and a copy sent to the Bureau of Investigation, where a search is made of the single fingerprint file. If the driver of the car happens to be a "public enemy," his exact identity can now be determined; and, when he is caught, he can be definitely connected with and prosecuted for the Oklahoma crime.

The general appearance file consists of photographs and complete physical descriptions of these 13,528 "public enemies," indexed in such a manner that complete information concerning all persons of a given description can be obtained within a few minutes. The *modus operandi* file describes how different bank robbers act in their approach, hold-up, and escape. On July 1, 1936, 699 bank robberies had been analyzed, indexed, and cross-indexed. The nickname file provides another means of identification.

The Bureau is an important link in a system of international exchange of fingerprint records. In 1936, the superintendents of identification bureaus in 79 foreign countries, as well as similar officials in the territories and possessions of the United States, were co-operating in this activity. The record of a citizen of any participating country received at the Bureau in Washington is forwarded to the identification bureau of the country of which he is a citizen; and the record of a citizen of the United States received in the identification bureau of any foreign country is forwarded to the United States. This international exchange contributes to the combating of crimes with international ramifications and particularly to the suppression of the so-called international confidence rings.

Voluntary or non-criminal fingerprinting started in

1933. In 1934, the file included only 600 prints; but two years later the number had increased to about 150,000.[1] They are expected to be of value in cases of amnesia, kidnaping, missing persons, and accidental death.

The searching of identification files is work that must be done at high speed. Suspects can not be held indefinitely, sometimes no longer than forty-eight hours. The Bureau, therefore, maintains a thirty-six-hour service; that is, replies go back to police departments within thirty-six hours after receipt of inquiries. To increase speed, a machine, capable of handling 375 prints a minute, is used for the more common classifications. Arrangements have been made for the telegraphic transmission of photographs of fingerprints. The classification of a fingerprint can also be sent by telegraph. When this is done, in an emergency, a police department may get the desired information within ten or fifteen minutes. For the receipt of communications from law-enforcement agencies, the Division of Identification is open night and day.

Most of the other federal crime-control agencies are in the habit of filing identification material on a comparatively small scale. The Secret Service maintains an identification file of single fingerprints of all known makers of counterfeit money and their associates arrested since 1928. The names of these offenders and their aliases are arranged alphabetically for convenient reference. The Service also maintains an identification file of regular fingerprints of persons arrested and convicted for counterfeiting, which also contains the photographs and previous criminal records of such offenders. The Enforcement Division of the Alcohol Tax Unit operates an

[1] Not including the Civil Service fingerprints, mentioned below.

elaborate filing and cross-reference system for identification and classification purposes. An identification file is maintained in the Bureau of Narcotics. Included are the fingerprints, photographs, and criminal records of persons arrested for violation of the federal narcotic laws. The field offices of the Customs Agency Service, including the Customs Patrol, maintain identification files of individuals and also indexes of various known smuggling vessels. In the case of persons arrested or indicted for violations of the postal laws, the Post Office inspectors file all available descriptive information; but the only criminal index is by names and aliases. The Immigration Border Patrol keeps a file containing material descriptive of aliens and alien smugglers. Fingerprint files maintained in the Mexican border districts include about 84,000 records of deported aliens and fugitives from justice.

Federal agencies, like the state and local, send fingerprints to and receive information from the Bureau of Investigation. Thus, the Bureau of Narcotics furnishes the Bureau of Investigation with the fingerprints of persons arrested for narcotic violations; and, in return, the latter agency gives to the former, when requested, the complete criminal records of those already in the file. The same sort of interchange occurs with other agencies.

From June 1928 to July 1932 the Civil Service Commission kept the fingerprints which it takes when appointments are made in the government service; but comparisons of these fingerprints were made at the Bureau of Investigation. In accordance with an agreement between the Director of the Bureau of Investigation and the Civil Service Commission, arrangements were made on June 30, 1932 for the searching of all Civil Service fingerprints by the Bureau of Investigation. More than

140,000 fingerprints were at that time transferred to the Bureau. It was agreed that, in the future, prints would be sent to the Bureau in triplicate, one copy to be retained, one copy to be immediately initialed and returned to the messenger as proof of delivery of the prints, and the third copy to be returned to the Commission with notations on the results of the searches. The Bureau of Investigation reports to the Investigations Division of the Civil Service Commission whether any criminal record is found by comparison with fingerprints previously on file. The Bureau now has on file about 350,000 Civil Service fingerprints. In December 1934, an arrangement was made by which the Bureau of Investigation receives from the War Department for searching and comparison, the fingerprints of persons applying for enlistment in the Army. Of about 47,000 checked to date, more than 3,000 were found to have had police records. The same service has been performed for the Navy and Marine Corps since March 1936. The fingerprints sent by the military establishments are not retained and filed in the Bureau. They are merely compared and returned. Each military branch maintains its own file. The Army's collection is said to include about 5,000,000 fingerprints.

EXPERT SERVICE

A technical laboratory was established in the Bureau of Investigation in the latter part of 1932 to perform certain kinds of work which require special expertness or the use of special instruments. The laboratory makes examinations of questioned documents, and has collections of typewriting standards, fraudulent checks, handwriting examples, and index cards descriptive of watermarks. For the study of documents, the Bureau uses delicate balances, binocular microscopes, a synchrisiscope, paper-thickness gages, micrometer calipers, precision rulers, color charts, special lamps for detecting indented writing with light beams, and ultra-violet and infra-red apparatus. In its practice of the science of ballistics, the Bureau uses microscopes, a helixometer, and special photographic equipment, and maintains a reference collection of bullets, cartridge cases, and firearms.

For the examination and analysis of bloodstains, pieces of skin, fragments of clothes, poisons, and soil, the Bureau presents the following inventory:

A research microscope providing magnifications up to 2,250 times, reference collections of mounted specimens of hairs and fibres, chemical benches equipped with necessary service for gas, electricity, water, and air, centrifuges, sterilizers, a microspectrometer, an ultra-violet microscope lamp, animal cages, refrigeration facilities, a metallurgical belt grinder, a petrographic microscope, a vertical illuminator, a microphotographic camera, vacuum pumps, an electric muffle furnace, and a blast burner.[2]

For the identification of tire impressions the Bureau has a file of the treads of all manufactured tires. The Bureau's experts do moulage work, making casts of footprints, tire impressions, faces of dead persons, or other similar perishable clues which can be preserved in this manner for laboratory study and court use.

Ten experts are engaged in document examinations; three specialize in ballistics; and several in chemical analyses. These scientific aids, while primarily for the use of the Bureau's own investigators, are available to and are utilized by state and local police departments, as well as by federal law-enforcement agencies. The number of different examinations made during a year mounts into the thousands; and, in a large number of cases, results

[2] 75 Cong. 1 sess., *Department of Justice Appropriation Bill for 1938*, Hearings before H. Committee on Appropriations, p. 75.

of high evidential value are obtained. In some cases, convictions, either in federal or state courts, are due solely or largely to the work of the Bureau's technical laboratory.

Some other agencies of the federal government possess comparable facilities in certain phases of scientific detection. The Secret Service, with some assistance from other agencies, is technically well equipped to deal with counterfeiting. The Alcohol Tax Unit specializes in analyses, tests, and measurements essential to the control for revenue purposes of the alcoholic beverage business. The Bureau of Narcotics is equipped for the analytical detection of dangerous drugs. The facilities of the Bureau of Standards, the Bureau of Chemistry and Soils, the Food and Drug Administration, and the Public Health Service are used at times in special phases of crime detection work. For the examination of questioned documents, and for certain other aspects of laboratory crime detection, the Bureau of Standards is probably the most efficient of all federal agencies. When the Post Office inspectors were running down fake eye-doctors, it was essential to have expert testimony on optics and on eye diseases. For the former, the Bureau of Standards was called upon; and for the latter, the Public Health Service. A remarkable demonstration of expertness in detection was provided at the Hauptmann trial by a wood expert from the United States Forest Service Laboratory at Madison, Wisconsin.

OTHER AIDS

In the operation of its fingerprint, alias, and *modus operandi* files, the Bureau of Investigation serves as a clearing-house of information about criminals. The Bureau has installed a stolen-property file for the purpose of recording data concerning thefts of property. At present, the Bureau is receiving and recording in its files for the information of law-enforcement agencies (1) any stolen property which may be described by name, model, and serial number, such as watches, firearms, bonds, typewriters, or similar office equipment; and (2) all stolen property involved in thefts amounting to an aggregate value of $5,000 or more, such stolen property, of course, being described in detailed nomenclature as to individual items involved. From the time of the announcement of the inauguration of this file on April 1, 1936 until July 1, 1936 over 19,000 index cards had been made for inclusion in the file.

The Bureau issues each month a booklet known as the *Law Enforcement Bulletin* to those law-enforcement officials and agencies throughout the United States who contribute fingerprints. In the *Bulletin* are listed the names, aliases, descriptions, and fingerprint classifications of persons whose apprehension is desired, a statement of their alleged crimes, the names of the law-enforcement officers to be notified of apprehension, and a photographic reproduction of one fingerprint of each individual so that police departments may include such data in their own identification records. This bulletin also includes articles dealing with methods and procedures in scientific law-enforcement work.

JURISDICTIONAL OVERLAPPINGS

Overlapping, as the term is here used, means that two or more agencies work in the same general field, deal with the same offenses, persons, or things, operate in substantially the same way in the same territory, or have in general the same objectives. Overlapping must be carefully distinguished from duplication. Duplication means that two or more agencies are doing precisely the same thing and that, with respect to this particular matter, all except one of them are wasting their efforts. Some overlappings are significant; others are not. Some actually contribute to administrative efficiency; others invite duplication and conflict.

The Bureau of Investigation presents a list of more than fifty different matters which have been placed within its jurisdiction. Alphabetically, they start with admiralty-law violations and end with white slavery. Some of them do not appear to involve, at least directly or to any important extent, any other federal agency. Such, for example, are anti-trust cases, bankruptcy frauds, contempt of court, racketeering, intimidation of witnesses, interstate flight to avoid prosecution or testifying, automobile thefts, stolen property, obstruction of justice, peonage, perjury, Red Cross violations, treason, sabotage, and the white-slave traffic. Other cases may bring the Bureau of Investigation into the field of almost any other federal agency. Of this nature are cases of bribery, claims, condemnation, conspiracy, frauds against the government, illegal wearing of service uniforms, impersonation, the assaulting or killing of a federal officer, and destruction, theft, or embezzlement of federal property.

Other cases present more definite overlappings. Thus, the Coast Guard, as well as the Bureau of Investigation, has jurisdiction over admiralty-law violations and crimes committed on the high seas. The Bureau of Prisons, as well as the Bureau of Investigation, is concerned with offenses involved in federal penal administration, the capture of escaped federal prisoners, and violations of federal parole and probation regulations. Crimes on government reservations are also within the jurisdiction of the Office of Indian Affairs and the National Park Service. Espionage concerns the War and Navy Departments; neutrality, the War, Navy, and Coast Guard; kidnaping and extortion, the Post Office Department (if the mails are used); interstate transportation of explosives and larceny from interstate shipments, the Post Office Department and the Interstate Commerce Commission; passport and visa frauds, the Department of State; and crimes against banks, the Federal Reserve Board and the Federal Deposit Insurance Corporation. In general, the Bureau of Investigation has primary investigative jurisdiction over all those offenses against the laws of the United States which are not specifically assigned to other governmental agencies for investigation.

ADMINISTRATIVE AND OPERATIONAL OVERLAPPINGS

In addition to the jurisdictional overlappings there are others that occur in actual administration and operations. These take the form pretty largely of investigative services performed by one agency for another. For example, when Congress established the Federal Deposit Insurance Corporation, it appeared necessary to provide protection both for the Corporation and the banks against such offenses as false statement, willful overvaluation, forgery, counterfeiting, embezzlement, theft, and robbery. Since the Bureau of Investigation and the Secret Service Division had investigators skilled and engaged in the detection of these crimes the criminal-law enforcement work of the Corporation was assigned to and divided between the two investigative agencies. Both of them are now charged with rendering service to the Corporation and both overlap the Corporation's administrative field. Incidentally, each was made, in this connection, to overlap the other's jurisdiction; and accordingly each runs some risk, at this particular point, of duplicating the other.

INTER-AGENCY CO-OPERATION

Where overlapping occurs, duplication or conflict may be avoided or minimized either by one agency's leaving the work to another, by a jurisdictional agreement, or by co-operation between the agencies concerned.

Though both the Secret Service and the Bureau of Investigation are charged with protecting the President, the two agencies do not duplicate or conflict. Primary responsibility is left to the Secret Service; and, when assistance is desired, agents of the Bureau of Investigation cooperate.

As we have seen further, the Bureau's identification files are contributed to and used by federal enforcement agencies generally. "Wanted" notices issued by the Bureau are sent to other federal agencies and transmitted by them to their respective field offices. The Bureau's technical laboratory may be used by federal as well as by state and local agencies. The declared policy of the Bureau is to give to any other federal agency information which is obtained by the Bureau in the course of its investigations and which appears to be pertinent to the investigative jurisdiction of such other agency. Likewise, each of the other agencies declares that its policy in this respect is essentially the same. For example, when the Bureau of Investigation was investigating the kidnaping of Guilliaume Rozen of New York City, information was developed concerning the traffic in narcotics by various persons involved in the kidnaping. The Bureau of Investigation passed this information on to the Narcotics Bureau of the Treasury Department and received from the Narcotics Bureau information relative to the contacts and associations of the persons in whom the Bureau of Investigation was interested.

Relations between the Bureau of Investigation and the Immigration Border Patrol provide several specific illustrations of the extent and fruitfulness of reciprocity. It occasionally happens that a deported alien whose fingerprint record has been filed by the Immigration Service with the Bureau of Investigation will re-enter the United States unlawfully. When subsequently arrested by a police agency or picked up on a vagrancy charge, he is fingerprinted by such agency and the record forwarded to the Bureau of Investigation. The latter thereupon identifies him as an alien who has been deported; and the Immigration Service is notified of the presence of the alien and the place of his detention. In the Labatt kidnaping case, the Immigration Border Patrol furnished personnel and transportation for a search of the down-river area at Detroit. The Border Patrol force at Detroit in 1936 apprehended and turned over to Department of Justice agents a United States citizen who had stolen merchandise in interstate commerce. In the St. Paul district, immigration officers patrolled an area through which a notorious kidnaper was expected to pass in attempting his escape. Similarly, in the Spokane district, the Patrol maintained a watch on the Canadian border for William Mahan, kidnaper of the Weyerhauser boy. In the Los Angeles district, Border Patrol officers apprehended a man who had escaped from Leavenworth Prison.

The Bureau of Investigation states that it furnishes to the Post Office inspectors information obtained pertaining to the various misuses of mails. Agents of the Bureau qualified as accountants perform accounting investigations in those mail-fraud cases in which an analysis of the books and records of a particular company is necessary. This service is rendered to the Post Office inspectors without charge; and the special agents who conduct such an investigation are also available, when needed, to testify at the trial of the case. The Post Office Inspection Service is sometimes called upon by the Bureau of Investigation to make mail tracings, and to furnish data concerning return addresses appearing upon mail addressed to the relatives or friends of fugitives being sought by the Bureau. In the case of the notorious counterfeiter, "Count Lustig," who had escaped from a federal prison, both the Bureau of Investigation and the Secret Service had jurisdiction; and his apprehension was due, it is said, to their joint efforts.

The Coast Guard seems rarely to have been in a position to render service to the Bureau of Investigation, beyond occasionally furnishing transportation or information. From time to time, in cases involving crimes on the high seas and violations of presidential proclamations pertaining to the export of munitions of war to foreign countries, the Bureau of Investigation asks the Coast Guard for the use of its facilities. In the Lindbergh case, the Coast Guard rendered tangible assistance. Following the payment of $50,000 to the supposed kidnaper through Dr. John A. Condon, a party consisting of Colonel Lindbergh, Colonel Breckenridge, Dr. Condon, and the Chief of the Intelligence Unit of the Bureau of Internal Revenue, proceeded to Woods Hole, Massachusetts, to look for the 28-foot boat *Nelly* on which the supposed kidnaper reported the infant. On its arrival at Woods Hole, the party arranged for an organized search by the Coast Guard destroyer *McDougal* and several patrol boats from the Coast Guard base at Woods Hole. In addition, the Coast Guard intelligence office investigated the activities of John Curtis of Norfolk; and Coast Guard vessels participated in the search for a boat off the Virginia coast reported to have the kidnaped infant on board. The Bureau of Investigation reports that it furnishes to the Customs Patrol information concerning individuals believed to be attempting to leave the United States through ports at which the Customs Patrol has representatives. The Customs Patrol reports in turn that it has assisted the Bureau of Investigation in extortion and white-slave cases, in cases involving interstate transportation of stolen automobiles, and in the location of criminals sought by the Bureau. The Alcohol Tax Unit has at times informed the Bureau of Investigation of violations of the Motor Vehicle Theft Law; and the Intelligence Unit of the Bureau of Internal Revenue has co-operated with the Bureau of Investigation in the apprehension of fugitives. With the Military Intelligence Unit and the Naval Intelligence Section, the Bureau of Investigation co-operates in such cases as sabotage, espionage, desertion, and illegal wearing of a service uniform.

CONFLICTS

One should not gain the impression, however, that the federal crime-control agencies live and work together like members of a happy family, each zealously observing the Golden Rule. As a matter of fact, each is busy trying to dig out from under its own work; and, naturally, each thinks of itself first.

All law-enforcement activities deal with persons and personal behavior in relation to rules laid down by government. The present federal law-enforcement structure has been built up, in large part, by the allocation of laws or provisions of laws, at the time of their enactment, to those departments or bureaus which have seemed appropriate enforcement instrumentalities. Each law or provision of law may create a new offense or a variation or particularization of an old offense. When offenses are allocated to more than one federal agency, much overlapping, of a sort, is inevitable; for, as we have seen, the criminal, especially the adult, repeating, high-powered criminal is not ordinarily a specialist. Different offenses are frequently commingled in the same person; and an individual sought by one agency for one offense is often wanted, or even actively pursued, by another agency for a different offense. Such a situation may result in duplicate, wasted, and even conflicting effort; and rival claims to a wanted man or to the credit for his capture may easily engender jealousies and open recriminations.

A case in point is that of Alvin Karpis; and, to perceive what happened, one need only read between the lines of the official reports of two Cabinet officers.

In the annual report of the Attornel General for the fiscal year 1936, we read:

Included in the Bureau's accomplishments in the field of kidnaping investigations during the year were the apprehension of Alvin Karpis, Harry Campbell, William Dainard, commonly known by the alias Mahan, and Thomas H. Robinson, Jr., in the brief period of eleven days from May 1 to May 11, 1936. Karpis, Campbell, and Robinson were subsequently sentenced in federal courts to life imprisonment for kidnaping and William Dainard received a sixty-year sentence for the same offense.[3]

For the same period and on a similar subject, the Postmaster General reported as follows:

On the afternoon of November 7, 1935, in a spectacular machine-gun hold-up of an Erie Railroad mail train at Garrettsville, Ohio, by five bandits, registered mail containing $34,000

[3] *Annual Report of the Attorney General*, fiscal year ended June 30, 1936, p. 128.

in currency and $11,650 in bonds was stolen. Alvin Karpis was found by Post Office inspectors to have been the leader of the bandits perpetrating the mail-train hold-up. This brought into view the end of the trail for Alvin Karpis and other members of his gang. In March 1936, Post Office inspectors and a member of the Kansas State police apprehended one of the gang. Several weeks later Karpis and two more of the gang were arrested. Post Office inspectors have established the identity of the fifth bandit, and they hope to take him into custody in the near future.[4]

Thus, conflict among federal agencies is evidenced by an unwillingness on the part of one agency to give credit to another; by feverish bursts of self-advertising; by a lack of cordial personal contacts among officials; by indirect attacks of one agency upon another; in at least one case a year or two ago, by an attempted "investigation" by Secret Service agents of certain activities of the Bureau of Investigation; and by the frequent use of other petty "sniping" tactics. The situation is generally recognized to be unwholesome and to militate against maximum efficiency. Actual operating conflicts appear to be rare; but antagonisms and misunderstandings among agencies are bound in the long run to affect operations, if they have not already done so. Lack of cordiality is most apparent between the Bureau of Investigation on the one hand and the Secret Service and Post Office inspectors on the other. Among these three agencies, continuous co-ordination has never been established, apparently never seriously discussed. Their chiefs have no luncheon meetings. Indeed, they seem to have little contact of any kind. At the Attorney General's Conference on Crime in December 1934, addresses were made by seven officials of the Department of Justice, by an expert from the Bureau of Standards, by the Commissioner of Narcotics, by the

---

[4] *Annual Report of the Postmaster General,* fiscal year ended June 30, 1936, pp. 77-78.

Superintendent of St. Elizabeth's Hospital, and by the Chief of the Children's Bureau. No other federal agencies were represented on the formal program, though they may have participated in the discussions.

FEDERAL-STATE-LOCAL RELATIONS

In many, perhaps a majority, of the cases handled by the Bureau of Investigation, a federal offense constitutes also a violation of some state law. Overlapping jurisdictions permit and demand co-operation; and overlappings have been deliberately created to remedy the inadequacies of local enforcement and to permit more effective federal assistance to local governments.

In its identification work, the Bureau appears most clearly as an agency for co-ordination and service. Assistance is also rendered by the training school of the Bureau; and *Uniform Crime Reports* is compiled from statistics sent in by state, county, and city law-enforcement officers.

Through personal contacts established by special agents of the Bureau in the field, the Bureau and its work are known to state and local agencies. The Bureau's field offices maintain contact with such agencies and keep up-to-date mailing lists which are used for sending to state and local departments identification orders, apprehension orders, and other material of general interest. The Bureau furnishes free of charge to all law-enforcement officers in the United States cards to be used in taking fingerprints and penalty envelopes for use in forwarding fingerprints to Washington. At the request of any law-enforcement officer, the Bureau will post a "wanted" notice against the fingerprints of any criminal indexed in the Bureau's files, in order that the interested officer may be notified of the arrest of this person by any other police department in the United States. The Bureau distributes each month the *Law Enforcement Bulletin*. Finally, the facilities of the technical laboratory are available without charge to other agencies; and Bureau experts are also available for testifying in state courts.

INTERNAL AND AUXILIARY ACTIVITIES

As we have seen, the Bureau of Investigation was relieved of most of its internal enforcement functions in 1936, when the work of examining judicial offices was transferred to the administrative branch of the Department. In other agencies which we are studying, the combination of internal with external enforcement presents a difficult problem. It is well, then, to note the reason why the Bureau of Investigation was divested, apparently at its own request, of the bulk of its internal enforcement functions. The action was recently explained as follows:

The principal difficulty, Mr. Chairman, under the plan of having the Bureau of Investigation make judicial examinations, was the fact that the Bureau primarily had the duty of the investigation of crime. As I understand their policy, it is to emphasize the importance of having all their men qualified investigators of violations of the law.

But they have been shorthanded. With a vast number of complaints, they could not run them all down and it was difficult for them to handle this examination work along with their other work. . . . They were unable to assign, because of a lack of an adequate force of agents, any definite group of men to make a study of this work and to work under the supervision of the administrative assistant. Primarily the work of the examiners is closely connected with and supplements the work of the administrative assistant; and in order to carry on this work the persons assigned to it must be not only general investigators and general accountants, but they must understand the fee bills, the rules of practice of the courts, and the administrative requirements of the Department. They must also understand the system of bookkeeping that has been developed in the course of years for the offices of court officials. All of these matters are of a specialized nature that a general accountant would not be familiar with.[5]

The Bureau of Investigation continues to make, from time to time, investigations of applicants for positions in the Department of Justice and in the federal courts. The Bureau investigated 432 applicants in 1936; but the volume of this work, compared with all other, is insignificant.

On the other hand, the auxiliary enforcement work of the Bureau is relatively important. This work constitutes, indirectly, the performance of services for federal agencies outside the Department of Justice; but the latter Department is itself, in large part, a service agency, since, in addition to its own general jurisdiction, it prepares for trial and prosecutes many cases which grow out of the enforcement activities of other departments and establishments. In addition, there are laws which the Department of Justice is specially charged with enforcing, such as the bankruptcy and anti-trust laws and the recently enacted criminal laws, already referred to, which have brought the Department directly into the field of general criminality.

Many cases handled by the Department of Justice are civil cases; and certain criminal prosecutions, for example those involving taxation and the anti-trust laws, are not directed at raw criminality. In many of these cases, the Bureau of Investigation checks the facts and collects evidence. Says a Department of Justice official:

---

[5] Testimony of Mr. Finch, chief examiner, 75 Cong. 1 sess., *Department of Justice Appropriation Bill for 1938*, Hearings before H. Committee on Appropriations, p. 131.

The way we work on these things is that the lawyers think out what you might call the plan of campaign. They raise what seem to them to be pertinent questions and then those questions are transmitted to the Bureau of Investigation which makes contact in due course, conducts interviews, and brings the results back to the lawyers.[6]

War-risk insurance investigations have taken a considerable amount of time. Since September 11, 1933, the Bureau has investigated over 8,000 such claims. It likewise works on general claims cases pending in the Court of Claims. Thus, the Bureau of Investigation is to be credited with a considerable volume of essentially noncriminal work. Much of this work and much of the Bureau's criminal investigative work may be considered auxiliary to the general operations of the Department of Justice.

DEPARTMENTAL POSITION, TIE-UP, AND SET-UP

For its auxiliary enforcement work, the Bureau of Investigation is, without doubt, properly located in the Department of Justice. At the present time, for example, the Bureau initiates investigations of violations of the anti-trust laws only upon the request of an assistant attorney general; and when complaints are received at the Bureau or through the field offices of alleged violations of these laws, the facts are referred to an assistant attorney general before investigation is undertaken. For general enforcement and service operations, the Bureau's present location is logical but it does not appear to be absolutely necessary. Of course, questions of policy are, from time to time, referred by the Director of the Bureau to the Attorney General or one of his assistants. Such questions occasionally arise, for example, in cases which

[6] Testimony of Mr. Dickinson, assistant attorney general, the same, p. 117.

overlap state and local jurisdictions. New statutes, assigned to the Bureau for enforcement, frequently require, not only interpretation, but also departmental policy determination. It is understood, further, that all complaints of administrative irregularities by employees of other governmental departments are referred to the Attorney General or a designated assistant for advice and instructions before investigation is begun. Finally, when a criminal case raises some question whether the facts constitute a violation of existing federal statutes, the facts are referred to the assistant attorney general in charge of the Criminal Division for consideration of the legal question; and investigation is undertaken only after the Bureau has been advised that the alleged facts, if established by investigation, constitute a violation of federal law.

The set-up of the Department places the Director of the Bureau immediately under the Attorney General. Below the Director are two assistant directors, one in charge of investigations and the other in charge of administration, identification, and training. Under the Assistant Director in charge of investigations are three divisions: Division One, Criminal Investigations; Division Two, Civil Investigations; and Division Three, Accounting Investigations. The other Assistant Director supervises Division Four, Administrative; Division Five, Identification; and Division Six, Inspection and Training. The Director has under his immediate control the 47 field offices, each under a special agent in charge. The appropriation for 1937 provided for 761 positions in Washington and 1,105 in the field. Of the field personnel 743 were special agents. The 1937 appropriation carried $1,181,500 for the Washington staff and $3,198,260 for the field personnel. The Bureau, therefore, is preponderantly a field organization; and the field force is primarily concerned with general crime control.

TRAINING

Visitors to the Bureau of Investigation—there are thousands yearly—are likely, at two or three points on their tour, to glimpse through an open door something that looks like a college class, a roomful of young men listening to a lecture. Privileged visitors are shown a sound-proof shooting gallery where marksmanship is practiced. For the maintenance of physical fitness, a well-equipped gymnasium is just around the corner.

In the recruitment of its personnel, the Bureau calls for youth, health, intelligence, good character, and, as a general rule, legal education. Most of the staff are either college students or college graduates. Eighty per cent are lawyers.

The special agents are not in the Civil Service; but they are under a merit system. Following their appointment, they are put through a 14-week training period at Washington with about 600 hours of class work, for the most part under experienced agents and officials of the Bureau. In addition to hearing lectures and seeing demonstrations, the student agents do practice work on hypothetical cases, pick up clues in a room where a corpse-like figure stretches on the floor, or surround a house where fugitives are supposed to be hidden. They are shown how to block highways, how to take fingerprints, how to preserve evidence, how to use tear-gas bombs and flares, and how to practice other techniques—especially how to shoot. The Bureau now requires its agents once every three months to qualify on the range as experts, sharpshooters, or marksmen, firing from the right and left hand and also from the hip. A special retraining period is given approximately every two years.

In connection with the training schools for special agents, the Bureau has conducted since July 1935 the National Police Academy for law-enforcement officials, covering administrative features of police work, discussion and consideration of every-day police problems, and practical training in enforcement duties. Sessions of the Academy are held concurrently with training schools for special agents; and the services of the training school faculty, as well as the services of visiting lecturers of national prominence who serve without pay, are made available to those in attendance at the Academy. The Bureau also renders assistance to local police training schools. Up to January 1937, the National Police Academy had graduated 81 representatives of local police departments.

The Director of the Bureau of Investigation explains the purpose of the Academy as follows:

It removes the argument for the establishment of a national police, which I think is impractical and undesirable. It gives to the local authorities the same control they have now, plus the benefit of additional training, and does not superimpose upon them any bureaucracy from Washington. Added to that fact, it bridges over that gap between local and federal law-enforcement officers, which is very important. It eliminates the jealousies that sometimes exist and helps to do away with friction which may develop.

We feel that if a man will come here and live with us for three months, go to Quantico and camp there for a week and take our gun training, that man will go back thoroughly conversant with our problems. He will be able to speak our language and we will be able to speak his language so that when the time comes that we have a kidnaping case in a particular city, let us say Boston, Captain Sheehan, who was our first outside trainee, would be designated as the officer to act as liaison between the local department and our agency, and we would in that way be able to get the assistance that we needed and accomplish certain things which we could not do otherwise.[7]

SUMMARY AND CONCLUSIONS

The federal government during the last eight years has given official cognizance to general criminality as a national problem and has taken definite steps to promote preventive and enforcement work. These federal steps have assumed the form partly of organized research, conference, and public addresses, and partly of definite administrative arrangements for co-ordinating and assisting state and local authorities in their law-enforcement efforts. These promotive, co-ordinative, and service efforts have tended to emanate from or find their location in the Department of Justice and, more specifically, in the Bureau of Investigation. If it is the policy of the federal government to continue to view crime as a national problem, and, in the future as in the recent past, to co-ordinate and assist so far as possible state and local law-enforcement agencies, logic would seem to dictate a centralization in the Department of Justice of all the *general* law-enforcement activities of the federal government. In the face of criminal elements, division of leadership or of responsibility is not desirable. Certain of such activities may be nominally or traditionally auxiliary to the functions of some department other than the Department of Justice; but, if they are essentially or predominantly *general* activities, they should be logically transferred to the Department of Justice.

The Bureau of Investigation is the only federal law-enforcement agency which is centrally equipped for co-operation with and assistance to other law-enforcement agencies, especially the local police departments. The

[7] Testimony of J. Edgar Hoover, the same, p. 82.

basic principle in the recent development and in the present organization and policy of the Bureau is to maintain in Washington an agency adequate for the co-ordination of the multiplicity of separate police forces throughout the country. Other federal law-enforcement units may be more successful in enlisting the co-operation of state and local officers; but the Bureau of Investigation operates on a plan of comprehensive and continuous co-operation. It has become in many respects a continuously operating service agency in the field of law-enforcement. But it is more than this: it is an operating agency in the field of general crime control; and it is, embryonically, a research and promotive organization. If there is to be further nationalization of crime control or any consolidation of federal law-enforcement agencies, it is to the Bureau of Investigation that functions will inevitably and logically be transferred. The heart of the problem probably lies in federal-state-local relationships. For the determination of sound policy in this connection, research is essential and a redirection of promotional effort may be necessary. But in this vital aspect of its problem, the Bureau, as we shall later point out, may find itself in a dilemma.

CHAPTER VI

THE SECRET SERVICE

It was said of the Holy Roman Empire that it was neither holy, nor Roman, nor an empire. Somewhat similarly, one might say of the United States Secret Service, that its functions are no secret, that it is not designed to be a *service* agency, except to the Treasury and related establishments, and that the inclusion of the term *United States* in its official title is somewhat misleading. As the then head of the Secret Service Division explained in 1935:[1]

> The duties of our service are clearly shown in law. We never go over the line into any other bureau's functions. We attend strictly to our own functions, and in the main the other investigative bureaus do the same thing. The Bureau of Investigation of the Department of Justice is authorized to deal with crime generally, but not to conflict with other investigative bureaus' operations specifically provided in law.
>
> They can deal with any violation of a federal statute, but they would not undertake, for instance, to investigate a case of counterfeiting or forgery of a government obligation or security, or any other of these functions specifically allotted to us. There is no conflict; there is no duplication of work; there is no overlapping of work.

The Secret Service is by no means wholly unaffected by overlapping, duplication, or conflict; but the problems presented by this agency are relatively clear cut.

JURISDICTION AND OVERLAPPING

The Secret Service Division enjoys practically exclusive jurisdiction over counterfeiting and forgery, in

[1] 74 Cong. 1 sess., *Treasury Department Appropriation Bill for 1936*, Hearings before H. Committee on Appropriations, pp. 241-42.

116   FEDERAL CRIME CONTROL

whatever administrative area these examples of clandes-
tine craftsmanship may be discovered. More specifically
the Secret Service shares with the Mint the detection of
debasement of coinage; with the Customs Bureau, prevention of importation of counterfeits and enforcement
of the Gold Reserve Act; with the Post Office inspectors,
jurisdiction over forgery of money orders and counterfeiting of postage stamps; with the Division of Disbursements, investigation of the forging of government pay
checks and frauds by contractors; with the Veterans'
Administration, activities directed against the forging
of adjusted service certificates and certain other perver-
sions of penmanship; and, with the Internal Revenue
Bureau, jurisdiction over counterfeiting of internal
revenue stamps. We have seen that at certain points the
Secret Service overlaps the Bureau of Investigation.

It is an important duty of the Secret Service, as it is
nominally of the Bureau of Investigation, to protect
the President, his family, and the President-elect. In the
discharge of this duty, members of the Secret Service
supervise itineraries, arrange with local officers for the
President's safety outside of Washington, accompany
him on trips, investigate crank letters, and exercise, in
general, a tactful but effective surveillance over all those
who come into contact with the Chief Executive. The
permanent police force, known as the White House Police, is placed by law under the control and supervision
of the Chief of the Secret Service. Threats against the
life of the President sent through the mails may by law
be investigated either by the Post Office inspectors or by
the Secret Service; and, if they are extortion threats, they
may be investigated also by the Bureau of Investigation.

The Secret Service is given general jurisdiction over
all offenses against laws relating to the Treasury De-

partment, and is required to perform any duties which may be delegated to the Division by the Secretary of the Treasury. Thus, the Division is, to some extent, a service agency for the entire Treasury Department, as well as for the President and his family, the Federal Deposit Insurance Corporation, the War Finance Corporation, the Farm Credit Administration, the Federal Farm Loan Board, the Veterans' Administration, the Works Progress Administration, and the Federal Reserve Board. In connection with the Works Progress Administration, for example, Secret Service agents investigate such matters as collusion of employees to defraud the government, deception or attempted deception by contractors, forgery, alteration or counterfeiting of checks, and padding of payrolls. Investigations under the Federal Farm Loan Act relate to such irregularities as false statements by applicants for loans, embezzlement or misapplication of moneys or credits by officials of the banks, false book-keeping entries, and attempted deception by examiners and others.

TRAINING

All permanent employees of the Secret Service Division have Civil Service status. An applicant for the examination must show that he possesses extended experience in high-grade investigative work requiring tact, judgment, resourcefulness, and initiative. The appointee is placed under specialized instruction for a week or two at the district headquarters to which he is assigned. An intensive specialized course of study is given at the Bureau of Engraving and Printing, the Office of the Chief in Washington, and the Mint in Philadelphia or other cities, relating to the manufacture of genuine obligations and securities, counterfeit money, the methods of counterfeiters, and the examination of questioned documents. According to the Chief of the Secret Service Division in 1936, the Secret Service agents in general "are not specialists. They are supposed to be able to investigate any criminal enterprise assigned to them."[2]

STATE RELATIONS

Various offenses within the jurisdiction of the Secret Service Division are also within the jurisdiction of the states. Overlapping is indicated by such designations as "Fraudulent Conversion," "Forgery," "Money," "Counterfeiting," and the like. The Division depends materially on the co-operation of police departments and other local law-enforcement agencies in the apprehension of criminals, raids on counterfeiting plants, protection of the President, and enforcement work of an emergency nature. In a number of cities, especially the larger ones, police detectives are said to be in daily attendance at the district offices of the Secret Service; and, in some, police officers are detailed to give their entire time to the work of this federal agency under the supervision of the Secret Service operatives in charge. This co-operation is not the result of any formal agreement, and it does not consist of an elaborate and continuous exchange of services, as is largely the case with the Bureau of Investigation. It is a kind of relationship that can not be statistically measured and it is not advertised; but it is said to be accorded to Secret Service agents everywhere whenever requested. The Division could not function as effectively as it does without the full co-operation of state and local agencies; and its officials believe that it would require a field personnel ten times as great as the present Secret

---

[2] 74 Cong. 2 sess., *Treasury Department Appropriation Bill for 1937*, Hearings before H. Committee on Appropriations, p. 583.

Service force if it were to operate without the assistance rendered by local agencies.

RELATIONS WITH OUTSIDE FEDERAL AGENCIES

Whenever in the course of their work Secret Service agents discover information relevant to the investigative duties of another law-enforcement unit, they are expected to turn the information over to the unit concerned. If, however, the different criminal activities in a case are so intermingled as to preclude a division of the investigative work, the agents of the interested units are supposed to work in co-operation until the conclusion of the case.

An example of overlapping jurisdictions and of steps taken to avoid duplication is offered by *Bulletin No. 389* issued by the Chief Inspector of the Post Office Department on September 15, 1936, which took notice of duplication of work by Post Office inspectors and Secret Service agents in connection with the loss or theft of mail containing government checks, followed by the forging and cashing of such checks. The bulletin provides that the postal investigation

. . . should proceed with the knowledge of local Secret Service authorities since that Service has jurisdiction over investigations of the forgery of government checks.

If the forgery was committed by other than a postal employee our investigation should be limited to the postal feature of the case with such information as might be of assistance to the Division of Secret Service concerning the forgery being communicated to representatives of that Service.

Where postal employees are chargeable with the forgery, it will be proper for inspectors to endeavor to make recovery from the forger but the question of prosecution for the forgery is, of course, for attention by the Secret Service.

A vivid instance of co-operation between the Secret

Service and the Post Office inspectors is recounted by the
Chief Inspector as follows:

Silver valued at $25,000,000 was moved from the United
States Mint at Philadephia to the Treasury Department in
Washington from July 29 to August 30, 1935, inclusive. Mail
trucks were driven inside the gates of the Mint, and the gates
closed. A convoy of city police and Secret Service agents waited
outside the gates, while Post Office inspectors directed the load-
ing of the trucks. Sacks, each weighing 60 pounds, were placed
on trucks which were wheeled into the mail trucks. When the
mail trucks were loaded, the gates were opened, the convoy
assumed positions, and the trucks drove through the streets of
Philadelphia to the railroad station, where the individual trucks
were wheeled into cars and unloaded. During this operation and
until departure of the train, railroad police and railway mail
service employees armed with machine guns stood guard.
Inspectors and railway mail service employees accompanied the
car to destination. Similar arrangements prevailed at Washington. The entire movement proceeded precisely on schedule and
without mishap.

Examples of co-operation between the Secret Service
Division and the Bureau of Investigation have been
mentioned previously.[3]

SET-UPS, TIE-UPS, AND RELATIONSHIPS WITHIN THE TREASURY

The Secret Service Division is directly under the Secretary of the Treasury. It depends on the General Counsel's Office of the Department for interpretations of laws
and for contact with the Attorney General, on the Con-
sulting Chemist of the Secretary's Office for experimental work in operations against counterfeiters and other
criminals, and on the Examiner of Questioned Documents for opinions on handwriting.

The Division has two branches, the Field Force and

[3] P. 100.

the White House Police. The Field Force is distributed among fifteen districts. In the headquarters office in Washington, the regular personnel in 1936 numbered fifteen. The permanent field force totaled 182. Of these, 142 were agents and forty were clerks or clerical assistants. The White House Police numbered sixty officers. The total amount appropriated for the Secret Service Division for 1937 was $1,053,610.

This agency renders a variety of services to different bureaus in the Treasury Department. In the main, such activities are classifiable as internal law-enforcement work, since they have to do largely with the inspection or supervision of buildings, equipment, personnel, and operations. Thus, the Bureau of Engraving and Printing, a Treasury agency, manufactures government paper currency, securities, and stamps. Perhaps nowhere else in the world would men and women be subjected to such overwhelming temptation, were it not for the safeguards and deterrents that constantly surround them. In this Bureau, Secret Service agents are responsible for the prevention of thefts. Investigations are made of "overages" and "shortages" and all other apparent discrepancies, so that the total daily output, less the spoilage, will check with the quantity of distinctive paper issued. Investigations are made of employees suspected of theft or mishandling and occasionally of persons who spread propaganda inimical to good discipline. Secret Service agents are expected to be familiar enough with the mechanical and manual operations of the Bureau to recommend when necessary more economical procedures or better protective devices. A watch is kept over the handling of moneys and stamps in the Bureau's vaults. The Federal Reserve vault contains about 3 billion dollars in negotiable notes. The Bureau has at all times approximately 11 billions in currency in course of handling. A portion of it is completed, while the remainder requires only some final process such as the addition of seal and numbers.

To the Register's Office of the Treasury, bonds come from the banks for exchange or cancellation. Some 445 employees are engaged in handling these securities; and the Secret Service is charged with preventing or investigating thefts and losses. To the Loans and Currency Division, coupon bonds come for registration, and registered bonds for exchange. About 2,200 clerks are engaged in these processes; and it is the duty of the Secret Service to see that no employee purloins a bond, either "on his own" or in collusion with someone outside.

In the Redemption Division of the Treasurer's Office, mutilated and soiled currency and securities, sent by individuals and banks, are received and redeemed. After an elaborate system of checking, the Division reports to the Secret Service any shortages that are revealed. Occasionally, a bank reports that some stated amount was forwarded to the Treasury but a smaller amount was shipped back. Investigations in such cases are made in the Treasury, the bank, or the shipping agency, or in all three, and must be made promptly before the thief, if there is one, covers his tracks. False claims for redemption are also submitted. Individuals send in fragments of notes, asking redemption at full value and submitting an affidavit relative to the destruction or loss of the missing portions. Later, the missing portions turn up with another request for redemption. If there is a willful attempt to defraud in such a case, the collection of evidence against the guilty person may involve considerable first-rate detective work. Opportunities for theft also occur in the destruction of worn and soiled bills, mutilated money and stamps, and currency spoiled in the process of manufacture.

Irregularities, questionable currency, and suspicious persons appearing in the Cashier's Office are attended to by the Secret Service. The mints and assay offices call upon the Secret Service for confidential investigations of their employees and of a variety of irregularities. For the Procurement Division, which does much of the federal government's purchasing, Secret Service agents look into the reputation, character, and financial standing of firms offering to bid. During the recent past, many investigations under the Gold Reserve and Silver Purchase Acts have been made relative to the nature of the operations of those licensed to deal in gold or silver, suspected hoarding of gold certificates, illegal exporting or importing of gold or silver, legitimacy of mining projects, and other aspects of mining operations. Such investigations have involved much travel, sometimes on snowshoes, in mountainous regions.

In the main Treasury building at Washington, about 3,000 employees are working. Apart from its administrative conduct, such a community daily creates situations which require investigation. Reported thefts of personal property must be investigated; for a sneak thief is not considered a proper person to be employed in the Treasury Department. Measures for the protection of the Department as a whole must be kept in constant and effective operation. Study and supervision must be given to the watch force, access to the building, security of the vaults, and the working of the alarm systems. It is also the duty of Secret Service agents to accompany and protect the trucks which carry payroll money from the Treaury vaults to the other government departments and establishments in Washington.

Apparently, the Secret Service Division has a closer working relationship with the operating units of the Treasury Department than with its law-enforcement units. The Alcohol Tax Unit has the same legal right as the Secret Service to investigate counterfeiting or misuse of liquor strip stamps. In practice the Unit makes the preliminary investigation and turns the information which it obtains over to the Secret Service. The Secret Service and the Coast Guard work together only occasionally. During the summer of 1936, the Coast Guard Cutter *Pontchartrain,* carrying Secret Service agents, helped guard the President during his vacation in Maine. The Coast Guard also furnished a boat at Houston, Texas, to carry Secret Service agents on a similar mission. From September 23 to October 18, 1936, a Coast Guard patrol boat and a speed boat worked with the Secret Service, investigating the activities of counterfeiters near New Rochelle, New York. The Customs Agency Service in 1936 rendered assistance to the Secret Service through the arrest of an individual wanted for forging government checks, through the submission of counterfeit coins and bills to Secret Service operatives, and through the furnishing of men and cars used in arresting offenders. Illegal exporting and importing of gold are within the cognizance of the Customs agents who seize and deliver to the Secret Service illegal reproductions of the currency, obligations, and securities of the United States.

The Treasury Department proposed early in 1936 to centralize its various law-enforcement units and activities. For this purpose, the Secret Service Division was to be reorganized so as to consist of five sections: a Liquor Enforcement Section, a Counterfeiting Section, a Customs Section, a Section of Personnel, and a Section of

Narcotics. The Coast Guard was not included; but the Secretary of the Treasury wished authority to detail to the enlarged Secret Service Division up to three commissioned officers of the Coast Guard. A bill to obtain these ends was introduced in Congress but failed of enactment. During the hearings before the Committee on Ways and Means, one member doubted "the advisability of reorganizing these bureaus under the name 'Secret Service.' The people identify the Secret Service with a particular purpose, the safety of the President."

"We do not like to have any secrecy about our legitimate activities. Personally I think the name is very, very objectionable."[4] Opposition also developed to the inclusion of the Bureau of Narcotics in the new organization.

ANALYSIS OF FUNCTIONS: CONCLUSIONS

Some of the functions of the Secret Service Division depend on the policy or discretion of the Secretary of the Treasury. In this class are investigations relating to the Treasury Department and the several branches under its control, co-ordination with other law-enforcement agencies in the Department, investigations of violations of the Gold Reserve Act, investigations to establish the responsibility of bidders on government contracts, supervision and safeguarding of the money-handling divisions of the Treasury Department, and the like. Other functions are specifically assigned by law. In this class are those activities which are the direct responsibility of the Secret Service Division and are presumably performed with a minimum of supervision by the Secretary and with little reference to Treasury policy. Such activi-

[4] 74 Cong. 2 sess., *Secret Service Reorganization Act*, Hearings before the H. Committee on Ways and Means, p. 17.

ties include the suppression of counterfeiting, protecting the President and his immediate family, and investigations under the Banking Act relating to irregularities within the Federal Deposit Insurance Corporation.

The Chief of the Division estimated in 1936 that counterfeiting cases were taking about 55 per cent of the time of Secret Service agents. The Division was established and charged with the detection, arrest, and prosecution of counterfeiters long before crime assumed its modern aspects. At that time, no doubt, the suppression of counterfeiting appeared an intrinsic feature of Treasury administration, rather than an integral part of general crime control. It is known now, however, that counterfeiters are likely to be all-round criminals. It appears that at least one out of three persons sentenced for counterfeiting has a previous criminal record of a serious nature. It could hardly be argued that these cases are so highly specialized as to require an agency distinct and apart from the general law-enforcement agency of the government. Any branch of criminal-law enforcement work is in a sense specialized; and the detection of counterfeiting is analogous to other work now done by the Bureau of Investigation. Counterfeiting is, of course, a "crime against the currency," and the maintenance of the integrity of the currency is traditionally held to be a responsibility of the Treasury Department. The detection of counterfeiters may be facilitated by contact with the Bureau of Engraving, the Mint, and possibly other branches of the Treasury Department; but, in the absence of information to the contrary, the location of anti-counterfeiting work in the Treasury Department does not seem indispensable either to the full efficiency of that work or to the proper administrative functioning of the Department.

Protection of the President, his family, and the President-elect is hardly a logical function of the Treasury Department. This duty is said to take about 12 per cent of the time of Secret Service agents. No reason is seen why this duty could not be performed by a unit of the Bureau of Investigation. Substantially the same duty is already assigned by law to that Bureau.

It is reported that Secret Service agents give about 8 per cent of their time to the investigation of offenses which are specifically placed by law within the jurisdiction of the Secret Service. The Bureau of Investigation is engaged in the investigation of similar offenses. In connection with the Federal Deposit Insurance Corporation questions have arisen concerning the respective jurisdictions of the Bureau of Investigation and the Secret Service, indicating the possibility in certain cases that the two agencies will either duplicate their investigations or fail to take any action at all.[5]

Nevertheless, a part of the work of the Secret Service Division seems to be, in the main, really auxiliary to Treasury administration or closely identified with the internal conditions and operations of the Department. Such is that done by direction of the Secretary; that which deals with violations of "other laws" relating to the Treasury Department; that involved in the guarding of Treasury buildings; police supervision of the Bureau of Engraving and Printing, the Register's Office, the Loans and Currency Division, and the Redemption Division; and that concerned with miscellaneous irregularities of Treasury personnel. It is understood that these activities which may be properly de-

[5] See Opinion of the Attorney General, *Jurisdiction of Secret Service Division, Treasury Department, under Sec. 12B of Federal Reserve Act,* June 30, 1936.

nominated auxiliary or internal take about 25 per cent
of the time of Secret Service agents, while those activities which are of the nature of general law-enforcement
or inter-agency service take about 75 per cent.

It would seem logical and practicable that a division
be made of the activities of the Secret Service and that
those activities which relate to counterfeiting, forgery,
protection of the President, and government agencies
outside the Treasury be transferred, with a proportion-
ate number of Secret Service personnel, to the Bureau
of Investigation.

CHAPTER VII

THE POST OFFICE INSPECTORS

The Post Office Department is socialized "big business." It is one of the largest of American public service enterprises. Its regular employees numbered on November 30, 1936 more than a quarter of a million. Measured by personnel, it is by far the largest of the civil departments of the federal government.

Postal revenue amounted in 1936 to about two-thirds of a billion dollars; expenditures were about three-quarters of a billion. Income and outgo are not the only money-handling features of the Post Office Department. The domestic and international money orders, issued in 1936, amounted to almost 2 billion dollars. The value of registered mail and parcel-post packages must have been as much, possibly more. The Postmaster General is also something of a banker. The total liabilities of the postal savings system on June 30, 1936 were more than a billion and a quarter.

The postal service blankets the entire country. In 1936, only 0.5 per cent of the Department's employees were stationed in Washington. Operations are decentralized among 45,000 post offices and numerous substations. Transportation and delivery of mail proceeds on foot and in railroad trains, airplanes, pneumatic tubes, automobiles, motor boats, and ships. The postal system is your next-door neighbor. It is in a constant service relationship with practically every individual in the country. Because we have grown up to view this service as a routine of daily living, we are little concerned with its vastness, its ramifications, and its fiduciary responsibilities. In such an enterprise, policy is not usually of major import; but good organization and efficient management are fundamental.

Though the Post Office Department performs services for other federal agencies, it is, on the whole, our most conspicuous example of unifunctionalism. Its work is homogeneous. It has one job, which it does, for the most part and at most times, with celerity and economy. Its task is not to meet national emergencies. It is, in the main, a constant load agency. To be sure, it is required at times, but not often, to do the unexpected; for example, when it was called upon a year or two ago to distribute and cash the veterans' adjusted compensation certificates. Neither is the work of the postal service seasonal, except for the annual Christmas rush, which can be and is fully anticipated. Superficially viewed, the postal service appears to be a changeless, or at least a very slowly changing, institution. But, as a matter of fact, if it is to function efficiently, it must be in constant process of adjustment. It must adapt itself to the growth of towns and cities, to the shifting of population, and to new transportation facilities, such as automobiles, trucks, and airplanes. Every day, it must absorb new personnel. When the forty-hour-week law was passed by Congress, the Post Office Department was forced to make quick changes in its work routines and labor shifts. To make adjustments, either gradually or quickly, in a vast and far-flung organization calls for experienced management at the center, armed with the results of expert studies in the field. Efficiency demands considerably more than nominal supervision and remote control. Frequent field inspections are indispensable.

But something more than resourceful management is required. In the postal service, honesty is as necessary as efficiency. In this machine, the parts are human; and occasionally a cog slips. Thefts and losses occur. Sometimes a postal employee is at fault; sometimes, an outsider; sometimes, an employee and an outsider working in collusion. The mails themselves are used to circulate obscenity, defraud the public, and commit crimes. When the postman delivers a package concealing counterfeit money, a bomb, or a poison, or an envelope containing a threat, an insult, or some other illegal communication, Uncle Sam becomes an accessory to the crime, unless he proceeds vigorously to do something about it. For the United States government insists that it shall monopolize the carrying of the mails. Its monopoly serves, not a class or a section, but the whole country and all the people. Its constituency or clientele is all inclusive. It is the government's peculiar responsibility, therefore, to preserve the "sanctity of the mails." If the postal service were unsafe or could be used with impunity by criminals, the service would be socially inefficient and socially uneconomical, even were it to show a substantial annual surplus. Well-played "politics," as well as ordinary morals and good business sense, demand that the nation's channels of communication should be kept free of hazards and pollution.

Consequently, the Post Office Department must have the aid of efficiency engineers, expert contrivers of operating economy, inspectors of office lay-outs, equipment, operations and accounts, and detectors of crime. These are now grouped in the Office of the Chief Inspector. The Post Office inspectors are the Department's eyes, ears, and long arm.

JURISDICTION AND FUNCTIONS

The general functions of the Post Office inspectors were stated by the Postmaster General in his 1935 report as follows:

Post Office inspectors are employed for the purpose of obtaining and supplying the Postmaster General and his assistants authentic and comprehensive information concerning the condition and needs of the postal service in every part of the country, and for the purpose of enabling the Postmaster General to deal with mail losses, mail depredations, and all other criminal offenses arising under the postal laws.

The investigations of Post Office inspectors can be broadly grouped under two general headings; namely, the predominantly criminal and the non-criminal. The non-criminal investigations are those dealing with postal organization, procedure, personnel needs, sites, quarters, equipment, and the fitness for retention in the service of the postal personnel.[1]

More specifically, the internal or non-criminal activities of the Inspector include the following: to act as the special representative of the Postmaster General, and as such to stand in a supervisory relationship toward postmasters, postal employees, and contractors; to keep the Department advised of the condition and needs of the postal service; to make surveys to be used as bases for formulating sound postal policies; to deal with service emergencies within the postal system; to instruct and advise persons connected with the postal system with reference to the application of departmental regulations; to conduct systematic inspections and audits of post offices; to supervise the induction into office of postmasters at presidential offices; to investigate the advisability of proposed consolidations of rural routes; and to make investigations relative to the negotiation of leases, reduction of rents, improvement in postal quarters not owned

[1] P. 70.

by the government, selection of sites for federal buildings, negotiations for purchase of sites, determination of space and equipment required or alterations needed, rearrangement of Star routes, protection of registered mail and funds at particular points, violations of second-class mailing privileges, misuse of franking privilege, Navy mail clerks' accounts, and other matters.

The above-mentioned activities are illustrative rather than inclusive. The activities of the inspectors are diversified. Anything which affects the postal service or concerns the Postmaster General may be the subject of an inspector's assignment.

In the field of criminal-law enforcement, the Post Office inspectors, generally speaking, have jurisdiction over all acts which involve wrongful use of postal facilities, mail losses, mail depredations, and other offenses arising under the postal laws. Within this limited sphere, their jurisdiction runs the whole gamut of criminality: assaults, robberies, burglaries, thefts, embezzlements, frauds, forgeries, counterfeiting, impersonation, lotteries, obscenity, extortion, treason, and traffic in poisons, narcotics, alcohol, contraceptives, firearms, explosives, and inflammables.

Altogether, according to the Chief Inspector, 145 different kinds of investigations are made regularly.

SET-UPS AND TIE-UPS

The Office of the Chief Inspector is directly under the Postmaster General and serves the entire postal organization. There is no other inspectional or enforcement unit in the Department.

A close working relationship exists between the Office of the Chief Inspector and the Office of the Solicitor. The latter office adjudicates the claims of private individuals arising from losses or damages and of postmasters on account of losses by fire, burglary, or other casualty. Prior to adjudication, these claims are investigated by the inspectors. The Solicitor decides whether matter is obscene, scurrilous, or extortionate.

Fraud orders are issued by the Postmaster General on the recommendation of the Solicitor. In a fraud case, the Department acts as a quasi-judicial authority. For example, the Ritholy optical case came to the Solicitor's Office on a report from the Chief Inspector. An attorney

... examined the report of the inspector and the exhibits that it was necessary to see to verify the findings of the inspector. When he had made up his mind that a *prima-facie* case of fraud was developed, he drew up a memorandum calling upon the respondents to show cause why a fraud order should not issue. ... At the same time the Chief Inspector's Office was notified of the date set for the matter so the inspector could come in and be heard. ...

On the date finally set the parties appeared in the office of the Solicitor. We have a regular hearing room for that purpose. The attorney for the Post Office Department had given thought to what he might need in the way of expert advice. He contacted the Bureau of Standards and secured the co-operation of the expert on optics and lenses out there, a very capable man. ... The attorney also procured the services of an optician from the Public Health Service. ... We had specialists from the government service, as well as some in private practice, to testify in the case also. ... I think it took the government about a week to present its case, the exhibits being numerous and the witnesses many.

The inspector, representing himself as somebody needing glasses, wrote the respondent under different names on dozens of different occasions and sent money for spectacles. Witnesses, used as guinea pigs, so to speak, also testified as to results of dealings with respondent. After the government had put in its evidence, the attorney for respondent, of course, cross-examined all our witnesses. There followed redirect examination by government counsel. Then the respondent put in its case. It put on experts, or alleged experts, and the attorney for the government cross-examined them. . . .

Then the attorney who tried it and the officer who heard it got together and agreed on the findings of fact and conclusions. That was prepared in the form of a memorandum to the Postmaster General. . . . When the Postmaster General signed the order it was published in the *Daily Bulletin*, and the particular postmaster involved . . . was given a special letter and copy of the order. From that time on the respondent receives no mail except official penalty mail or franked mail. Then, in some cases there is a court proceeding that follows. The respondent, not satisfied with the action the Department has taken, may apply to a federal court for an injunction. . . .[2]

In the present organization of the Chief Inspector's Office, the Chief Inspector and the Assistant Chief Inspector have under their immediate supervision the Library, the Superintendent of the Departmental Office, and the fifteen field divisions. Under the Superintendent of the Departmental Office are the Accounting Section and two assistant superintendents. One assistant superintendent has under him the Service Section, the Miscellaneous Section, the Fraud Section, the Criminal Investigation Section, and the Mail and Supply Section. The other has charge of the Public Funds Collection Section, the Mail Matter Collection Section, the Depredation Section, and the Foreign Section.

The duties of four of these sections should be carefully noted. Those of the Fraud Section are to receive and examine complaints relative to the use of the mails for alleged fraudulent purposes, and the mailing of lottery and other prohibited matter. The Criminal Investigation Section receives and examines complaints relative to the mailing of obscene, scurrilous, and defamatory

[2] 75 Cong. 1 sess., *Post Office Department Appropriation Bill for 1938*, Hearings before H. Committee on Appropriations, pp. 102-03.

matter, poisons, explosives, inflammables, narcotics, intoxicants, firearms, and letters of extortion. It examines claims for reward for the arrest and conviction of postal-law violators, and maintains criminal records and indexes. The Depredation Section handles complaints and inquiries relative to postal robberies, fires, wrecks, accidents, and depredations upon the domestic mails, including loss, rifling, damage, wrong delivery, and interception. The Foreign Section is concerned with the disposition of and depredations upon the international mails, including loss, rifling, damage, delay, and wrong delivery.

It was suggested as long ago as 1853 that the inspectors be divided into two classes: one to perform service functions and the other to handle matters arising from mail depredations. An examination of the present organization of the Chief Inspector's Office shows that the idea of dividing the functions of the Office into two classes has had some influence; but the organization does not now embody any clear-cut differentiation of the two classes of functions. It is evidently difficult to accomplish in organization and operations any clear-cut distinction between criminal and non-criminal investigations.

TRAINING

All Post Office inspectors, including the Chief Inspector, are under Civil Service. In order to qualify for examination, an applicant must have had at least four years' experience in the postal service. Appointments are apportioned among the states according to population and are also said to be divided between the two major political parties. Post-entry training is wholly individual. The new appointee is assigned to an experienced inspector who acts as instructor. There is no fixed period of training; but six months is the usual probationary period. All inspectors have the same basic training and each is expected to be competent to handle any kind of investigation. If during the course of his career, it becomes apparent that an inspector is especially qualified for a particular line of work, he may be assigned for some time to a field of activity in which that kind of work predominates. But any inspector so assigned is available for and intermittently performs other kinds of work. The fact that the appointment of Post Office inspectors is of the nature of a promotion from other branches of the postal service would seem to indicate a conviction that their qualifications should be preponderantly for internal and auxiliary enforcement.

OVERLAPPING AND CO-OPERATION

Inevitably, the Post Office inspectors overlap from time to time the Bureau of Investigation, the Secret Service, the Customs Agency Service, the Bureau of Narcotics, the Alcohol Tax Unit, the Food and Drug Administration, the Securities and Exchange Commission, and other federal agencies.

For example, a fraudulent use of the mails, particularly a fraudulent sale of securities or sale of worthless stock, may involve a violation of laws enforced by the Securities and Exchange Commission. In such cases, the Chief Inspector has ruled:

When the matter appears to be one in which both the Securities and Exchange Commission and the Post Office Department have jurisdiction there should be co-operation between the representatives of both departments and the inspector should confer with the local representative of the Securities and Exchange Commission.

If the Post Office Department lacks jurisdiction, the evidence in that Department is turned over to the Securities and Exchange Commission.

A fraudulent use of the mails, if it involves the sale of cure-alls or other nostrums or quack treatments, may fall within the jurisdiction of the Food and Drug Administration. If it constitutes an illegitimate trade practice, it will probably be of interest to the Federal Trade Commission; and, if the trade practice happens to be in the alcohol industry, the Federal Alcohol Administration may enter the picture.

Importation from foreign countries by common carrier of lottery or obscene material is a matter over which the Customs Bureau may exercise jurisdiction. When such materials are made the subject of interstate shipments by common carrier, the Bureau of Investigation and the Interstate Commerce Commission also may be interested. Mailing of threats against the President is a matter for joint investigation by the Post Office inspectors and the Secret Service Division. When untaxpaid alcoholic liquor is sent through the mails, both the Post Office Inspection Service and the Alcohol Tax Unit are involved. When narcotic drugs are mailed, the Post Office inspectors divide jurisdiction with the Bureau of Narcotics. Other cases of overlapping, co-operation, or conflict, with particular reference to the Bureau of Investigation and the Secret Service, have been referred to in preceding chapters.[3]

For technical assistance in handwriting and optical matters, the inspectors depend on the Bureau of Standards; and for chemical analyses on the Department of Agriculture. The Forest Service has helped in at least one postal case, much as it did in the Hauptmann kid-

[3] See pp. 101-02, 104-05, 119-20.

naping case. The postal case involved the mailing of bombs. "They took the wood of the box in which these bombs were placed, and . . . established the fact that a piece of wood found in the cellar of this man was from the same piece of wood used in the box."[4]

In general, like other agencies, the Post Office Department expresses its desire "to foster the enforcement of all of the laws of the United States, and when information comes into the hands of an inspector which indicates a violation of any federal law proper co-operation should be extended to the government official having jurisdiction."[5] The Chief Inspector's Office has a definite co-ordinative arrangement, either formal or informal, with the Securities and Exchange Commission, the Federal Trade Commission, the Federal Communications Commission, the Bureau of Investigation, the Secret Service, the Bureau of Narcotics, the Food and Drug Administration, the Civil Service Commission, and the Intelligence Unit of the Bureau of Internal Revenue. The Post Office inspectors receive numerous requests from other agencies for tracing of mail. During a recent twelve-month period, the office in New York City received 665 such requests. Of these, 102 were from the Bureau of Internal Revenue, 52 from the Bureau of Investigation, 42 from the Immigration and Naturalization Service, and 41 from the Passport Service.

In their internal enforcement work, the Post Office inspectors have no significant relations with state and local authorities. With respect to criminal violations of the postal laws, co-operation with such authorities is essential and is, in practice, continuous and mutually help-

[4] *Post Office Department Appropriation Bill for 1938*, Hearings, p. 153.
[5] *Post Office Department Miscellaneous Bulletin No. 99.*

ful. Of the 665 requests for mail tracings mentioned
above, 332 came from state and local agencies.

ANALYSIS OF FUNCTIONS: CONCLUSIONS

Historically, and in large part actually, the Office of
the Chief Inspector is an essential instrumentality and an
integral feature of departmental administration. In the
performance of their internal inspectional work, the inspectors act as an essential and inseparable service arm
of the Post Office Department. In addition to their internal administrative inspections, however, they have,
as we have seen, other duties which may be considered
either as loosely auxiliary to the operations of the Post
Office Department or as analogous to general law-enforcement work. If it would be logical and advantageous
to transfer certain functions of the Secret Service to the
Bureau of Investigation, the arguments would appear
quite as strong for transferring to the same Bureau the
general law-enforcement functions of the Post Office
inspectors; for example, those involving robberies, burglaries, thefts, frauds, obscenity, counterfeiting, forgery,
assaults, and arson. Indeed, these so-called postal crimes
and depredations seem to overlap the jurisdiction of the
Bureau of Investigation more decidedly than do those
offenses which are now handled by the Secret Service;
and postal crimes seem to be just as closely linked with
the general problem of criminality as are counterfeiting
and forgery. But, before we come to a definite decision,
we must ask and answer two questions: Would it be possible and beneficial to separate administratively the criminal investigative work of the Post Office inspectors from
their non-criminal duties? Is it possible and practicable
to divide the personnel now engaged in the two classes
of work?

It has been repeatedly emphasized by postmasters general that the work of the inspectors relates predominantly to internal administration rather than to the detection and apprehension of criminals. It is asserted by Department officials that

Post Office inspectors are essentially postal specialists and regularly in close contact with all of the various postal operations. They are expected to possess, and, as a whole, do possess expert knowledge on postal matters. . . .

As we have seen, the inspectors are appointed from the ranks of the postal personnel. The following excerpts from the House hearings illustrate the varied nature of the criminal investigations undertaken by the inspectors:

The criminal investigations are not of a uniform type but cover an extremely varied field. The inspector investigating a fraud case must deal with the suave, educated, well-trained director of gigantic business enterprises, who often holds a respected and powerful place in the business community until his dishonesty is exposed as a result of the inspector's work. The inspector investigating the hold-up and robbery of a mail train or post-office truck must cope with the shrewd and oft-times politically entrenched underworld gangster, reckless of human life and often represented by able and unscrupulous members of the legal profession. An inspector investigating the mailing of an infernal machine is obliged to cope with the vagaries of a mind stimulated to ingenuity through malice inspired by some real or fancied grievance. In the investigation of the embezzlement of government funds and mail matter, the inspector deals with the lives of postal employees who, yielding to temptation, have fallen into habits of dishonesty which cost them their standing in their communities and bring disaster and suffering on their innocent families.[6]

It is common knowledge that many "outside" crimes have been handled with marked success by the Post

[6] 74 Cong. 2 sess., *Post Office Department Appropriation Bill for 1937*, Hearings before H. Committee on Appropriations, p. 138.

Office inspectors. Their qualifications, experience, and training, however, would not seem, in general, particularly appropriate for general criminal-law investigative work.

The percentage of time devoted to criminal investigations by the Post Office inspectors varies from year to year; and in any one year, it cannot be precisely determined. With reference to the situation in 1935, the following excerpt from the House hearings is interesting:

Mr. Ludlow: What would be the relative proportion of your work as between running down violations—

Mr. Aldrich: You mean as between the conducting of examinations and violations of the postal laws?

Mr. Ludlow: I mean between what you might call the criminal branch and the administrative branch.

Mr. Aldrich: The time put in in investigating, the time spent at court, and that would include time spent before grand juries, and conferring with United States attorneys—we would lump that all in and it would take about 30 per cent of our time. That would include everything relating to a violation of law, and the time spent in going to court. Seventy per cent of our business really relates to postal engineering, and the operating and management of the Post Office.[7]

During the fiscal year 1936, the Chief Inspector estimates that 35 per cent of the time of his personnel was given to criminal investigations. It is his estimate also that about 60 per cent of the complaints in criminal cases originate within the postal service; and in most, if not all, of the criminal cases, a portion of the evidence and some of the investigative operations are located inside the postal service. On the other hand, the statistics issued by his office indicate that a high percentage of the persons arrested for postal crimes, in the categories of crime

[7] The same, p. 152.

usually associated with general law enforcement, were persons outside the service.

Let us understand, so far as possible, in what manner and to what extent the so-called postal crimes and their investigation are linked with the internal operations of the Department. We shall let the Chief Inspector himself furnish most of the testimony. On the general problem, he says:

The criminal cases handled by inspectors are not a distinct class. The criminal features are inextricably interwoven with the administrative problems of the postal service.

For example, in the inspection of post offices, which is primarily an accounting and efficiency measuring activity, embezzlements are discovered and falsification of records disclosed; in the investigation of fraudulent use of the mails, while the primary object is to obtain information to enable the Postmaster General to determine whether matter should be admitted to or excluded from the mails, criminal elements are found and the inspector prepares the case for trial by the United States attorney, without additional expense. The investigation of depredations on the mails at first glance may appear to be purely criminal, but in every such case a large proportion of the effort of the inspector goes into a careful scrutiny of the internal operating conditions of the postal service at the point of loss; the character of supervision, the suitability and arrangement of postal equipment and working conditions, the fitness of employees, and the accuracy of the records kept are studied in connection with a view to devising safeguards against recurrences and removing from employees as well as from professional criminals the opportunity and the temptation to steal.

The Post Office Inspection Service made 130 arrests for robbery in 1936. The hold-up of a mail train at Rondout, Illinois, involved a loss of $2,050,000 in registered mail. As the Chief Inspector explains it:

The operations involved in the detection and apprehension of the persons responsible for this offense included a technical study of the manner in which registered mail was actually handled on that train and between the various post offices of origin and the train; a study of the schedules and rules under which the mail was due to have been handled; and an investigation of the standing, character, and habits of all postal employees who might under the organization and procedure have been in a position to know or obtain advance information as to the date and manner of the shipments. It was necessary also to contact through postal channels the senders of the 2,188 pieces of registered mail stolen to verify the fact of mailing, and ascertain accurately the contents. This was necessary alike to the detection of the offenders and the adjudication of claims for indemnity. Later, as securities stolen in the hold-up were negotiated, it was necessary not only to trace them through previous holders to ascertain the identity of the persons attempting to realize on the fruits of the robbery but also to identify the individual securities with the various registered letters from which they had been taken with a view to their restoration to the sender and the securing of refunds for indemnities paid by the Department for the loss of the mail. These operations related entirely to the internal affairs of the Post Office Department; at the same time these activities were an integral part of the operations involved in the detection and apprehension of the guilty persons.

The inspectors made 517 arrests for burglary in 1936. In most of these, the losses included government funds, stamps, blank money order forms, and mail matter. Investigation involved an audit of the postmasters' accounts, determination of the quantity and serial numbers of the stolen money order forms, and notification of all postmasters and others to prevent cashing of money orders bearing such numbers. Correspondence was necessary with the senders and addressees of missing mail. Still other investigative activities were internal; and the Chief Inspector believes that

. . . an attempt to separate these phases of the same investigation between different classes of investigators would produce an inefficiency and a duplication of work and of expense which does not now exist.

According to the Chief Inspector, nearly 300,000 complaints are made yearly concerning loss and rifling of unregistered letters and parcels. Prior to investigation, he says,

. . . it is usually impossible to surmise, much less to know, whether the loss was caused by the dereliction of a post-office clerk, a railway postal clerk, a letter carrier, or a hall letter box thief. To confer upon one set of investigators the investigation of losses occurring in post offices and upon another the investigation of losses from letter boxes would give rise to an overlapping and conflict of effort perhaps without parallel in the federal service.[8]

No doubt exists that most postal crimes and their investigation show both internal and external aspects. It might also be impracticable, as a general rule, to assign the internal investigation to one set of operatives and the external to another. In many instances, however, it might be feasible and economical for the internal auditing and checking to be done by the Post Office inspectors, the remainder of the work to be done by the Bureau of Investigation.

There appears to be no compelling reason why an investigation in a post office should not be done by an agency outside the Post Office Department. According to the Chief Inspector, the post-office hold-ups "are mostly in small post offices and contract stations. These people go into drug stores where we have post offices and they will go in there when the clerk in charge of the office or station is going to count the funds and put them away, and they get the funds generally at the point of a

[8] The statements quoted above are taken from a letter from the Chief Inspector to The Brookings Institution, dated Jan. 13, 1937.

gun. . . ."[9] To be sure, the Postmaster General is held responsible for the "sanctity of the mails"; but this responsibility is not his alone. It appertains to the entire federal government. It would seem that a competent federal agency outside the Post Office Department could be depended upon, quite as fully as the Post Office inspectors, to observe and preserve the sanctity of the mails. The Postmaster General is, and should be, held responsible for the honest and efficient operation of the postal service; but this responsibility would not be seriously impaired if certain postal crimes were handled by another federal agency. Other federal departments and establishments depend on outside agencies, partly or wholly, for enforcement service. Hotels, railroads, and insurance companies employ detectives; but these operatives usually deal with relatively narrow and mostly "inside" cases, and do not assume exclusive responsibility for every irregularity that originates in or touches their respective institutions. My home is my castle; and generally speaking, I am responsible for what happens in it; but, when a burglar has carried away my silver, I do not stand on my dignity or presume self-sufficiency; I call in the police.

As a matter of fact, the Post Office inspectors already share their jurisdiction with other law-enforcement agencies, including the Bureau of Investigation; and the inspectors are called upon at present to co-operate with such agencies. The Bureau of Investigation now handles extortion threats sent through the mails; the Bureau, it is understood, makes all accounting investigations in mail fraud cases; and the inspectors supply mail tracings to other law-enforcement agencies.

[9] *Post Office Department Appropriation Bill for 1938*, Hearings, p. 143.

Notwithstanding the interweaving of the internal and the external, it appears that in many criminal cases investigated by the inspectors, the evidence and the investigative operations are located predominantly outside the postal service and call, not so much for postal specialists, as for men trained in detective and general criminal-law enforcement work. This would be true, one would assume, of many, though probably not all, post-office burglaries, mail robberies, and thefts from mail receptacles. Indeed, even now all such crimes are not and can not be handled by the inspectors. In many cases, they are handled and can probably be better handled by local law-enforcement officers. The Chief Inspector estimates that nearly 300,000 complaints are made yearly concerning loss and rifling of unregistered letters and parcels. Yet, the total number of cases in all categories issued to the inspectors in 1936 numbered only 109,752; and the cases issued which involved loss and rifling of unregistered letters and parcels could not have exceeded 35,000 and were probably much fewer. The inspectors made only 1,365 arrests for theft and rifling of mail. One of several conclusions is possible: that the Chief Inspector's estimate of total complaints was exaggerated, that most of the complaints were unfounded, that the efforts of the inspectors were almost a total failure, or that the bulk of enforcement work was done by local police agencies.[10]

The investigation of such matters as fraudulent use of the mails and the sending of objectionable matter through the mails is not confined rigidly within the bounds of the postal service. It is probable that many such cases, though originating in connection with the postal service, possess,

[10] The figures used above are derived from letter of the Chief Inspector, Jan. 13, 1937; and *Post Office Department Appropriation Bill for 1938*, Hearings, pp. 137-39.

from the point of origin, not much more of a postal character than an ordinary murder or kidnaping. The persons who commit post-office and train robberies are frequently the same as the perpetrators of bank robberies. For example, a group attempting the burglary of a post office at Dendron, Virginia were said to be responsible for more than forty burglaries in the eastern sections of Virginia and North Carolina. Alvin Karpis was both a kidnaper and a mail robber. But why have two different federal agencies pursuing him?

It is believed that jurisdiction over most, if not all, of the general "postal" crimes should be transferred to the Bureau of Investigation. The offenses which seem appropriate for transfer would include: theft and rifling of mail; burglaries and burnings of post offices, stations, and other mail repositories; hold-ups and robberies of letter carriers, mail trucks, and mail trains; mailing of obscene matter, of extortion letters, and of poison, inflammables, explosives, alcohol, narcotics, and other prohibited substances; and use of the mails to defraud or for the promotion of lotteries. It may be true that not more than a quarter or a third of the work and personnel of the Post Office Inspection Service could be practically transferred; but there is some reason to believe that, because of the preponderance at present of internal inspectional work, the criminal portion of its work tends to be neglected. The suggested transfer, if carried out, will not diminish the need of co-operation between the Post Office Department and the Department of Justice in criminal-law enforcement work. On the contrary, a reorganization of the kind suggested would increase the number of offenses within the jurisdiction of the Department of Justice which are discovered in or by the Post Office Department; and the Bureau of Investigation would have greater need than at present for the co-operation of the Post Office inspectors in the obtaining of evidence available only within the postal service.

Matters which are transferred from the Post Office inspectors to the Bureau of Investigation should, so far as practicable, be transferred also from the Solicitor's Office of the Post Office Department to the legal branches of the Department of Justice. If it were not practicable to place in the latter Department the legal and quasi-judicial work preliminary to the issuance of fraud orders, such work could be kept where it now is; and the agents of the Bureau of Investigation would maintain in fraud cases much the same relationship with the Solicitor of the Post Office Department that they now maintain in other cases with attorneys of the Department of Justice and the district attorneys.

Substantially the same recommendation for a reallocation of the work of the inspectors was made by the Postmaster General in his annual report for 1920-21, based on a study made by a commission consisting of the Chief Inspector, the Solicitor of the Department, and a group of outside experts. This commission divided the functions of the inspectors into three groups: one to be assigned to the Bureau of Investigation; one to be retained by the Post Office Inspection Service; and the third to be handled in co-operation by the two agencies. It was the commission's opinion that if activities were thus reallocated, losses from mail depredations would be "very materially reduced," and the division of Post Office inspectors would be able to "bring about a more effective and efficient administration of the postal service by giving attention to a great volume of business not now promptly performed solely because of the inadequacy of its force."[11]

[11] *Annual Report of the Postmaster General*, fiscal year ended June 30, 1921, pp 119-22.

CHAPTER VIII

THE MARITIME POLICE

When the Great Administrator undertook the first sweeping reorganization of all time and transformed Chaos into Cosmos, He is said to have issued the following instruction: "Let the waters under the heaven be gathered together unto one place, and let the dry land appear." When this reallocation was accomplished, He took up matters of terminology. He "called the dry land Earth; and the gathering together of the waters called he Seas: and God saw that it was good."[1] Water, super-abundant and eternally restless, is an immense fact in history, science, and civilization. In public administration, it is both a problem and a force. The conditions associated with water—or with the lack of it—have from the earliest times called for social co-operation. Government seeks to control and utilize its interior water resources; and one of its age-old duties has been to look outward on the seas, guard its coasts, protect its ships from storms, scrutinize those who enter and leave the ports, regulate commerce and navigation, and gather toll from goods, persons, and ships. Byron exclaimed that man's control stops at the shores. Perhaps partisanship does (sometimes) but control does not.

Naturally, public administration is, for the most part, organized for operations on dry land, for that is where the population itself resides and, in the main, functions. On dry land, administration is a fairly pliant thing; and it can be quite readily divided and subdivided according to such factors as subject matter, activities, objectives,

[1] *Genesis*, Chap. I.

areas, and population groups. A relatively logical organization on land is made easy by the fact that transportation facilities are numerous, flexible, largely individual, and relatively cheap. On the water and especially
on the high seas, the determinant of organization is not
so much its subject matter, its function, or its objective,
as it is the medium in which it must operate and the basic
transport equipment which it must use. Ships are not
individual but group facilities. Vessels and crews are
technical and expensive instruments. So long as it is
necessary to maintain and operate them, it is economical
to keep them as busy as possible. Out of these obvious
facts, the United States Coast Guard has emerged, and
its peculiar rôle in law enforcement has taken tangible
form. On the seas and in peace, it serves as the eyes and
ears and long arm of the federal government. In war, it
joins the Navy.

ENFORCEMENT JURISDICTION AND OVERLAPPING

In the jurisdiction of the Coast Guard, overlapping is
the rule rather than the exception. In fact, the Coast
Guard is on the sea what a really consolidated law-
enforcement agency would be on land. Its specifically
granted jurisdiction covers smuggling and other violations of the customs laws, all of which are naturally within the purview of the Customs Bureau. Other laws or
regulations which are enforced by the Coast Guard are
listed below, and the agencies overlapped are indicated
in parentheses:

Navigation (Bureau of Customs and Bureau of Marine Inspection and Navigation, Commerce Department. Apparently
also the United States Maritime Commission).

Anchorage of vessels and oil pollution (Corps of Engineers,
War Department).

Regattas and marine parades (Department of Commerce).

Alaskan fisheries, fisheries on the high seas, and sponge fishing (Bureau of Fisheries, Department of Commerce).

Immigration (Immigration and Naturalization Service, Department of Labor).

Quarantine (Public Health Service, Treasury Department).

Neutrality (State Department, Bureau of Customs, Treasury Department, and Bureau of Investigation, Department of Justice).

Mutinies on merchant vessels (Department of Justice).

An act approved June 22, 1936 assigned to the Coast Guard general criminal-law enforcement powers, authorizing commissioned, warrant, and petty officers of the Guard:

. . . to make inquiries, examinations, inspections, searches, seizures, and arrests upon the high seas and the navigable waters of the United States, its territories, and possessions, except the Philippine Islands, for the prevention, detection, and suppression of violations of laws of the United States.[2]

When acting under the authority of this act, the officers of the Coast Guard are deemed "to be acting as agents of the particular executive department or independent establishment charged with the administration of the particular law"; and they are subject "to all the rules and regulations promulgated by such department or independent establishment with respect to the enforcement of that law." Within this general jurisdiction, therefore, the Coast Guard overlaps all other federal agencies that are charged with either general or specific law-enforcement duties.

Contrasting with the federal land agencies already discussed, the Coast Guard, so far as its enforcement

[2] This general authority does not extend to the "inland waters" of the United States, other than the Great Lakes and their connecting waters, "inland waters" being construed not to include "harbors, bays, sounds, roadsteads, and like bodies of water along the coasts of the United States, its territories and possessions, and shores of the Great Lakes."

operations are concerned, acts largely as a patrol force. It has its "intelligence" officers, to be sure; and Coast Guard boats are frequently engaged in the trailing or pursuit of suspected craft. For example, the present so-called "drive" on the illicit narcotic trade is expected to last for some years. As the Commandant of the Coast Guard explains it:

It is the plan that the Coast Guard will trail vessels from the Orient, both into port and out of port. They also trail them from port to port. A vessel at Seattle unloads a part of its cargo and goes on to Tacoma and unloads a part of its cargo, and then goes possibly to Bellingham and up to Vancouver. While in the waters of Puget Sound, we endeavor to keep that vessel constantly under surveillance to see that no narcotic packages are thrown overboard. . . .[3]

But the deterrent and preventive function of the Coast Guard is probably much more important than its detective and apprehension activities. If no smuggler were actually caught by this agency, it would still be engaged, and necessarily engaged, in anti-smuggling operations; for in the absence of the Coast Guard or a similar organization, the coasts would be left wide open to smugglers and smuggling would greatly increase. A Coast Guard boat acts much like a policeman on his beat, who, if his suspicions are aroused, will stop and question you and, if they are verified, will arrest you. Therefore, following the passage of the act of June 22, 1936, which in effect assigned general law-enforcement jurisdiction on the seas to the Coast Guard, this agency instituted a more extensive boarding campaign. During the months of July, August, and September, 1936, coast guardsmen are said to have boarded over 20,000 vessels, reported over 2,000 for violations of law, and seized six.

[3] 75 Cong. 1 sess., *Treasury Department Appropriation Bill for 1938,* Hearings before H. Committee on Appropriations, p. 616.

SAFETY WORK

While the primary function of the Coast Guard is the suppression of smuggling and related law-enforcement work, its function of saving life and property and rendering general assistance to shipping is almost equally important. The Coast Guard is made by law the maritime life-saving and protective arm of the federal government. Its duty, according to law, is to save life and property, to assist vessels in distress, to give relief and assistance on the Mississippi and Ohio Rivers and their tributaries in times of flood, to destroy and remove wrecks, derelicts, or other dangers to navigation, to maintain a service of ice observation and ice patrol in the North Atlantic Ocean, to extend medical and surgical aid to United States vessels engaged in deep-sea fishing, and to care for and transport shipwrecked and destitute persons. The Coast Guard is also charged with examining merchant seamen for certificates as lifeboatmen and with the collection and compilation of statistics of marine disasters. During the Ohio Valley floods in January 1937, the Coast Guard sent to that area about 1,300 men, over 260 boats, several planes and trucks, and a number of portable radio sets.

Life saving and rescue work is done not only from the shore stations and by and from small boats but also, near the shore and out at sea, by the largest vessels. Coast Guard airplanes also do this work. They take ill or injured persons from vessels at sea, carry medical supplies to ships and to isolated victims of storms and floods, and warn commercial and pleasure craft which lack radio facilities of approaching storms. After the hurricane which swept the Atlantic coast from Florida to New Jersey in September 1936, Coast Guard planes made a quick survey of the coast; and their reports enabled the

authorities to dispatch relief immediately to the points
where it was urgently needed.

MILITARY FUNCTIONS

Although the Coast Guard is required by law to operate under the Treasury Department in time of peace, it
constitutes "a part of the military forces of the United
States" and must "operate as a part of the Navy, subject
to the orders of the Secretary of the Navy, in time of
war or when the President shall so direct." Accordingly,
the Coast Guard must keep prepared to serve, when
necessary, as a part of the Navy. These preparatory activities are in part an inherent feature of the peace-time
organization and work of the Coast Guard and are in
part performed concurrently with its normal work. It is
maintained by Coast Guard officials that military organization and discipline are well adapted to a maritime law-
enforcement agency; and they state that military training, including target practice with small arms and short-
range battle practice with naval guns, interferes but little
with the major peace-time duties of the Coast Guard.
Nor do naval requirements regarding ship construction
and armament appear to diminish the serviceability of
the Coast Guard for civilian operations.

SERVICES AND CO-OPERATION

Throughout the statute law, the Coast Guard is, either
specifically or generally, charged with the duty of assisting other branches of the Treasury Department as well as
various other agencies, departments, and establishments.

Circular Letter No. 126, issued by the Commandant
on October 16, 1936, directs all responsible officers of
the Coast Guard to

. . . keep in close contact with the senior officials of all bureaus,
agencies, services, and other activities of the government for

which the Coast Guard performs duty. This includes the following: the Bureau of Customs, the Customs Agency Service, the Narcotics Bureau, the Alcohol Tax Unit, the Secret Service, the Public Health Service (Quarantine), the Bureau of Fisheries, the Biological Survey, the Bureau of Marine Inspection and Navigation, the Department of Justice (U. S. attorneys and Federal Bureau of Investigation), the Army (Engineers), the Immigration Service. Conference between the Coast Guard representatives and the local officials of those activities will be held sufficiently often to assure that the Coast Guard is co-operating in so far as practicable to their satisfaction in the enforcement of the laws administered by them.

The intelligence work which precedes anti-smuggling operations is usually performed by customs agents, the Coast Guard Intelligence Unit, or both working together. Following an arrest by Coast Guard officers for a violation of the customs laws, customs agents take over the investigation of the case preliminary to prosecution and prepare the case for trial by obtaining statements from witnesses, discovering new witnesses, and correlating evidence. The Customs Patrol participates with the Coast Guard in joint patrols, lending equipment or facilities when requested, and furnishing information. An example of the co-operation of Treasury units occurred in March 1936 when the British steamer *Hillfern* loaded a bulk cargo of alcohol in Antwerp to be smuggled into the United States. The activities of this vessel were under close surveillance before the cargo was loaded, and a lookout for the vessel or its cargo was maintained along the entire Atlantic seaboard. A part of the cargo was transferred at sea to the American tank vessel *Charles D. Leffler*. This vessel, with a bulk cargo of 49,000 gallons of alcohol, was seized on April 25 at New York. The *Hillfern* returned to Antwerp with the remainder of its alcohol cargo. In this successful skirmish, Coast Guard, Customs, and Alcohol Tax personnel co-operated under the supervision of the Commander of the New York Division of the Coast Guard. In addition to preventing the smuggling of alcoholic liquors, the Coast Guard aids the Alcohol Tax Unit by employing aircraft for the location of stills. It is stated that, in one co-ordinated drive on illicit stills in Florida, in which two planes were used, seventy-eight stills were seized and thirty-four arrests made. The manner in which the Coast Guard serves the Bureau of Narcotics has already been referred to.

The Coast Guard co-operates with the Immigration and Naturalization Service of the Department of Labor by helping to prevent the illegal entry of aliens. Division commanders and other field officers of the Coast Guard work in close co-operation with immigration officers, furnishing transportation by plane or boat and information. Coast Guard and immigration officers occasionally make joint seizures of aliens and of smuggled merchandise. The seizure of foreign vessels for smuggling usually involves the delivery of the alien crews of such vessels to immigration officers. The Coast Guard, in the summer of 1936, furnished an airplane, with pilot and mechanic, to be used jointly by the Immigration Border Patrol, the Customs Patrol, and the Royal Canadian Mounted Police to apprehend an airplane which was smuggling alcohol into Canada and aliens and merchandise into the United States. In the Jacksonville district, Immigration Border Patrol as well as other immigration officers have been invited to attend, and have apparently been in the habit of attending, the conferences held by field officers of the Treasury Department for the discussion of smuggling problems. Along the coast, for example in the Jacksonville district, valuable assistance has been extended by the Immigration Border Patrol to the Coast Guard.

For the Bureau of Marine Inspection and Navigation of the Department of Commerce the Coast Guard inspects vessels to enforce laws and regulations pertaining to equipment and operation, this work being concerned mainly with craft such as yachts, fishing vessels, and motor boats, rather than with large steamers, which have a regular annual inspection by the Bureau of Marine Inspection and Navigation. The Coast Guard patrols boat races and marine regattas, such as the Harvard-Yale boat races at New London, the Inter-collegiate boat races at Poughkeepsie, and the America cup races; takes charge of the closing of channels by authority of the Secretary of Commerce for such purposes as launching of ships, fleet reviews, and marine parades; and patrols the St. Mary's River from Lake Superior to Lake Huron to enforce regulations promulgated by the Secretary of Commerce.

For the Bureau of Fisheries of the same department, the Coast Guard conducts a patrol of the fur-seal herd from Washington to Alaska each spring, and in Bering Sea every summer; and enforces each season the international convention limiting the halibut catch off the North Pacific coast of the United States, British Columbia, and Alaska. During 1936 seven vessels were seized for violation of the fishing regulations. Incidentally, the Coast Guard observes and reports the activities of Japanese fishermen in Alaskan waters. In enforcing regulations relative to sponge fishing, little work is necessary; but the Coast Guard has prevented clashes between rival sponge fleets from Key West and Tarpon

Springs, Florida. The Whaling Treaty Act passed in
1936 aims at the conservation of whales and lays down
stringent regulations relative to the taking of these mam-
mals and the operation of whaling stations. The act is
enforced by the Coast Guard, the Bureau of Customs,
and the Bureau of Fisheries of the Department of Commerce.

For the Corps of Engineers of the War Department,
the Coast Guard enforces anchorage regulations in the
ports of New York, Norfolk, Charleston, Galveston,
San Diego, San Pedro, San Francisco, and Chicago, and
War Department regulations governing Vineyard and
Nantucket Sounds, Buzzards Bay, and Narragansett
Bay.

For the Department of the Interior, which has a Di-
vision of Territories and Island Possessions, the Coast
Guard furnishes transportation to Puerto Rico and the
Virgin Islands, and to Jarvis, Baker, and Howland
Islands, in the Pacific Ocean near the equator. The Coast
Guard has been visiting the last-named islands quarterly
to replenish the supplies of the Americans living there.
In Alaska the Coast Guard obliges the Office of Indian
Affairs by transporting personnel and freight.

With the Department of State, as well as the Department of Justice, the Coast Guard co-operates in the enforcement of the neutrality laws. During the Cuban
Revolution of 1933 twelve Coast Guard vessels, serving
temporarily under the Navy Department, took stations
at Cuban ports to assist refugees and to co-operate with
consular officers. During the Spanish Civil War which
began in 1936, the Coast Guard Cutter *Cayuga*, serving
temporarily under the Navy Department, assisted refugees in Spanish ports, and for about a month acted as a
floating embassy for the American Minister to Spain.

Early in 1937, when a ship, supposedly loaded with munitions for the Spanish government, left hurriedly while the new neutrality act was being enacted, it was a Coast Guard vessel that followed it to the high seas. The State Department helps the Coast Guard, as well as the Customs Service, by obtaining information through consular officers for use in the suppression of smuggling.

The Coast Guard furnishes planes and boats to the Biological Survey of the Department of Agriculture for the annual census of migratory wild fowl, carries agents of the Biological Survey to various places, and patrols certain bird sanctuaries. Under an act for the protection of game in Alaska, Coast Guard officers are empowered to enforce the law and the regulations issued by the Secretary of Agriculture.

Each summer, a Coast Guard cutter transports the judge and court officials of the United States District Court in Alaska from Valdez, Alaska to villages along the Aleutian Peninsula and bordering Bristol Bay. This service, of about one month's duration, enables the court to cover an area not served by commercial transportation. Officers on certain Coast Guard vessels in Alaska are given commissions as United States commissioners and United States deputy marshals to enable them to make arrests and hold suspects for trial before court.

The Coast Guard maintains close co-ordination with the Navy in such matters as regulations, training, supplies, communications, construction, and repairs. On rare occasions the Navy assists its maritime cousin in operations on water.

The Coast Guard communication system is used by the Bureau of Customs, the Public Health Service, the Immigration and Naturalization Service, the Bureau of Lighthouses, the Post Office Department, the Weather

Bureau, and other federal agencies which require such service.

Co-operation with the Bureau of Investigation, the Secret Service, and the Post Office inspectors is occasional and is not, as a rule, particularly significant.[4]

In general, then, the Coast Guard is in large part a service agency of the federal government,[5] doing work for, and giving assistance to, other branches of the executive organization. From this point of view, the organization is analogous to many other police forces, which, in addition to their ordinary police functions, are charged with special types of public safety work and also with certain regulatory and inspectional duties. In fact, a former commandant of the Coast Guard called attention to what he considered the similarity of duties between his agency on the waters of the United States and the Royal Canadian Mounted Police on land.[6]

The Coast Guard, particularly in its life saving and rescue work, gives service directly to the public. Says the Commandant:

I could give you innumerable instances of demands made upon the Coast Guard for new or additional services, but I believe a few examples will suffice. Last summer we were called upon from many sections to place men and boats along the beaches, both on the coast and on the lakes, for the protection of bathers at summer resorts and watering places, a service that is normally performed by paid civilian life guards; we have been called upon to place boats and men in inland lakes and streams, both for the protection of life and enforcement of law; we have been asked to send our ships into the center of hurricanes, to send out weather reports, and chart the course of hurricanes; we have

---

[4] For instances of such co-operation, see pp. 98-99, 102-03, 124.

[5] The statutory duties of the Coast Guard in relation to the states are not important. It is charged with assisting the states in the enforcement of their health laws (U. S. Code, Title 42, Sec. 97).

[6] 73 Cong. 2 sess., *Treasury Department Appropriation Bill for 1935*, Hearings before H. Committee on Appropriations, p. 243.

been called upon to police wharves and docks during labor troubles; our services have been demanded in the rôle of escorts to vessels during such disputes; we have been asked to extend our airplane emergency medical relief activities to residents of coastal cities and even inland villages, in addition to vessels and fishermen.[7]

PERSONNEL

The regular personnel of the Coast Guard numbers nearly 10,000. The training of cadets is by the Coast Guard itself in its Academy at New London, Connecticut. The air pilots are trained at the Navy Air School at Pensacola. The nature of the qualifications and training required by the Coast Guard may be gathered by perusal of the *Personnel Instructions* issued by the Service. For example, in the examinations for District Commander the following general subjects appear: boatsmanship, navigation, and coast pilotage; gunnery and drill regulations; navigation, customs, and motor boat laws; military law; communications; engineering. The personnel is, with minor exceptions, a technically specialized and technically trained force. Specialization not only applies to a variety of ranks and positions; but there is also a rather sharp line dividing the personnel into two parts. About three-fourths of the men on shore are assigned to life-saving work; and a man is seldom transferred from the life-saving service to the other branch or *vice versa*.

PROPERTY AND EQUIPMENT

To understand fully what the Coast Guard is, what it does, what it should do, and where it belongs, one must look at its properties and equipment, particularly its boats, ship-building and ship-repair facilities, airplanes and landing fields, radio transmitting stations, and tele-

---

[7] *Treasury Department Appropriation Bill for 1938*, Hearings, p. 700.

graph, telephone, and cable lines. The only other law-enforcement agencies possessing similar equipment are the Bureau of Customs and the Immigration and Naturalization Service. In fact, the Coast Guard is probably the only crime-control agency in which equipment is an important determinant of functions, organization, and relationships.

The total value of the Coast Guard fleet, not including the shore life-saving boats, was put in 1937 at $60,000,000. The 1,500 shore structures were valued at $12,000,000; and the 4,900 miles of telephone line at $3,000,000.

The floating equipment in commission on September 30, 1936 included thirty-seven cruising cutters, fifty-two harbor cutters and harbor launches, seventeen 165-foot patrol boats, twenty-three 125-foot patrol boats, eleven 100-foot patrol boats, six 78-foot patrol boats, fifty-eight 75-foot patrol boats, thirty-nine miscellaneous patrol and picket boats, and four special craft.

The cruising cutters, from 165 to 327 feet long, are designed primarily for deep-sea operations in any weather. They are rugged and capable of towing large vessels, and are used to do various interchangeable kinds of work. They may be employed for several months continuously on patrol—seal, halibut, ice, or anti-smuggling —and then be employed for a like period on rescue work, destruction of derelicts, or breaking open icebound harbors. The patrol boats from 125 to 165 feet in length are seaworthy; but they do not have the ruggedness or general capabilities of the cutters. They are used in the main for law enforcement, but perform rescue work on occasion. Inshore patrol boats, 70 to 80 feet long, are capable of operating at sea in good weather and are used primarily for law-enforcement duty. Picket boats, about 38 feet long, are used mainly for law enforcement in bays, sounds, inlets, and other protected waters; and, under favorable conditions, they operate at sea near the coast. Harbor tugs from 100 to 110 feet long and AB boats about 60 feet long are used to transport customs, immigration, and other officials to meet incoming ships, take customs guards to and from their stations at the various ports of entry, and enforce anchorage and harbor regulations. The special life-saving equipment includes gasoline-driven boats about 36 feet long and open boats 26 feet and under, gasoline driven or pulled with oars. In all, about 1,750 of these small boats are used for life saving.

The Coast Guard maintains construction and repair facilities on a small scale; but repair work on harbor boats is nearly all done at commercial shipyards, and practically all the major repairs to Coast Guard ships are made at commercial or Navy yards. Most, if not all, of the life-saving boats are built by the Coast Guard itself at Curtis Bay, Maryland.

Air stations were in operation on October 15, 1936 at Miami and St. Petersburg, Florida; Cape May, New Jersey; Salem, Massachusetts; Charleston, South Carolina; Biloxi, Mississippi; Port Angeles, Washington; San Diego, California. A new air station is authorized at Floyd Bennett Airport, New York; and, when it is completed, the present air station at Cape May, New Jersey will be discontinued. On that date, one air patrol detachment[8] was established at Del Rio, Texas. In 1936,

[8] The Coast Guard differentiates between "air stations" and "air patrol detachments." Air stations are permanent, located on government-owned ground, and on the seacoast, and have hangars, with machine shops and other repair and maintenance facilities, barracks for enlisted personnel, and radio stations. They engage both in law enforcement and in assistance and rescue work. Air patrol detachments are less permanently located. They operate fewer planes and land planes only, have few repair and overhaul facilities, and are in leased quarters.

the Coast Guard had assigned to its air stations forty-six airplanes. It will have fifty-one in 1938.

The Coast Guard maintains and operates a coastal communication system consisting of telephone and telegraph wires, aerial, underground and submarine, with a total mileage of nearly 5,000. It operates also a number of radio stations.

CAN THE COAST GUARD BE UNSCRAMBLED?

The Coast Guard's grotesque assortment of functions has not escaped the attention of administrative logicians. Nor have they failed to notice the odd fact that this miniature navy is located in the Treasury Department. Surely, it seems that our aquatic orphan has been placed in the wrong home and given too many different toys to play with. Why should armed ships and life-saving boats be under the ultimate command of a custodian of cash and credit? Why should captains, boatswains, and other sea-dogs be quartered with bookkeepers? Let us separate the strange bed-fellows. Away with irritating disharmony between booming guns and jingling coins—decks and deficits! But pause a moment. Is it not possible that the superficial disharmony which some sensitive ears have detected may be in reality nothing worse than a stimulating dissonance? Is it not more a matter of hair splitting than ear splitting?

To help us answer these questions, let us ascertain, if we can, the degree to which Coast Guard equipment is specialized and segregated. Harbor boats are used mainly for customs and regulatory work; and the shore life-saving boats are used almost exclusively for life saving; but the cutters and patrol boats perform a variety of duties, chiefly law enforcement, but also life saving, rescue work, and miscellaneous services. As a whole, the Coast

Guard is not a grab-bag; it is reasonably integrated in its operations; and each unit in the organization is more or less dependent on other units. The variety of its functions gives it added flexibility, and enables it to take up the slacks and level off the peaks. Except for certain classes of small boats used in shore life-saving work, all Coast Guard craft are used in varying measure for law enforcement as well as for other work. As the present Commandant of the Coast Guard has said: "There is no vessel of the Coast Guard that performs one and only one type of duty. All our vessels are available for various duties, such as enforcing navigation laws, boarding vessels, and so forth."[9]

A similar blending of functions occurs in the use of aviation equipment. Coast Guard airplanes do life-saving, assistance, and anti-smuggling work. As was explained by a Coast Guard official at the House hearings on the 1937 appropriation bill:

In addition to our law-enforcement duties, we use our planes in searching for derelicts, locating yachts that are lost or stolen, taking sick persons off merchant vessels and transporting them to the hospital, hurricane warnings to small craft at sea and to persons in isolated areas who are in danger, and assistance to persons in distress as a result of storms and floods.[10]

A large Coast Guard vessel is built for more than one purpose. Let the Commandant explain it:

In the construction of any vessel so many factors enter into it that the vessel is bound to be a compromise. If one desires high speed in a vessel he must have construction of a comparatively light type, which means that the vessel is not so good for working around shoals, wrecks, and so forth. If one desires a vessel for towing a disabled vessel, he cannot have it a speedy vessel also.

---

[9] 74 Cong. 2 sess., *Treasury Department Appropriation Bill for 1937*, Hearings before H. Committee on Appropriations, p. 512.
[10] The same, p. 548.

We try to get a vessel that is a composite, one that will make speed and at the same time have considerable towing ability, so that it can tow in a distressed vessel. Moreover, in addition to these qualities, it is desirable that the vessel be constructed so as to be of service to the Navy in time of war....[11]

During the last ten years, the Coast Guard has been steadily reducing the number of its small boats. The 75-foot patrol boats numbered 201 in 1926 and 58 in 1937. There were 195 miscellaneous patrol and picket boats as late as 1932, but only 39 in 1937. This change in the size of boats has been due to a desire to obtain more speed. "The length of a ship has a direct bearing on its speed."[12] Since each floating unit of the Coast Guard performs, during the year or even at one time, a variety of functions, it is practically impossible to estimate precisely the percentage of time given to the different classes of work. Even if it were possible, it would be futile to do so. You can reapportion a large number of small boats which perform a variety of functions; but, when the boats are few and large, they cannot be distributed among several different agencies and segregated to different uses without building more. If you build more ships and restrict each ship to a more specialized function, some of the craft will be idle a good part of the time, unless their work is expanded for the purpose of keeping them busy. An attempt to dismember and reallocate the coastal and deep-sea fleet would be wasteful both of construction and of operating funds. I am inclined to agree with the following statement made by a former commandant of the Coast Guard:

The economy and efficiency in having one federal police force on the seas to enforce the complexity of laws relating to customs,

---

[11] *Treasury Department Appropriation Bill for 1938,* Hearings, p. 636.
[12] The same, p. 635.

navigation, shipping, fisheries, immigration, quarantine, neutrality, oil pollution, and other miscellaneous laws, as well as to carry out other miscellaneous duties of the federal government are obvious. One vessel when patrolling the water of any locality can board a fishing vessel, motor boat, or other merchant craft and can enforce all these laws simultaneously, and at the same time be ready to render assistance to vessels in distress. Likewise, a shore station, while ever ready to save life and property, can readily exercise the necessary supervision over motor boats, fishing vessels, and other water craft in the immediate vicinity to see that all federal laws are obeyed. . . .[13]

On the recommendation of his Commission on Economy and Efficiency, President Taft proposed in 1911 that the Revenue Cutter Service should be transferred to the Navy Department and the Life-Saving Service to the Department of Commerce, where the Bureau of Lighthouses was, and still is. Instead, Congress consolidated the Revenue Cutter Service and the Life-Saving Service to create the Coast Guard, which was left in the Treasury Department. Nevertheless, in 1923 and 1924 when general administrative reorganization was in the air, it was again urged that the Life-Saving Service be joined with the Bureau of Lighthouses in the Department of Commerce and the remainder of the Coast Guard be turned over to the Navy.[14] At this time, however, the Coast Guard, because of the necessity of dealing with rum-runners, had become a conspicuous factor in the enforcement of national prohibition; and prohibition enforcement was a general responsibility of the Treasury Department. It was further pointed out in the joint congressional committee that the American philosophy of government demanded a separation of civil and mili-

[13] *Treasury Department Appropriation Bill for 1935*, Hearings, p. 243.
[14] 68 Cong. 1 sess., *Reorganization of Executive Departments*, Hearings before Joint Committee on the Reorganization of the Administrative Branch of the Government, pp. 95-98.

tary functions, that "a coast guardsman is a policeman in some ways," and that it would be "terribly offensive" to the people if the Navy were to be used "as a civilian policeman."[15]

Whether these points were well taken or not, the practical advantages of the proposed assignment of civil functions to the Navy may be seriously doubted. How it would work out is a matter of speculation, into which we need not now enter. The Coast Guard is, in many striking ways, *like* the Navy; but, in time of peace, the two services have few close operating relationships.

There is, perhaps, no decisive objection to a transfer of the shore life-saving branch of the Coast Guard to the Department of Commerce, where the life-saving service would operate in close conjunction with the Bureau of Lighthouses. Generally speaking, the personnel, buildings, boats, and other equipment of the shore life-saving service are not interchangeable with corresponding units of the enforcement branch of the Coast Guard. On the other hand, life saving and rescue work are functions of the large ships and airplanes, as well as of the smaller boats that operate from shore. To an extent, the thread of life saving and rescue runs through the entire fabric of the Coast Guard. Lighthouses, too, are static and preventive, while life saving and rescue work are dynamic and recuperative. This latter type of humanitarianism frequently demands the co-ordination of mobile units of all kinds and sizes, on shore, at sea, and in the air; and it is reasonable to suppose that such co-ordination can be most promptly effected under unified command.

It has been suspected, furthermore, that something ought to be done about unifying or co-ordinating the en-

[15] The same, p. 97.

forcement of navigation and port regulations; and the suggestion has been made that this function should be exercised by a single authority, the Department of Commerce or the Interstate Commerce Commission. If this suggestion were approved, the harbor boats of the Coast Guard and the various odd jobs that they perform would be turned over, say, to the Bureau of Marine Inspection and Navigation, which, we may infer, would be placed with other agencies that are primarily concerned with the regulation of transportation. These boats are now used at the ports by customs and immigration officers; but, of course, they could continue to be so used were they operated by an agency other than the Coast Guard. Nevertheless, unless harbor boats are to be duplicated, the authority that operates them will have to be a "good neighbor" to the other federal agencies that function at the ports. It must give service, much as the Coast Guard now does. On the whole, it is not yet clear what sort of reorganization, if any, should be attempted in the ports and harbors. There, we are still somewhat at sea.

TREASURY CO-ORDINATION

The Coast Guard, apparently, is one of those peculiar multi-functional federal agencies, such as the Census Bureau and the Office of Indian Affairs, which can be located with about equal logic in any one of three or four departments. From a purely theoretical standpoint, the Coast Guard could be attached to Treasury, Navy, Justice, or Commerce. From a practical standpoint, Justice would be immediately ruled out. Smuggling, however, is a concern of the Treasury, not the Navy; and anti-smuggling work bulks larger in volume than any other general class of Coast Guard enforcement operations. Moreover, the Coast Guard performs more services for the Treasury than for any other department or establishment.

In any event, an agency like the Coast Guard will inevitably be *attached* to, rather than *merged* in, the department to which it is allocated. It is of such a nature that, wherever placed, it will have to be set up and administered as a practically independent unit. Such is its present position in the Treasury Department. Its Commandant, an admiral, is directly responsible to the Secretary of the Treasury; and the Coast Guard organization is in no sense inextricably interwoven in the Treasury organization as a whole. There are tie-ins, of course, with the General Counsel's Office, the Division of Disbursements, the Procurement Division, and the Public Health Service; and there is much co-operation, as we have seen, with the Treasury enforcement agencies. Theoretically, most of these relationships could be maintained if the Coast Guard were outside the Treasury. On the other hand, the tendency in the last few years has been to tie in the Coast Guard more closely with other branches of the Department.

Steps have been taken to eliminate duplication of equipment and division of responsibility between the Coast Guard and other Treasury agencies. Some time ago, the Secretary of the Treasury transferred to the Coast Guard the customs boats which were engaged along the coast of Maine in law-enforcement work, as well as customs boats in the harbors of the United States engaged in harbor patrol. This transfer did not, apparently, include customs boats on the Detroit River where, it is understood, there are no Coast Guard craft. At about the same time (March 9, 1934), the Secretary of the Treasury instructed that all flying activities under the jurisdiction of the Treasury Department be consolidated with and placed under the jurisdiction of the Coast Guard; and the Commissioner of Customs was directed to turn over to the Coast Guard all airplanes and aviation equipment operated by or in possession of the Bureau of Customs. Ten airplanes were transferred. Eight were found unfit for service and were destroyed; one crashed on December 5, 1935; and one was still in service as late as October 24, 1936. The Coast Guard's communication system serves the entire department, as well as outside federal agencies.

The Coast Guard was also directed in 1934 to undertake the instruction in the use of small arms of all Treasury Department personnel whose official duties require use of firearms. Coast guardsmen now give marksmanship training to custom-house employees, the Customs Border Patrol, the Narcotics Bureau and Alcohol Tax Unit agents, and Secret Service operatives, and the guards at the mints, at the Bureau of Engraving and Printing, and at other Treasury buildings.

When the Secretary of the Treasury was eliminating duplications in 1934, he was also endeavoring to establish co-ordination. He placed under the supervision of the Coast Guard all activities of the Treasury Department having to do with the prevention and detection of the smuggling of liquor and narcotics on the seacoast between ports of entry. The Commander of the Norfolk Division of the Coast Guard, for example, was charged with the direction of all activities of this character on the coasts of Maryland, Virginia, and North Carolina. Under the Division Commander were placed the resources, not only of the Coast Guard, but also of the Customs Service, the Alcohol Tax Unit, the Bureau of Narcotics, and the Secret Service. The Division Commander was instructed to call into conference the responsible local officers of these several agencies for the purpose of formulating a concrete program of co-ordinated action. The Division Commander was further directed to submit to the Secretary's office at the end of each week, through the Commandant of the Coast Guard, a report of progress with any recommendations that might be considered appropriate. In other areas, the field co-ordinator is usually a Coast Guard officer. Meetings of the representatives of Treasury enforcement agencies are held in the field monthly, or oftener when necessary; and these meetings are presided over by the area co-ordinator. In order to bring the several units into close proximity in the field, some of them have re-districted their territory, so that the several field offices may be, to the greatest possible extent, in the same cities. In Washington, the heads of the various Treasury enforcement agencies meet weekly in conference, presided over by the Assistant Secretary in charge of co-ordination.

Though two or three different attempts at legislation have been made, the Treasury co-ordination machinery has not yet been established by law. What has been done thus far, however, constitutes probably the most significant of recent improvements in federal law-enforcement organization.

MARINE CENTRALIZATION

The navigational equipment and personnel used by the federal government for civil purposes are not yet completely segregated in the Coast Guard. Even in the Treasury Department, the Bureau of Customs and the Public Health Service maintain a number of small boats. The customs boats operate on inland waters and along the Florida coast. The Public Health Service craft are for quarantine and inspection purposes.

The Bureau of Lighthouses of the Commerce Department has a considerable fleet of lightships, tenders, and relief ships. The Coast and Geodetic Survey of the same department operates specialized vessels, with some tenders and small craft, for oceanographic and hydrographic work. A few vessels and a number of patrol boats are operated by the Bureau of Marine Inspection and Navigation. The Corps of Engineers of the War Department presents an impressive inventory of barges, tugs, towboats, launches, dredges, and other floating equipment. The Inland Waterways Corporation has a considerable fleet of tow and tug boats and barges, with a few motor boats. Floating equipment is also operated by the Bureau of Fisheries, the Immigration and Naturalization Service, and a number of other federal agencies.

Some of the mail is carried for the Post Office Department by powerboats, under contract. Incidentally, we may note some interesting excerpts from the latest appropriation hearings. It seems that in December 1936 there was in the harbor of New York a mail-carrying service by a certain steamship called the *President*,

. . . which belongs to the government but is being operated under contract by the New York Central Railroad. The boat goes down to quarantine and meets incoming steamers, takes off the mail and brings it up in advance of the steamers. . . . The present contract expires next July, and we do not know what it is going to cost us to renew it. The present contract calls for $115,000 a year, and the railroad company says it is losing $60,000 a year. In accordance with the contract, the government is required to stand the expense of all repair to the *President* in excess of $500. . . .[16]

---

[16] Testimony of Mr. J. W. Cole, deputy second assistant postmaster general.

. . . The *President* is getting old and the repairs are costing much more progressively. We want to know whether we can get a contractor who will furnish his own boat.

Mr. Ludlow: Would you save any money if the government should operate this boat at night only, I mean as a government operation?

Mr. Triem:[17] We could not do it ourselves.

Mr. Ludlow: You do not have the personnel to operate a boat?

Mr. Triem: The Post Office Department has not the personnel which could operate a boat. The *President* is a large boat, and we would have to rely upon a contract. We thought possibly we might get some railroad company owning a boat that was used in the harbor to perform this service on a trip basis, or between certain hours only. . . .[18]

We can easily imagine that the Coast Guard had already been asked by the Post Office Department to relieve the aging and expensive *President*. Such are the problems of government bureaus that "go down to the sea in ships." This digression suggests that Coast Guard services, in certain directions, might properly be expanded, rather than contracted or redistributed. In general, however, the civilian craft, not now under the Coast Guard, are either small, highly specialized, or, like the mail-boats, operated under contract. Many of these boats are used on inland waters. To transfer all of them to the Coast Guard for the sake of centralizing navigational equipment would be hopelessly impractical. Navigation is like certain other facilitating activities that are carried on in the various federal agencies, which are amenable neither to absolute centralization nor to extreme decentralization. Perhaps the Coast Guard, at present, represents close to the maximum of centralization. Until some intensive, technical, and localized studies are made, one

[17] Assistant superintendent.
[18] 75 Cong. 1 sess., *Post Office Department Appropriation Bill for 1938*, Hearings before H. Committee on Appropriations, pp. 194-95.

can not say whether further centralization is feasible or whether, on the contrary, decentralization is clearly indicated.

SUMMARY AND CONCLUSIONS

The tendency has been for the Coast Guard, in its civil aspects, to monopolize a fairly definite territorial jurisdiction; in general, the high seas and the coasts. It is a multi-functional service agency. As a problem in administrative organization, it suggests a number of intriguing possibilities. It has grown "like Topsy"; but, decidedly, the burden of proof is on those who would change substantially its present set-up, functions, and relationships. It is a law-enforcement agency; but we must dismiss as obviously impractical any idea that the Coast Guard should go to the Department of Justice, where it would be co-ordinated more closely with the Bureau of Investigation. But it has been seriously proposed in the past that all federal patrolling on sea and land should be unified. A proposal of this nature, which would fundamentally involve the Coast Guard, can be properly appraised only when we thoroughly understand the organization and functions of the federal land patrols. These will be discussed in the next chapter.

CHAPTER IX

THE BORDER PATROLS

In the federal law-enforcement organization, patrolling, like Caesar's Gaul, is divided into three parts. Our marine outpost is the Coast Guard; while the national gateways are watched on land by the Customs Patrol and the Immigration Border Patrol.

SET-UPS

The two land patrols are in different departments. The Customs Patrol, formerly scattered among the forty-eight collection districts, is now grouped in only four large districts under the central direction of the Customs Agency Service, which is a subdivision of the Bureau of Customs of the Treasury Department.[1] The Customs Agency Service has three units: (1) the Administrative Unit, which handles personnel, financial, and administrative matters; (2) the Investigative Unit, which supervises field offices in the United States and foreign countries and includes the Port Examination Commission and the Customs Information Exchange; and (3) the Enforcement Unit, with a chief, assistants, and clerical staff in Washington and the Customs Patrol in the field.

[1] "You see, for example, Maine is one customs district. We had a separate patrol in Maine. Vermont is another customs district, and we had a separate patrol there. New York is another one, and we had a patrol there. Likewise, we had one in Buffalo and another one in Detroit. They were all separate and distinct. Now we have consolidated all of those into one unit, one district, and have the headquarters at Buffalo, the idea being, of course, that we would have more mobility in transferring the men around and also greater use of the equipment." 75 Cong. 1 sess., *Treasury Department Appropriation Bill for 1938*, Hearings before H. Committee on Appropriations, p. 260.

The Immigration Border Patrol is under the Commissioner of Immigration and Naturalization, who is directly responsible to the Secretary of Labor.

FUNCTIONS AND ACTIVITIES

Neither of the land patrols is a general crime-control or a general service agency. Each is charged with specialized auxiliary law enforcement. In this respect, both are different, on the whole, from the Bureau of Investigation and the Coast Guard. Generally speaking, both operate in the same areas; but one is primarily concerned with the movement of commodities; the other, with the movement of human beings.

Incidental to their primary function, Customs Patrol inspectors, as they are officially designated, guard and watch the highways adjacent to the international boundaries. This they do in automobiles, snowmobiles, and snowcycles, on horseback, and on foot. In some regions, they operate in speedboats and outboards. They get in touch with "informers" to obtain information regarding smuggling operations. They examine the ground along the boundary for tracks of persons, animals, and vehicles. They check the brands of legally imported livestock, livestock at dipping vats, railroad shipping points, and stock pens, and also animals that are returned to the United States by customs officers of Canada or Mexico. Members of the Patrol pursue and detain automobiles that fail to stop for examination by the customs inspectors at the points of entry. When smuggled goods are found, they are seized by the Patrol. This agency is also charged with preventing the exportation of articles from the United States without the filing of proper export declarations. Members of the force board and search suspected craft in bays and inlets, and keep a watch over vessels thought to be carrying contraband merchandise. The Patrol exercises surveillance over landing fields in order to detect airplanes entering or leaving the country illegally.

The Immigration Border Patrol operates in a somewhat similar manner for a quite different purpose. It patrols, guards, and searches highways, trails, rivers, bridges, ferries, wharves, railroad and ship yards, and open country along the international boundaries and certain parts of the coasts. Members of the Patrol use every appropriate means of locomotion and transport. They stop and inspect vessels, trains, automobiles, and other conveyances. They halt and question persons who are on foot or on horseback. They arrest aliens and alien smugglers, and convey persons under arrest to examining officers or places of detention. They conduct investigations concerning the unlawful entry or smuggling of aliens and concerning legality of residence, gather evidence and prepare reports for use in deportation proceedings and prosecutions, and make character investigations in naturalization cases.

Incidentally, both patrols render first-aid to persons injured or in distress; and each performs various other duties which need not be detailed here.

OVERLAPPING, DUPLICATION, RELATIONSHIPS, AND CO-OPERATION

All three federal patrols—the Coast Guard, the Customs Patrol, and the Immigration Border Patrol—are, in a measure, overlapping forces. Functionally, the Coast Guard markedly overlaps each of the land patrols. Geographically, the land patrols overlap each other; that is, their operations take place side by side in much the same territory. Thus, we find among the three agencies two different and significant types of relationships.

If we discover in the three forces, or in any two of them, needless duplication, ineffectiveness, or waste, and if these conditions are due to the separateness of the patrols, on what basis shall we attempt to reorganize? Shall we adopt geography or function as our rule-of-thumb? Or may we use both of these criteria? Would it be wise to consolidate two, or all three of the patrols? Or may efficiency be achieved merely by a reallocation of activities? Or by a better co-ordination of operations?

In probing this problem, investigations in the past have tended to emphasize the similarities, rather than the differences, between the smuggling of goods and the illegal entry of aliens. To cope with either type of ir-regularity, the government must have inspectors stationed at points of entry; and, when persons—or per-sons and commodities—are crossing the boundary be-tween points of entry, agents of the government must, whenever possible, stop, question, and inspect. In the smuggling either of goods or of persons, the crime has its inception in a foreign country. To cope with either type of law-breaking, therefore, it is desirable in as many cases as possible to do detective work and set up preven-tives at the places of origin. Accordingly, both the Customs Agency Service and the Immigration and Natu-ralization Service have agents working in foreign coun-tries.

Disregarding, for the moment, the apparent duplica-tion of inspection officials at points of entry and of in-vestigative officials in foreign countries, let us now examine more particularly the operations of the patrol-men along the border.

On land, commodities in any considerable number or quantity usually follow the traveled routes. In most cases, when goods are smuggled, they soon lose their identity in the great mass of similar commodities within the country. Generally speaking, if they are not detected at or near the boundary at the moment of entrance, their detection anywhere else or at a later date is well-nigh impossible.

On the other hand, an alien or a group of aliens is not bound to follow a road or trail. A smuggled or smuggling person does not readily lose his identity. He may die, but he is not consumed. And he is not detectable merely by uncovering and inspection. The process of detection in his case always involves questioning; and it may require an intricate tracing of his movements over a considerable period of time, a comparison of photographs and fingerprints, and a searching of documents such as certificates of birth, of registry, or of naturalization.

Consequently, the Immigration Border Patrol is accustomed, more than its companion organization, to work along the less frequented routes and even away from roads and trails altogether. Members of the Immigration Border Patrol, moreover, work farther back from the boundary, sometimes a hundred miles or so. The difference between goods and persons helps to explain also why the Immigration and Naturalization Service has no separate "intelligence unit," like the Coast Guard, and the Customs Agency Service.[2] Because of these and other facts, it appears that the Immigration Border Patrol must be more flexible and more mobile than the Customs Patrol.

Operating side by side, jealousies have appeared and

[2] The Immigration and Naturalization Service, however, has had for some time a special prosecution staff and a special investigating staff working on frauds at New York City. There are also special investigators working in other places.

conflicts have occasionally occurred between members of the two patrols; but jealousies and conflicts have not apparently been serious.

On the whole, there is considerable informal co-ordination between the two forces. It is true that in fifteen places along the border the Immigration Border Patrol has a field office and the Customs Patrol has none; but both patrols have either district headquarters or sub-offices in Buffalo, Detroit, El Paso, Havre, International Falls, Jacksonville, Laredo, Miami, New Orleans, Pembina, Seattle, and Tampa. These places include the most important operating centers.

The field officers of the Immigration and Naturalization Service have long been under instructions to aid in the enforcement of federal laws against the introduction of contraband; and it is said that such co-operation with the Customs Service is well established and practically continuous. Members of the Border Patrol apprehend and deliver to the Service persons who have violated the customs laws. When information regarding the smuggling of commodities is obtained by the Border Patrol, it is turned over to appropriate customs officials. Such information, in a number of instances, seems to have resulted in the seizure of substantial quantities of smuggled goods; and considerable quantities of such goods have been seized at various points by the Immigration Border Patrol itself and turned over to the Customs Service. Automobiles and other conveyances have been taken by the Patrol and delivered to collectors of customs or their deputies. An arrangement is in effect at Detroit between the Immigration Border Patrol and the Customs Patrol to avoid duplication and overlapping of patrol work by boat on the Detroit River. At St. Paul, the two patrols have entered into a co-operative agreement. In one district, at least, Immigration Border Patrol units are given a written assignment as they start on each tour of duty; and these schedules are available to Customs Patrol units, if they wish to use them, to avoid duplication.

The policy of the Customs Patrol relative to co-operation is stated in the *Manual of Instructions for the Guidance and Use of Customs Patrol Inspectors* (May 28, 1932) as follows:

Border Patrol officers should, so far as possible, co-operate with officers of other branches of the government service and with state and local officers.

However, Border Patrol officers, in their official capacity are not authorized to make arrests in other than customs cases. The same is true of violations of federal criminal statutes involving other than the customs laws. Such action, if accomplished, would be in their capacity as private citizens and upon their own responsibility. It is suggested, therefore, in order to obviate situations whereby Border Patrol officers may be subjected to civil suits for damages, that action by them in such instances be limited to a close co-operation with the local, state, or other federal officers, who are by virtue of their official capacity and authority, authorized to apprehend offenders.

Whenever a Customs Patrol inspector apprehends any foreigner or alien entering, attempting to enter, or who appears to have recently entered the United States by rowboat, speedboat (or, in fact, by any boat other than an established ferry or steamship line), by automobile, by aircraft or by walking across the ice or over any land boundary, or in any other unusual manner, such foreigners or aliens should not be released until such aliens and their cases are presented to the nearest immigration officers on duty. If the alien is accompanied by an American citizen he likewise should be turned over to the immigration authorities.

Both patrols co-operate with other federal law-enforcement agencies. The Intelligence Unit and the Alcohol Tax Unit of the Bureau of Internal Revenue and the Bureau of Narcotics are the only ones not already discussed in previous chapters.[3]

For the Alcohol Tax Unit, the Customs Patrol has seized stills, distilling equipment and supplies, and non-tax-paid liquor; has loaned men, cars, and equipment to assist in seizures and arrests; and has given information regarding violations of the liquor laws. It is stated that in 1936 the Patrol apprehended or assisted in the apprehension of about 106 offenders for the Alcohol Tax Unit.

It is the duty of the Bureau of Customs, under the provisions of the Narcotic Drugs Import and Export Act, to detect, prevent, and punish unlawful importation and exportation of narcotic drugs. It is also the duty of that Bureau to handle the importation of crude opium and coca leaves at the ports of entry, pursuant to a permit issued by the Commissioner of Narcotics; to arrange for the trans-shipment of any narcotic drugs or preparations arriving at a port of the United States from a foreign country destined to another foreign country; and to handle the exportation of narcotic drugs from the United States to a foreign country, pursuant to an export authorization issued by the Commissioner of Narcotics. In addition to these duties performed by the Bureau of Customs as a whole, assistance has been rendered by the Customs Patrol to the Bureau of Narcotics similar to that extended to the Alcohol Tax Unit.

It is estimated that 79 per cent of the cases handled by the Customs Patrol originate in the Patrol itself, 12 per cent are referred to it by other branches of the Customs Service, 4 per cent by the Immigration Border Patrol, one per cent by the Coast Guard, one-half of one per cent by the Bureau of Investigation, and none by the Secret Service.

[3] For co-operation with agencies already discussed, see pp. 101, 103, 138, 156-58, 160-61.

The Immigration Border Patrol has recently seized and turned over to the Alcohol Tax Unit several loads of alcohol en route to Canada; and the Patrol has given the Alcohol Tax Unit information concerning the location of stills and of contraband liquor. Likewise, the Patrol has made seizures for the Bureau of Narcotics; and the narcotic district supervisors furnish to immigration officials information with respect to aliens charged with violation of the federal narcotic laws, for use in determining whether or not such alien violators are subject to deportation. The Border Patrol in the Los Angeles district has assisted the Bureau of Narcotics by fingerprinting and photographing persons arrested by narcotic agents.

Of the 12,406 persons apprehended during the fiscal year 1936 by the Immigration Border Patrol, 11,869 were held by immigration authorities; while 311 were delivered to Customs, 17 to the Alcohol Tax Unit, 16 to the Bureau of Investigation, 2 to the Army and Navy, one to the Bureau of Narcotics, and 190 to state and municipal officers. During the fiscal years 1925 to 1936 inclusive, the Patrol is reported to have arrested a total of 17,770 persons, other than violators of the immigration and Chinese exclusion laws. The offenses of these persons ranged from violation of the customs laws to robbery and murder.

A record of the number of aliens actually delivered to the Immigration Border Patrol by other enforcement agencies has been maintained only since September 1935. From then until the end of the fiscal year, 524 aliens were delivered to the Patrol—75 by the Customs Service, 71 by state and municipal authorities, and 378 by agencies not specified. No record is kept of the number of cases brought to the attention of the Immigration Border Patrol as distinguished from actual delivery of aliens. In some of the immigration and naturalization districts, inter-agency co-operation is more extensive, more cordial, and more fruitful than in others. Of course, co-operation is called for in some districts more than in others. It is interesting to note, for example, that in the Galveston district the Immigration Border Patrol received (or felt that it received) little or no co-operation from other federal law-enforcement agencies, except the Customs Patrol. On the other hand, in the El Paso district, 570 aliens were delivered to immigration officers by other services. Federal agencies delivered 115 and, of these, 110 were handed over by the Customs Service.

Beyond the field of law enforcement, strictly speaking, both patrols perform incidental and occasional services. For example, the Customs Patrol reports that during 1936 it assisted federal livestock inspectors in preventing violations of the livestock quarantine laws; the Forest Service, by reporting forest fires and assisting in locating monuments on the international boundary; and the Office of Indian Affairs, by helping to supervise livestock on Indian reservations.

Neither the Investigative nor the Enforcement Unit of the Customs Agency Service has extensive or significant relations with state or local officials. Neither unit is dependent on the co-operation of such officials, though state and local agencies have rendered assistance to and received assistance from the two units. The Immigration Border Patrol, at its request, has been placed on the mailing lists of many state and local agencies, receiving not only the more or less generally distributed lookout notices, but also requests for special action in the cases of wanted criminals. It is stated that these matters receive prompt attention, even to the extent in aggravated

cases of special details in the interest of the requesting
agency. Through this co-operative effort, various criminals have been apprehended by the Border Patrol for
state and local agencies; and the latter assist the Patrol
in like manner. Indeed, of the 570 aliens delivered to
immigration officials in the El Paso district in 1936, no
less than 455 were received from non-federal agencies.
Of these, 297 came from municipal police, 94 from
county sheriffs, 22 from county probation officers, and
one from state police.

RELATIVITY AND TIE-UPS

As of June 30, 1936, the personnel of the Immigration Border Patrol numbered 916, and that of the Customs Patrol, 589. During the fiscal year 1936, the Immigration Border Patrol cost $1,807,518; the Customs
Patrol, $1,581,323. The total civilian personnel of the
Department of Labor on September 30, 1936 was
14,520. That of the Treasury Department on the same
date was 72,910, five times the personnel of the Department of Labor. Relatively to its administrative environment, the Immigration Border Patrol is a big frog in a
little pond, while the Customs Patrol is a little frog
in a big pond.

Both the Bureau of Customs and the Immigration and
Naturalization Service are predominantly field organizations. In the latter agency, 97 per cent of the employees
are in the field.

The difficulty of dismembering an administrative
agency depends on the cohesiveness of its parts. The
Immigration and Naturalization Service and the Bureau
of Customs are both cohesive organizations. From either
agency, it would be difficult to pry loose its patrol force.
Is the effort worth the cost?

The Immigration Border Patrol is at present interlocked with other branches of the Service and there are good reasons for such interlocking. Section 16 of the Immigration Act of February 5, 1917 provides:

Said inspectors [immigrant inspectors] shall have power to administer oaths and to take and consider evidence touching the right of any alien to enter, re-enter, pass through, or reside in the United States, and, where such action may be necessary, to make a written record of such evidence; any person to whom such an oath has been administered, under the provisions of this act, who shall knowingly or willfully give false evidence or swear to any false statement in any way affecting or in relation to the right of any alien to admission, or readmission to, or to pass through, or to reside in the United States shall be deemed guilty of perjury and be punished as provided by Section 125 of the act approved March 4, 1909, entitled "An act to codify, revise, and amend the penal laws of the United States."

The immigrant inspectors, who are stationed at points of entry, act preliminarily in a quasi-judicial capacity; and in a large majority of cases, obviously, their decisions are final. The immigration patrol inspector cannot himself make a decision in doubtful cases. He must refer the suspected person to an immigrant inspector. As the late Commissioner of Immigration and Naturalization expressed it:

The two branches of the Service engaged in the enforcement of the immigration laws represent in their respective spheres a progressive sequence of interwoven actions which in the ultimate constitute a single duty of a single Service. The only real division is where the authority of the patrol inspector ends.

The Immigration Border Patrol depends almost wholly upon what might be termed the Immigration Service Division, for supervision and guidance; relies wholly upon other units for combined statistics, accounting, and all matters involving the securing and maintaining of supplies, equipment, and such like. All prosecutions and legal actions resulting from its work are handled by the officers of the Immigration Service Division, upon which it also relies for records concerning aliens who have been deported or refused admission to the United States. Unless the officers are made acquainted with rulings of the Department and court decisions bearing upon the immigration laws and keep abreast with immigration legislation, it cannot hope successfully to engage in the enforcement of immigration laws on our borders. Not infrequently, a force of immigrant and patrol inspectors is sent into isolated regions where the presence of immigrant inspectors is essential to carrying out the mission upon which engaged.[4]

Some light is thrown on the question of the proper location of the Immigration Border Patrol in a report made to the Secretary of Labor by Assistant Secretary of Labor White on April 28, 1933. In January 1932 the Patrol was partially separated from the Immigration Bureau, though remaining under the direction of the Department of Labor. On the basis of detailed reports from Bureau and field officials, Mr. White came to the conclusion that "the change [made in January 1932] was a mistake and destroyed to a great extent at least the effectiveness of both the Border Patrol and the Immigration Service in protecting the borders, and the morale of the Border Patrol Service." According to available information, the unified set-up decided upon in 1933 has been more satisfactory than the immediately preceding arrangement. While experience in this connection may not be conclusive by itself, it establishes a presumption that the Patrol should be left in the present set-up.

The Immigration Border Patrol exists because of the responsibilities which devolve upon the Immigration and Naturalization Service, of which the Patrol is merely one of several functioning units. The consolidation in 1933 of the Immigration and Naturalization Bureaus

[4] Report to Brookings Institution by Commissioner D. W. MacCormack.

into a single Immigration and Naturalization Service was a commendable achievement of co-ordinated administration. It resulted in the creation of a unified administrative agency empowered and equipped to deal with the alien from the time he enters the country to the time he becomes a citizen. There must, for example, be a single record of each individual showing all of his pertinent acts during the period of transition, since each such act has a bearing on the general question of the alien's status, rights, and obligations. Close co-ordination is required not only in records but also, as we have just seen, in actual operations.

The Customs Patrol, as previously pointed out, is under the Enforcement Unit of the Customs Agency Service. The Investigative Unit of the same Service has the general function of detecting and preventing frauds on the customs revenue. The customs agents, who operate under this Unit, investigate and report on all matters brought to their attention by the Commissioner of Customs, collectors, appraisers, surveyors, comptrollers, and others, relating to drawback, under-valuation , smuggling, dumping, personnel irregularities, customs procedure, tariff classifications, licensing of custom-house brokers, petitions for remission of additional duties, and other matters. Customs agents are authorized, both in the United States and abroad, to examine the books of exporters and importers and in certain cases to obtain subpoenas for books and records; and to make searches, seizures, and arrests. In addition, they investigate administrative practices and the conduct of customs personnel and audit the books and accounts of collectors of customs and of customs brokers. The customs agents, therefore, have internal, as well as auxiliary, enforcement functions. They operate throughout the United States and in foreign countries, but with a high concentration of work at the principal ports of entry. The Customs Patrol operates almost exclusively along the coasts and land borders, the larger part of its work being along the land borders.

Thus, the Customs Patrol and the customs agents are in the same Service, which is an integral part of the Bureau of Customs. The Patrol works in conjunction with the investigative officers. Actual policing is performed by the Patrol, while the intelligence work prior to seizures and the investigative work subsequent to seizures is carried on by the customs agents. The larger part of the work of the customs agents is non-criminal. The application of the customs laws is highly complex and technical; and efficiency in this work requires special training and previous experience in customs administration. From the standpoint of obtaining qualified men for customs enforcement work, it seems certain that a separation of the Customs Agency Service from the Bureau of Customs would be extremely prejudicial to efficient customs administration.

The Customs Agency Service, in addition to its auxiliary enforcement duties, has the function of internal enforcement, that is, it investigates the offices of the customs collectors. This duty of the Customs Agency Service might conceivably be separated administratively from external enforcement. Such a separation of duties would not be likely to result in any economy; and, even if the duties were thus divided, we should still find that the external enforcement duties of the Service were closely connected with the operations of the Bureau of Customs as a whole. In other words, the Customs Agency

Service, including both the customs agents and the Customs Patrol, should be looked upon as integral and essential features of the administration of the customs laws.

PERSONNEL TRAINING

Members of the Immigration Border Patrol are appointed after Civil Service examination and serve a probationary period of one year. New appointees are instructed in the use of firearms, immigration and naturalization laws, criminal law and court procedure, rules of evidence, Spanish (on the Southern border), investigation methods, interrogation of suspects, patrolling, smuggler's methods, first-aid, and so forth. Intensive training extends through the probationary period; but further training is given during an officer's entire service.

All employees of the Customs Agency Service are likewise under Civil Service. At times, appointments are made from an open Civil Service list or by transfer from other government departments. Usually, appointment is by transfer of selected employees from the Customs Service, after not less than five years' experience therein. In practice, most appointments are made only after ten years' or more experience in customs work. Because of this fact, post-entry training is individualized and varied. The training period is generally six months. Instruction is by observation of the various branches of the collector's organization and by study of customs laws and regulations. On completion of the training period, the student takes an examination. In all cases, new agents, when assigned to actual investigations, work in close association with experienced members of the Service. In addition, the Customs Bureau operates a correspondence school, open to customs agents as well as other customs employees.

Customs Patrol inspectors are given instruction in customs laws, enforcement methods, rules of evidence, court procedure, first-aid, personal hygiene, and use of firearms. From one to two weeks of training a year is given at district headquarters. Practically every member of the Customs Patrol is said to be enrolled in the correspondence school.

EQUIPMENT

The equipment used by the Immigration Border Patrol in October 1936 included 316 automobiles, twenty-four trucks, nine 18-foot river patrol speed boats, two 25-foot inshore cabin cruisers, two 26-foot harbor-patrol boats, and eighteen skiffs, canoes, and outboards.

For about two years, the Immigration Border Patrol has been engaged in studying, building, and installing radio communication facilities. Most of the equipment has been constructed in the radio laboratory located in the Immigration and Naturalization Service reservation at Detroit, under a WPA project. Half or more of the automobiles and a number of boats are now equipped with radio receivers. More than fifty fixed receiving stations have been established. About eighty automobile or boat transmitters for two-way communication have been completed or are under construction, and a number are in operation. The Patrol operates broadcasting stations at Marine City, Detroit, Buffalo, and El Paso. In October 1936 the erection of radio masts and the installation of radio transmitters was in progress at a number of other stations. When these various installations are completed, the Border Patrol will have a highly effective chain of radio communication stations over the entire land borders. In the Florida district, the Immigration Border Patrol uses Coast Guard radio facilities, and it is

not planned to install transmitters in that district so long
as the Coast Guard shares the use of such equipment.

The transportation equipment of the Customs Patrol
includes about seventy speed boats and outboards, over
300 automobiles, a few snowmobiles and snowcycles, and
a number of horses. Neither Patrol has airplanes.

SHALL ALL PATROLLING BE UNIFIED?

A bill was drafted in 1930 for the purpose of combining the two patrols and placing their administration under the Coast Guard; and hearings on the subject were
held on April 24 and 25, 1930, before the House Committee on Interstate and Foreign Commerce. A comprehensive and detailed survey had been made by the
Coast Guard and probably also by the two bureaus more
immediately concerned; and the bill was apparently approved, at least in principle, by both the Treasury and
Labor Departments. The plan of consolidation advanced
at that time was apparently motivated by a desire to
make prohibition enforcement more effective. Efficiency
in the regular work of the Immigration and Customs
Services appears to have been a secondary consideration.
No reduction in the cost or personnel of the patrols seems
to have been contemplated. Indeed, the Treasury Department proposed an actual increase in personnel of
924 employees and in annual expenditure of $3,414,496
for the patrolling work proper, together with increases
for overhead administration.[5]

It was stated in the 1930 hearings:

One of the essentials of an effective border patrol is that it
be organized upon a military basis, with an enlisted and commissioned personnel, and with military training and discipline.

---

[5] At a later date, however, the Department of the Treasury submitted
to the Bureau of the Budget a plan of consolidation under the Coast
Guard with an estimate of expenditures indicating considerable savings.

What I mean by that is that it is essentially a police force and that we are likely to get probably better men, a higher standard of morale, build up more rapidly a tradition of service, if we have a semi-military or military organization, than if we attempt to operate under civil service laws.[6]

Nevertheless, it was admitted at that time that even if a unified border patrol were placed under the Coast Guard

. . . it should be organized and maintained as a distinctly separate organization. The Coast Guard has other duties more important than the prevention of smuggling on our land borders. . . . Patrolling our land borders is essentially a police function. The Coast Guard proper is a naval organization charged with the duty of protecting life at sea and enforcing on our ocean boundaries the laws of the United States. We do not propose to make policemen of our sailors. But we do want to avail ourselves of their central organization.[7]

Consolidation of the border patrols with the Coast Guard would apparently tend to improve co-ordination of anti-smuggling work on land and water. It may be urged in this connection that both the Customs Patrol and the Immigration Border Patrol now operate to some extent on water as well as on land. While most of the floating equipment of the Customs Service has been turned over to the Coast Guard, no steps have been taken toward a like transfer of the floating equipment of the Immigration Service. Its boats are small and few; in fact, they are fewer than those which are still operated by the Customs Bureau. There is no evidence of duplication in the use of floating equipment; but, of course, the possibility of an unnecessary duplication on water could be obviated by the consolidation of land and water patrol work under the Coast Guard.

[6] Statement of Ogden L. Mills, 71 Cong. 2 sess., *Border Patrol*, Hearing before H. Committee on Interstate and Foreign Commerce, p. 5.
[7] The same, pp. 5-6.

Consolidation with the Coast Guard might be urged also as a means of avoiding duplication of aviation and radio equipment and operation. In this connection, no evidence appears of duplication at the present time. Neither land patrol has at present any airplanes; and, although the Immigration and Naturalization Service is extending its radio facilities, it continues to make use of Coast Guard transmitting stations in areas where such stations are operating.

While the question of operations on water and in the air is not important to the Immigration and Naturalization Service, it may be economical to maintain the policy of keeping water and air enforcement operations centralized so far as possible in the Coast Guard. This organization is already equipped for large-scale operations on water and in the air. Its activities are flexible; and it has had long experience as a service agency, rendering a variety of services to other agencies of the government, outside as well as inside the Treasury Department, and including the Immigration and Naturalization Service. In certain coastal areas, the Coast Guard, it is understood, now performs all of the functions of both the Immigration and Customs Patrols.

The principal reason for the expansion of the Customs Patrol was the need for enforcement of national prohibition; the principal reason for the original establishment of the Immigration Border Patrol was the enactment of the so-called Quota Act. It is apparent that conditions have materially changed since the original establishment of the two patrol forces. The most significant change has been brought about by the repeal of the Eighteenth Amendment. Prior to repeal, liquor smuggling was the major problem of the Customs Patrol on

all land and sea borders of the United States. Since repeal, liquor smuggling has gradually decreased; and at
the present time it is said to be at the minimum except on
the Mexican border. It is pointed out by customs officials,
however, that droughts in the United States and other
conditions have made the smuggling of livestock, wool,
and agricultural and dairy products profitable, and that
such commodities have in large measure replaced liquor
as the major problem of the Customs Patrol. The smuggling of narcotic drugs has also assumed outstanding importance; but narcotics smuggling, according to those
most familiar with it, is largely a coastal activity and the
smugglers, probably in a majority of cases, are found
among the crews or passengers of legitimate vessels. In
1935, it is true, the Immigration Border Patrol in California seized 310 tins of opium valued at about $50,000;
but this seizure was made over a hundred miles from the
border; and the evidence is said to have indicated that
the narcotics had been smuggled through a seaport and
not over the land border. Considering the work of both
patrol organizations, it appears that the major problem
of land border control is at present and probably will be
in the future the prevention of the smuggling of aliens.

To the placing of the Immigration Border Patrol
under the Coast Guard it may be objected, in short, that
the Coast Guard is a naval or quasi-naval organization;
that it automatically goes under the Navy Department
in time of war; that the clear-cut character of its present
geographical jurisdiction should be maintained; that
Coast Guard personnel, training, traditions, equipment,
and operations are not analogous to those of the Immigration Border Patrol; that the work of the latter is predominantly on land; that alien control is the major land

border problem; and that the operations of the Patrol are closely integrated with the general functioning of the Immigration and Naturalization Service.

Thus, it has been suggested, on the one hand, that the Coast Guard be transferred to the Navy and, on the other hand, that the land patrols be placed under the Coast Guard, but no one, apparently, has yet been rash enough to recommend that the land patrols be handed over to the Army. Note this bit from the appropriation hearings:

Mr. Ludlow: You are estimating $19,440 as you have just said, for guards at the Fort Knox bullion depository. How many guards do you expect to employ there and what is the necessity for them?

Mrs. Ross: We have twelve guards there; we want twelve more.

. . . .

Mr. Ludlow: They are civilian guards, I believe you have told us?

. . . .

Mrs. Ross: Yes, they are Civil Service employees.

Mr. Ludlow: Some of us have the impression, or had it, that this depository, being located where there was an Army post, would be guarded by soldiers.

Mrs. Ross: Many persons have had that idea, but the War Department has said positively that it does not do that kind of duty. It will, though, as I have stated, render assistance in case of emergency, but it will not be responsible for guarding the repository.

Mr. Ludlow: And the War Department does not propose to furnish any guard whatsoever?

Mrs. Ross: No; except in case of emergency. . . . . We are, in fact, quite remote from the Army post proper. We are a considerable distance away, and we depend upon our own guard system and the protective devices installed.[8]

----

[8] *Treasury Department Appropriation Bill for 1938,* Hearings, pp. 335-36.

Thus, the Coast Guard does not "propose to make policemen of its sailors"; nor does the Army intend to make watchmen of its soldiers.

SHALL THE LAND PATROLS BE CONSOLIDATED?

A good deal of discussion has revolved around the question of consolidating the Immigration Border Patrol with the Customs Patrol, the consolidated agency to be administered either by the Immigration and Naturalization Service or by the Bureau of Customs.

The first argument for this plan is based, naturally, on the fact of territorial overlapping and the appearance of duplication. The latter, however, relates chiefly to the customs and immigrant inspectors, rather than to the patrolmen. A person entering the country is inspected once from the standpoint of citizenship and again from the standpoint of taxation.[9] Why can not one man or one set of men perform both inspections at once? At a few unimportant points of entry, customs inspectors have for several years done the work of immigrant inspectors, or the latter have taken over customs work. In places where traffic is heavy, however, more inspectors are required; and specialization and division of work are not merely justified but indispensable. In such places, the fact that the immigrant inspector and the customs inspector work separately and are responsible to different agencies does not necessarily mean duplication, inefficiency, waste effort, or any added inconvenience to the public.

Consolidation of the two patrols would, theoretically,

[9] "It seems to me almost absurd to see on one side of a building at a small port the Immigration Service, and on the other side the Customs Service, one handling customs and the other handling immigration. In some places where the work is slack, there is not probably ample work for both." Testimony of James H. Moyle, commissioner of customs, *Treasury Department Appropriation Bill for 1938,* Hearings, p. 252.

produce a better coverage of the border with the present personnel or effect economies through reduction of personnel. It might make possible more elaborate organization. For maximum efficiency, the head of a district office should have an assistant, for it is impossible for an official to travel, maintain outside contacts, or take personal charge of important investigations and at the same time do his headquarters work as it ought to be done. Consolidation of field officers, by creating a larger field force in each district, makes possible the provision of assistants in the field headquarters offices. A larger force would presumably permit stronger concentrations in emergencies. The flexibility of the combined force, however, would depend somewhat on all of its members' having the same training. If it were necessary for part of the consolidated force to specialize in customs matters and the other part to specialize in immigration matters, the force as a whole would not be as flexible, as unified, or as economical as it might at first glance appear. Unfortunately, such specialization appears to be essential.

Consolidation might help to insure continuous co-operation between the two branches of patrol work and the elimination of such duplications and conflicts as now occur. Valuable co-operation now takes place between the two forces; and it is doubtful whether any serious jurisdictional or operating conflicts have occurred.

Each patrol is a means to an end. Neither can act as an independent agency. Both are established for auxiliary law-enforcement work. Co-ordination is of course necessary between them; but it is even more necessary that co-ordination should be achieved between the Customs Patrol and the other branches of the Customs Service and between the Immigration Border Patrol and the other branches of the Immigration and Naturalization

Service. If the field organization of the Bureau of Immigration and Naturalization were dismembered and if the Immigration Border Patrol were directed by some authority other than the Commissioner of Immigration and Naturalization, it would be necessary at once to establish a means of co-ordinating the Patrol with the inspection branch of the Immigration and Naturalization Service. The problem of co-ordination thus created might be more difficult than the present problem of co-ordinating the two separate patrols. It would seem that, inevitably, considerable damage would be done to the continuity and unity of operations within the Immigration Service. Moreover, the Commissioner of Immigration and Naturalization could hardly be held responsible for results if he were shorn of complete control over one of his indispensable instruments of enforcement. The relative importance of the Immigration and Naturalization Service in the Department of Labor and the fact that the Service is predominantly a field force suggest that any division of the field force or any transfer of functions and personnel to another department should be undertaken only after the most careful consideration.

Substantially the same line of argument may be used against a transfer of the functions and personnel of the Customs Patrol to the Immigration and Naturalization Service.

SHOULD PATROLLING GO TO THE BUREAU OF INVESTIGATION?

If it is granted that the Bureau of Investigation should be the general crime-control agency of the federal government, it might be argued that the Bureau, like municipal police departments, should be equipped for patrolling. If so, in what area is patrolling more necessary

than along the borders, where fugitives presumably
escape? If, from the standpoint of general law enforcement, the borders need patrolling, why not transfer the
Customs Patrol or the Immigration Border Patrol or
both to the Bureau of Investigation? Then, it may be
contended, we would have at last a well-rounded federal
crime-control agency.

Against this contention we must apply with redoubled
force the arguments which have just been adduced
against a consolidation of one patrol with the other. In
favor of a transfer to the Bureau of Investigation, very
little of an affirmative and practical nature can be said.
To be sure, some criminals wanted by the Bureau do
escape to foreign countries, just as fugitives from other
agencies similarly elude capture. As of October 10, 1936,
the Bureau was seeking the apprehension of 579 fugitives. Of these, forty-seven were known to be in foreign
countries from which extradition was for some reason
impossible. It is not without interest, too, that while the
Bureau of Investigation, Secret Service, and Post Office
inspectors are attempting to prevent our citizen criminals
from leaving the country, it is the duty of the Immigration and Naturalization Service to prevent alien criminals from coming in and to deport those who are found
here. During the fiscal year 1936, the Service deported
1,727 criminal aliens. Bruno Richard Hauptmann, by
the way, was an alien self-smuggler, who, unfortunately,
had not been caught and deported.[10] Whatever the ethics
of the matter may be, it is numerically much more important to get alien criminals out than to keep citizen

---

[10] It is not desired, of course, to support the rather common impression
that aliens as a class are largely criminal. Of the 9,195 aliens deported
in 1936, about 19 per cent were criminals; but approximately 4,000,000
aliens are in the country.

criminals in. In any case, the Immigration Border Patrol has a point of view quite different from that of the Bureau of Investigation and other agencies which operate in the interior. The chances are that a few domestic criminals will escape to foreign countries, whatever the border patrol set-up may be. A fugitive-proof patrol of land borders as extensive as ours could be maintained only at prohibitive expense. The problem does not seem to be of much relative importance; and it can probably best be handled, as now, through co-operative action by the Bureau of Investigation and other enforcement agencies with the passport authorities, customs and immigration inspectors and patrolmen, the Coast Guard, the steamship lines, and foreign police departments.

SUMMARY AND CONCLUSIONS

In spite of their superficial similarities, their parallel operations, and their apparent duplications, the two land patrols are different; and their consolidation with each other or with a third agency would be impracticable. The Customs Patrol should remain in the Treasury Department, where it is already fairly well co-ordinated with the Coast Guard and other Treasury enforcement agencies. The Immigration Border Patrol is and must continue to be an integral part of the Immigration and Naturalization Service. It is, perhaps, not administratively essential that this Service be located in the Department of Labor. It would not be illogical to transfer the entire Service to the Treasury Department; and such a reorganization would probably facilitate co-ordination with the Coast Guard and the Customs Patrol. But it is idle to pursue the fantasy further. The Immigration and Naturalization Service has been recently "humanized"; its character and reputation are now good; its traditional association is with labor interests; and the administration of naturalization, particularly, has a pronounced educational or social-welfare slant.

So, if something needs to be done, we must fall back on inter-departmental co-ordination. Perhaps there can be more interchanges of personnel and duties between the Customs Service and the Immigration and Naturalization Service and more division of territory between the two patrols than there are now. It is possible that the two agencies may jointly undertake a detailed study of their common problems, and find the best solutions. It is possible that they may require some leading, urging, or compelling.

CHAPTER X

REVENUE, ALCOHOL, AND NARCOTICS

In our survey of federal crime-control agencies, we have reached the Bureau of Internal Revenue and the Bureau of Narcotics. One of the situations now presented to us offers no particular difficulty: the use of detective techniques for the purposes of tax collection. The Investigative Unit of the Customs Agency Service of the Bureau of Customs, which we have already discussed, has its analogue in the Intelligence Unit of the Bureau of Internal Revenue. On the other hand, the Alcohol Tax Unit, of the same Bureau, and the Bureau of Narcotics, which is established separately, spring from composite, changing, and confused objectives and present correspondingly complex problems. Let us dispose first of the Intelligence Unit.

INTELLIGENCE UNIT

The Intelligence Unit is located in the immediate office of the Commissioner of Internal Revenue. At the end of 1936 the Unit consisted of three divisions: (1) the Personnel, Enrollment, and Records Division; (2) the Fraud Division; and (3) the Field Districts. The districts were fifteen in number; and the field force on June 30, 1936 numbered 196 men.

In addition to the investigation of violations of internal revenue laws, the Intelligence Unit is concerned with serious infractions of disciplinary rules or regulations on the part of officials and employees of the Bureau of Internal Revenue; and, when directed by the Secretary of the Treasury, the Unit investigates alleged irregularities by officials and employees of other branches of the Treasury Department. In addition, a large part of the work of the Unit relates to investigations of applicants for positions in the Bureau and in certain other branches of the Department. To the Unit is also assigned the investigation of applicants for admission to practice before the Treasury Department as attorneys and agents, and the investigation of charges against enrolled attorneys and agents.

This agency is closely tied in with the Bureau and the Department. In the initiation of many of its investigations, the Unit acts on instructions from the Commissioner of Internal Revenue, the General Counsel, or the Secretary of the Treasury. The Penal Division of the General Counsel's Office reviews the reports of the special agents of the Unit to determine whether action should be taken in accordance with the recommendations made. Tax fraud investigations are made in conjunction with internal revenue field agents or with deputy collectors who handle the audit features of cases under investigation. The duties of the Intelligence Unit relate primarily to obtaining evidence to determine criminal responsibility.

The Unit co-operates with other law-enforcement agencies of the Treasury Department and with agencies outside the Treasury.[1] Its relations with state and local law-enforcement agencies have assumed no continuing significance; though such co-operation was involved in the racket investigations at Chicago, New York, and other places, which resulted in the conviction and imprisonment of Al Capone, Waxie Gordon, and other notorious criminals.

The special agents are under Civil Service. A newly

[1] For references to such co-operation, see pp. 102, 139, 183.

appointed agent is given an outline of instructions and correspondence training courses covering accounting, income-tax laws, evidence, commercial law, and so forth; and he is assigned to work with one of the agents of long service and experience. The intensive training period is six weeks or less. At the end of the training period the student special agent receives assignments on his own responsibility, and his training is continued by means of the correspondence courses which are studied outside of business hours.

On the whole, the enforcement work of the Intelligence Unit is auxiliary and internal. Its basic functions belong where they are; and no other feature of this agency suggests that any of its activities or personnel should be transferred elsewhere.

ALCOHOL CONTROL: ORGANIZATION AND FUNCTIONS

The alcohol-control functions of the federal government are exercised primarily by the Federal Alcohol Administration and the Alcohol Tax Unit of the Bureau of Internal Revenue. The functions of the former agency are: to regulate, through the issuance of basic permits, the business of importing, producing,[2] and wholesaling alcoholic beverages; to prevent exclusive outlets and "tied houses"; to administer the labelling provisions of the law; and to make investigations and studies. The functions of the Administration, therefore, seem to lie primarily in the field of business regulation; incidentally, in the field of public health.

The Alcohol Tax Unit is charged with the administration of the internal revenue laws relating to the following subjects: (1) production, custody, and supervision of alcoholic liquors; (2) establishment, construc-

[2] Brewers are not included.

tion, operation, custody, and supervision, of distilleries, industrial alcohol plants, bonded warehouses, denaturing plants, wineries, bonded wine storerooms, breweries, rectifying houses, de-alcoholizing plants, cereal beverage plants, and other places where alcoholic liquors are produced or stored; (3) determination, assertion, assessment, and compromising of all internal revenue taxes and penalties pertaining to alcoholic liquors; (4) inquiries and investigations relating to the filing of returns for occupational and commodity taxes and penalties in respect to alcoholic liquors; (5) investigation, prevention, and detection of violations of laws pertaining to alcoholic liquors; (6) detention and seizure, for violations of laws, of liquors and other property, and the custody, control, sale, and disposition of property so seized; and (7) the discharge of liens.

For administrative purposes, the Alcohol Tax Unit has been divided into two divisions, Permissive and Enforcement, thus recognizing the two main functions with which it is concerned: supervision of the legitimate industry, and suppression of illicit traffic. The Enforcement Division distributes its work among four sections: the Examining Section, the Enforcement Files Section, the Pardon and Parole Section, and the Raw Materials Section. The Examining Section inspects the field offices, trains the enforcement personnel, prepares instructions, reviews reports of investigations, and exercises general supervision. The total personnel of the Alcohol Tax Unit on October 31, 1936 was 4,381. All but 204 were in the field. The personnel of the Enforcement Division numbered about 1,680, of whom 1,390 were investigators. Measured by manpower, it was the largest of the federal law-enforcement agencies operating on land.

The activities of the Enforcement Division include

those appropriate to an auxiliary enforcement agency: investigation of suspected persons, properties, and operations; serving of search and seizure warrants; arrest and arraignment of violators; collection and preparation of evidence; lending of assistance to United States attorneys; and giving testimony at trials. Agents of the Enforcement Division investigate petitions for remission of forfeitures; obtain evidence to support jeopardy assessments; investigate the financial responsibility of defendants; occasionally make statistical surveys and research reports with reference to the alcohol industry, lawful or illicit; and conduct investigations relative to applications for pardon and parole filed by offenders convicted of violating the internal revenue liquor laws.

All employees of the Enforcement Division are under Civil Service. The investigators receive training either by lectures or correspondence courses in criminal investigation and criminal and constitutional law. The lecture course covers a period of two or three weeks; the correspondence course, several months. Particular emphasis is placed on the subject of evidence. Investigators are assigned with inspectors, Secret Service operatives, internal revenue agents, customs agents or others; and the investigators' reports are reviewed in Washington by examiners. The Unit has personnel trained in radio, ballistics, photography, dictograph, wire-tapping, handwriting, fingerprinting, shadowing, cryptanology, law, and so forth. All are trained in the use of small arms and all are provided with comprehensive briefs on the law of conspiracy and the law of searches and seizures.

THE ALCOHOL TAX UNIT: ENFORCEMENT RELATIONSHIPS

The Alcohol Tax Unit is not equipped or inclined to radiate service throughout the federal, or even the

Treasury organization. It is specialized to its own perplexing and somewhat technical tasks. In the field of crime control, its officers are expected to confine themselves, so far as possible, to the prevention of illicit distilling, sale, and transportation of liquor, and other evasions of the liquor-tax laws. They are not encouraged to perform duties imposed upon other officers. Nevertheless, the Unit is a part of the Treasury co-ordinating system previously described.[3] Its investigators were instructed in 1934 to co-operate effectively with officers of the Customs Service, the Coast Guard, the Bureau of Narcotics, and the Secret Service Division. When the Alcohol Tax Unit discovers that an apprehended person is wanted by some other agency, it notifies such agency; and, if the Unit has evidence incriminating a person not yet arrested and if the offense is outside the jurisdiction of the Unit, it turns the evidence over to the agency having jurisdiction. In an emergency, Alcohol Tax agents may arrest an offender and detain him until a representative of the agency having jurisdiction can be notified and can arrive upon the scene.

The Intelligence Unit of the Bureau of Internal Revenue conducts personnel investigations for the Enforcement Division of the Alcohol Tax Unit. The Enforcement Division, in turn, aids the Intelligence Unit by providing investigative personnel, when requested, for the purpose of conducting particular kinds of investigations. The Alcohol Tax Unit on the one hand and the Customs Agency Service and the Coast Guard on the other overlap with respect to the smuggling of non-tax-paid spirits. Coast Guard airplanes have been used in rendering assistance to the Alcohol Tax Unit. The planes locate the stills; and the ground force, consisting of per-

[3] Pp. 172-73.

sonnel from the Unit, makes the seizures and arrests. The Unit in turn has aided the Coast Guard with automotive transportation.

The functions of the Federal Alcohol Administration dovetail into those of the Alcohol Tax Unit. The Enforcement Division of the Unit conducts for the Administration character investigations of applicants for permits to engage in the legitimate liquor industry; and the Division also makes investigations and reports for the Administration to support citations for the suspension and revocation of permits. Chemical analyses are made for the Federal Alcohol Administration in the laboratory of the Alcohol Tax Unit.

In some matters, the Alcohol Tax Unit overlaps and co-operates with the Food and Drug Administration of the Department of Agriculture, the Federal Power Commission, the Federal Trade Commission, and the Federal Communications Commission. The Unit has close working relations with the Consular Service and the Passport Division of the Department of State, the Taxes and Penalties Unit of the Department of Justice, the Bureau of Standards of the Department of Commerce, the Veterans' Administration, and the Bureau of Engraving and Printing.[4]

The Twenty-first Amendment, repealing the Eighteenth, contains, in addition to the repeal clause, the following:

The transportation or importation into any state, territory, or possession of the United States for delivery or use therein of intoxicating liquors, in violation of the laws thereof, is hereby prohibited.

If public opinion were again to swing toward state

[4] For other examples of inter-agency relationships involving the Alcohol Tax Unit, see pp. 92-93, 96, 103, 124, 138, 156-57, 172, 184.

prohibition, the federal obligation to protect the dry states would present a considerable administrative problem. But, according to Harrison and Laine,

> The once formidable task of protecting dry states has been steadily diminishing since repeal. After two years there remain only five states to be guarded against liquor shipments from outside their borders. . . .
>
> It is unquestionably true that the citizens of dry states are not of a single mind about vigorous enforcement of their prohibition laws. . . . Recognizing this situation, the federal government has taken a realistic view regarding its responsibility toward dry states. It proposes to undertake the control of liquor shipments into them only to the extent that they wish the shipments to be controlled. . . .[5]

The amount and kind of overlapping between the Alcohol Tax Unit and the states vary from state to state. The state laws are far from uniform; and most of them differ in various respects from the federal laws. The offenses within the jurisdiction of a particular state, that are also within the jurisdiction of the Alcohol Tax Unit, depend on factors that vary from absolute prohibition of the importation, manufacture, sale, transportation, or possession of intoxicating liquor in a dry state to a provision in a wet state that no distilled spirits shall be manufactured or sold without payment of tax. Even some of the states whose laws cover approximately all offenses within the jurisdiction of the federal agency have no adequate enforcement organization. Some state and local officials tend to look upon the traffic in non-taxpaid spirits as a federal problem; while other states have excellent enforcement units that make and prosecute their own cases and co-operate with federal agencies. Of the thousands of persons who annually violate the fed-

[5] *After Repeal*, p. 226.

eral liquor-tax laws, a relatively small number are arrested by state and local officers.

While the Enforcement Division of the Alcohol Tax Unit can operate independently of state and local authorities, complete elimination of the traffic in non-tax-paid spirits can not be accomplished unless each state has proper legislation and enforces its own liquor-control laws. The success of the Unit, therefore, is largely dependent upon the assistance it receives from state and local police authorities. Enforcement officers of the Unit are expected to co-operate with such authorities. The policy of the Unit is to encourage state and local officers to handle violations of state liquor or revenue laws which are also minor violations of federal laws, turning over to the Unit for investigation the major cases under state laws which are also major violations of federal laws.

ANTI-NARCOTIC ACTIVITIES AND ORGANIZATION

The Bureau of Narcotics has general supervision of the enforcement of the Harrison Narcotic Law and related statutes, including the administration of the permissive features of the Narcotics Drugs Import and Export Act; and the Bureau co-operates with the Customs Service in the enforcement of the prohibitive features of the latter act.[6] Under the Narcotic Drugs Import and Export Act, the Commissioner of Narcotics, with the advice of the Surgeon General of the United States Public Health Service, determines periodically the total quantities of crude opium and coca leaves which may be allowed to be imported for medical and scientific purposes. These quantities are then allotted among qualified importing manufacturers; and permits are issued to them

---

[6] For the functions of the Customs Service in narcotic control, see p. 184.

upon application for the importation of specific quantities against their respective allotments. The Bureau likewise issues formal authorization, upon appropriate application, for the export of narcotic drugs and preparations to a foreign country; and for the in-transit shipment through the United States of narcotics drugs and preparations consigned from one foreign country to another. Under the act of June 14, 1930, the Bureau issues permits for the importation of quantities of coca leaves additional to those admissible under the Narcotic Drugs Import and Export Act, but only for the manufacture of a decocainized coca extract. Incidental to such permission, it is incumbent on the Bureau to see that the cocaine content of these additional supplies of leaves is destroyed. Under the Convention for Limiting the Manufacture and Regulating the Distribution of Narcotic Drugs (supplementing the International Opium Convention of 1912), the Bureau compiles and submits annually, through the State Department to the International Supervisory Body, estimates for this country of the manufacturing requirements with respect to each narcotic alkaloid or salt covered by the Convention. Manufacture within the United States during any year is limited to the quantities of each narcotic alkaloid or salt actually required in accordance with the estimates previously submitted.

The Bureau is obliged, of course, to prepare, promulgate, and enforce various regulations to the end that the manufacture, sale, distribution, export, and use of dangerous habit-forming narcotic drugs may be limited exclusively to medical and scientific purposes. Necessarily, the Bureau supervises the amounts of raw material and manufactured drugs in the possession of each manufacturer and requires from each a quarterly report showing receipts of raw materials, and production of drugs and derivatives. The returns from manufacturers and wholesale dealers must be audited; and statistical compilations are prepared from them. To the Permanent Central Opium Board at Geneva, reports are transmitted through the State Department showing statistics of imports and exports, manufacture, stocks on hand, and quantities confiscated as contraband. The Commissioner of Narcotics also prepares an annual report on the working of the Convention in the United States, including statistical data and a comprehensive summary of enforcement activities and results obtained during the year.

The above-mentioned activities are, in the main, regulatory and statistical. They form a sequence of interdependent procedures which should not be administratively separated. In addition, the Bureau exercises promotional functions. It seeks to encourage state legislation for the suppression of the abuse of habit-forming drugs; and it endeavors in various ways to inform the public concerning the narcotics situation. A Uniform State Narcotic Law was approved about four years ago by the Conference of Commissioners on Uniform State Laws and by the American Bar Association, and, on June 30, 1936, had been adopted with little or no modification by twenty-nine states.

The Bureau's enforcement activities relate to two different, but not always distinct, types of law-breaking: smuggling from without, and illicit traffic within the country. The Bureau estimates that approximately 80 per cent of its time is spent in enforcement activities and that the remaining 20 per cent is devoted to permissive and other work. In the Bureau of Narcotics, the Commissioner has under his immediate supervision the Field Inspection and Special Representation Division and the

Enforcement Division. Under the Deputy Commissioner are the Administrative Division, the Returns Division, and the Drug Disposal Committee. Attached is the Narcotic Section of the General Counsel's Office of the Treasury Department. The field inspectors examine field offices, install uniform methods of organization and procedure, and report the condition of narcotic-law enforcement within the several districts. Special representatives act as liaison officers, making contacts with federal and state officials, civic organizations and others, in order to secure enactment of the Uniform State Narcotic Law, other effective narcotic legislation, and the co-operation of judges, prosecutors, parole boards, and state licensing boards in matters affecting narcotic-law enforcement. The Enforcement Division is responsible for the investigation of all violations of narcotics laws. The field force works through sixteen districts.

The total personnel of the Bureau on January 1, 1937 was 382.

All classes of employees in the Bureau are under Civil Service. An applicant, to be examined for an enforcement position, must have had:

(1) At least three years' experience in criminal investigations; or,

(2) A minimum education in medicine or pharmacy, one year's experience in medical or pharmacal work, and at least one year's experience in criminal investigation; or,

(3) A law education or admission to the bar, and at least one year's experience in criminal investigation. On appointment, a narcotic officer is assigned to a district where he works under the supervision and guidance of experienced colleagues. In this manner, he serves a six-month probationary period. He is required to take a

correspondence course in "Constitution and Law," and receives special training in the use of firearms.

BUREAU OF NARCOTICS: TIE-UPS AND RELATIONSHIPS

The Bureau of Narcotics is included in the Treasury's arrangement for the co-ordination of its law-enforcement agencies. In the regulatory and fiscal aspects of its work, the Bureau has a close relationship with the Public Health Service, the Customs Service, and the Bureau of Internal Revenue. On the enforcement side, assistance is rendered by the Coast Guard, the Customs Patrol, and the Alcohol Tax Unit. The Public Health Service makes such researches as may be necessary into the narcotic-drug problem and reports on the quantities of crude opium, coca leaves, and their salts, derivatives, and preparations that are necessary with suitable reserves to supply the normal and emergency medicinal and scientific requirements of the United States. These studies are used by the Commissioner of Narcotics in determining the amounts of crude opium and coca leaves to be permitted importation. The Division of Mental Hygiene of the Public Health Service is in charge of the United States Narcotic Farms. The Bureau of Internal Revenue handles all fiscal matters under the Harrison Narcotic Law, including the assessment and collection of taxes, the sale of commodity tax stamps, the receipt of applications from and the granting of registration under the same law to prospective taxpayers, the issuance of official order forms to taxpayers, and the receipt of and accounting for moneys offered in compromise of criminal and civil liability under that law. The Bureau of Narcotics refers to the Intelligence Unit any facts coming to its attention which indicate that a peddler of narcotics may have an unreported income which might be subject to income tax. The Customs Service is an essential link in the chain of enforcement.[7] The Alcohol Tax Unit and the Bureau of Narcotics exchange information obtained by one and of interest to the other.

The Department of State transmits to the Opium Advisory Committee at Geneva information regarding new laws and regulations governing narcotics put into effect in the United States; transmits opium import permits to consular officers in the foreign countries from which exportation is to be made; furnishes estimates and statistical reports to the Permanent Central Opium Board; sends to the Opium Advisory Committee the annual report of the government of the United States on the traffic in opium and other dangerous drugs; submits information and inquiries to the Bureau of Narcotics with respect to the international narcotic problem, particularly with reference to developments which might affect our system of narcotic drug control; passes along information to the Bureau regarding laws and regulations abroad on this subject; and supplies the Bureau with reports on opium prices in the principal foreign opium markets. The narcotic returns of manufacturers and dealers are made available to inspectors of the Food and Drug Administration of the Department of Agriculture, in order that they may obtain from such returns information regarding persons or firms receiving shipments of narcotic drugs in interstate commerce. Such information is useful in connection with the collection and examination of samples of drugs which have been shipped in interstate commerce, to determine whether or not they possess the ingredients claimed for them. The Bureau of Narcotics co-operates through the Division of Island Territories

[7] For the functions of the Customs Service in narcotic control, see p. 184.

of the Department of the Interior with the internal revenue authorities of Puerto Rico and the health officials of the Virgin Islands, in connection with shipments of drugs and the procuring of annual reports. Likewise through the Bureau of Insular Affairs of the War Department the Bureau co-operates with the Philippine authorities.[8]

In narcotics, as in alcohol control, federal-state-local relationships reflect an aspect of the problem that is fundamentally significant. Narcotics control lies within the police power of the states. It became a federal function because the states, in this connection, were unable to act with any degree of thoroughness. Opium and cocaine are produced in foreign countries. Inevitably, therefore, they are subjects of foreign commerce and constitute a clear-cut problem of international relations. Nevertheless, it is not the policy of the federal government to assume the whole burden. It has not attempted, for example, directly to control marihuana, which is domestically produced. The Bureau of Narcotics is required to co-operate with the states in the drafting of legislation for the suppression of the narcotic evil. It is charged with exchanging information with the states on this general subject; and at times it assists state and local authorities in the initiation and prosecution of cases before state courts and state licensing boards. To the licensing boards, the Bureau reports the names of licensees who are believed to be drug addicts or who have been convicted of narcotic violations. Such information is used in connection with the revocation or suspension of state licenses to practice a profession or engage in a business involving transactions in narcotic drugs.

[8] For other examples of co-operation with or by the Bureau of Narcotics, see pp. 93, 100, 138, 139, 153, 184.

Effective narcotic-law enforcement depends in large measure on the co-operation of state and local, especially municipal, police authorities. Each year a considerable number of cases are made jointly, by federal and local officers working in co-operation; and most of the joint cases involve unregistered persons, who are, for the most part, underworld characters.

NATURE AND INCIDENCE OF NARCOTICS ENFORCEMENT

The purpose of the federal government is to keep all narcotic drugs in legitimate channels. To accomplish this purpose, it must prevent the smuggling of drugs into the country and the diversion of drugs imported. If these were prevented, the evil would be under approximate control; though we should still have the problem of addiction among physicians and nurses, as well as the apparently growing menace of marihuana. Some half-dozen years ago, smuggling reached considerable proportions. In 1930, customs officers seized 23,836 ounces of morphine; and in 1931, 17,266 ounces of raw opium, 15,735 ounces of smoking opium, and 7,960 ounces of heroin. The total quantity of all narcotic substances taken in 1931 was 66,674 ounces. In no subsequent year has the figure reached 20,000. The decline of seizures does not indicate any diminution of anti-smuggling effort. On the contrary, the evidence is that smuggling itself has decreased, owing to the effectiveness of federal counter-measures. The Commissioner of Narcotics stated in 1935:

There is no doubt that there is some smuggling of narcotics by aircraft and by surface craft of the usual smuggling type, but the greatest narcotic-smuggling problem appears to be connected with the activities of individual members of the crews of legitimate vessels from the Orient. . . .[9]

In 1936, the Commissioner thought that smuggling on the Pacific coast was increasing.

The prevention and detection of smuggling from foreign countries is, in general, only a small part of narcotics enforcement work; and this part is performed in the main by the Customs Service, with continuous help from the Coast Guard and occasional assistance from the Immigration Border Patrol and other agencies. The Commissioner of Narcotics estimated in 1934 that about 5 per cent of the work of his Bureau related to the apprehension of smugglers. It is not probable that the percentage has increased since that time.

The effect of decreased smuggling is to reduce the supply in the domestic trade, raise prices, encourage adulteration, and stimulate diversions from legitimate to illegitimate channels. As stated by the Secretary of the Treasury in his annual report for 1935:

The decrease in the supplies of smuggled narcotics has forced peddlers and addicts to turn more and more to the channels of legitimate distribution for their supply. The robbery of wholesale and retail stocks, the forgery and false execution of narcotic prescriptions, and the improper prescribing and dispensing of narcotics are accordingly becoming more of an enforcement problem.[10]

Any person who legally handles regulated narcotics must register annually. An unregistered person may have the drugs in his legal possession, but only when they have been obtained upon a physician's prescription from a registered dealer for legitimate medical use

[9] 74 Cong. 1 sess., *Treasury Department Appropriation Bill for 1936*, Hearings before H. Committee on Appropriations, p. 421.

[10] P. 138.

and are in a container which bears various identifying marks and is sealed with an internal revenue stamp. Violators of the narcotics laws, therefore, fall roughly into two main classes: registered persons and unregistered persons. The registered persons are largely physicians and druggists. The unregistered violator may be an addict who uses and does not ordinarily seek to dispose of what he illegally obtains; or he may be a higher-up in a powerful wholesaling ring or gang which blends the smuggling, stealing, and selling of narcotics with other forms of vice and crime; or he may be the "dope" peddler—the ultimate petty retailer in this infamous business.

To make clear some of the peculiarities of enforcement in this field, the following table is offered:[11]

	Violations Reported		Convictions	
Year	By Registered Persons	By Unregistered Persons	By Registered Persons	By Unregistered Persons
1931	1,003	5,072	154	2,957
1932	703	4,405	104	2,944
1933	882	3,951	130	2,681
1934	1,373	3,270	140	2,231
1935	2,106	4,187	240	2,875
1936	2,424	3,435	150	2,809
Total	8,491	24,320	918	16,497

In every one of the last six years, reported violations by unregistered persons have exceeded those by registered persons. Since 1932, however, offenses by registrants have been increasing, while violations by others show no such trend.

While the number of violations is not necessarily the same as the number of violators, it appears that a rela-

[11] The figures are taken from 74 Cong. 2 sess., *Treasury Department Appropriation Bill for 1937*, Hearings before H. Committee on Appropriations, p. 445.

tively small number of registered violators are convicted. During the last six years there were 8,491 violations by registered persons; but the courts convicted only 918 or about 11 per cent of the violations. Of the unregistered violators, 16,497 were convicted, or about 68 per cent of the 24,320 violations. The fact is that, in the recent past, a large percentage of the registered violators have not been brought to trial. Many of these cases are technical, without willful intent to break the law; and they are settled with letters of admonition. Other cases besides these are dropped or compromised because of the difficulty of conviction. Perhaps there is some unjust discrimination in favor of the registered offender; but the important reason seems to be that a large part, perhaps 50 per cent, of the enforcement work of the Bureau of Narcotics is of a peculiar and specialized type, having to do with persons, chiefly druggists and physicians, who can not be successfully handled by ordinary criminal-law enforcement methods. To be controlled, they must be persuaded, bargained with, and brought into line without too much publicity.[12] In short, a substantial part of the so-called enforcement work of the Bureau is more analogous to regulation and tax collection than it is to crime control.

BASIC PROBLEMS

Alcoholic beverages and narcotic drugs affect in some degree, temporarily or permanently, the physical and mental health of the individuals who use them habitually or to excess. Protection of the public health is a local

[12] It must not be understood that these are all minor or technical violators. "Dr. Ratigan in Seattle, for instance, who was sentenced to eight years, bought 350 times the average purchase of a doctor, and his purchases amounted to 440,000 medical shots, for which he charged a dollar a shot." 75 Cong. 1 sess., *Treasury Department Appropriation Bill for 1938*, Hearings before H. Committee on Appropriations, p. 181.

and a state, as well as a federal function. In the federal organization, promotion of health is the primary objective of the Public Health Service in the Treasury Department; and it is either a primary or a secondary objective of numerous other federal agencies. For example, the care of the consumers' health has played an important, if not a decisive rôle, in the development and functioning of the Food and Drug Administration in the Department of Agriculture. This agency, it should be noted, deals, on the whole, with tangible, analyzable, and consumable substances which are bought and sold in interstate and foreign commerce. Experience has shown that an effective control of such substances necessitates a regulation of the businesses which produce or sell them. Thus, when it concerns itself with commodities, health protection inevitably becomes business regulation—another broad administrative field. Business regulation is interested, not only in the content and composition of goods and in the honesty of labelling and advertising, but also in trade practices, monopolies, and restraint of trade. The Federal Trade Commission is a fairly typical business regulatory agency.

Physical health is one thing; morality is another. Physical health and physical disease, nutrition and poisoning, can, to a remarkable extent, be scientifically proved. Diagnosis, test tubes, microscopes, and guinea pigs usually do the trick. Morality, on the contrary, is a matter of community opinion, feeling, or prejudice; and most of us, within our own lifetimes, have witnessed striking changes in our tribal taboos, immoral practices becoming moral and moral practices becoming immoral. Broadly speaking, the tendency in recent times seems to have been to liberalize the acts and relations of individuals and relatively small groups, with respect to personal habits, entertainment, recreation, religion, sex, and marital relations. The general inclination seems to be to shift the details of such matters from the field of morality to the field of health, esthetics, or social utilitarianism. On the other hand, more definite ethical standards and stronger moral barriers seem to have appeared, within our own country at least, in the large fields of industry, politics, administration, and international relations.

The historic crimes, such as murder, theft, and rape, were immoral long before they became illegal; and, viewing the modern picture of crime, we see in the background something like a double exposure. The legally defined crimes seem to be shifting in part from the field of morals to the fields of health and economics, from an area where emotion prevails to areas where tests, demonstration, measurement, and proof are possible.

Moreover, the modern disposition is to transfer the responsibility for crime from the individual to society. In other words, the individual conscience is being relieved through the imposition of new moral obligations on the community as a whole. To be sure, we are not yet prepared or preparing to treat the traditional crimes with toleration; for the adoption of such an undiscriminating liberalism would mean a relapse into anarchic savagery. Our attitude is that, for the protection of society, the criminal must be caught, no matter where the moral responsibility for his acts may lie; and it is the proper function of a police agency to catch criminals, whether they are viewed as morally culpable, mentally ill, or merely as victims of environmental maladjustments.

It is not so clear, however, that a crime-control agency can function effectively in the more recently established domains that are rather definitely dedicated to matters of health and morals. As a rule, police and investigative agencies have little to do with the public health; but they have much to do, locally, with the enforcement of morals legislation. Such matters as drunkenness, prostitution, gambling, and obscenity are commonly within local police jurisdictions. Even in the federal organization, we have seen that the Bureau of Investigation has primary jurisdiction over the interstate transportation of prize-fight films and of women for immoral purposes, while the Post Office inspectors are concerned with lotteries, obscenity, and related matters. We have also noted, in earlier chapters, the changes in public attitudes toward alcoholic beverages and the experiments with different federal set-ups for alcohol control.

It is interesting also to recall at this point that narcotic drugs were for a time closely associated administratively with alcoholic beverages. Though now separated at the bureau level, both classes of commodities are assigned primarily to the Treasury Department, which, though it includes the Public Health Service, is not a health department. Neither is it in any sense a morals department. The Treasury is a fiscal agency; and its fiscal function obviously explains why it has charge of alcohol and narcotics. The federal government, in the main, can protect morals or health only through its taxing power, its power to regulate interstate and foreign commerce, or its postal power. All three powers are applied to the control of alcohol and narcotics; but the taxing power is apparently viewed at the present time as the most immediately effective. Indeed, taxation has been resorted to for the control of certain dangerous firearms—commodities that are significant almost exclusively from the standpoint of crime control.

In the light of contemporary opinion and public policy, one should, of course, be cautious about speaking of narcotics and alcohol in the same breath. Drug addiction is uncompromisingly viewed as a serious menace to morals and health. In narcotics control, taxation is merely a means to an end. With respect to alcohol, on the contrary, the raising of revenue is now the chief consideration, so far as the federal government is concerned; and questions of morality and health are, for the time at least, subordinate.

National policy failed when it branded the liquor traffic as criminal and adopted a "puritanical" attitude with regard to the enforcement of the prohibition laws. It is possible that the laws were, from the start, out of harmony with the prevailing moral sense. If law and morality were harmonious in the beginning, they got more and more out of step as morality changed; and it is probable that the sweeping application of criminal-law enforcement to the liquor traffic was a strong, if not the strongest, influence in creating or solidifying the popular attitude of tolerance toward the traffic. The experiment with national prohibition taught us, or should have taught us, that criminal-law enforcement, when apparently indicated for a moral or a health condition, should be prescribed with extreme caution. Under certain conditions, the remedy may be worse than the disease. Criminal-law enforcement is unfortunately capable of undermining its own foundations.

Drug addiction is less general than drinking. The use of narcotics is demonstrably more dangerous to the individual; and the non-medical drug trade bears at present the full weight of social reprobation. Yet, criminal-law enforcement might easily prove a too inflexible instrument for successful use on the narcotics ulcer. It is conceivable, even in this situation, that the disease might destroy the instrument, or, at least, cause the patient to prefer the disease to the instrument.

The taxing of alcohol is not altogether simple. It has its disturbing implications and instabilities. On this phase of the problem, we have recent and good authority:

> Liquor is a luxury product and a commodity that is inherently susceptible of abuse. As such it is taxed for the dual purpose of raising revenue and placing a check on its use.
>
> . . . .
>
> The problem of law enforcement, encountered wherever liquor is sold, . . . can be aggravated by imposing severe limitations on sales, or it can be mitigated by liberalizing restrictions. The difficulties of preventing tax evasion are increased or reduced roughly in proportion to changes in the rate of the tax. Compliance with legal restrictions can be reasonably well enforced wherever the public honestly desires it.
>
> On the other hand, if restrictions are not well rooted in public acceptance, they cannot be enforced even by specially competent officials. These simple truths are readily acknowledged. The difficulty comes in determining what the public wishes or will stand for in liquor-law enforcement. . . .
>
> To the extent that limitations on selling and high taxes curb excessive individual consumption of liquor they are fully justified. When, however, they give rise to bootlegging and persistent violation of selling regulations, their value must be questioned. The important thing, therefore, is to determine the proper balance between evils connected with excessive drinking and evils arising directly from over-taxation and over-regulation.[13]

Alcohol control and narcotics control have points of similarity and of contrast. Each trenches on different fields of administration. Each represents a complex of activities, a bouquet of objectives. With respect to each, federal and state jurisdictions are concurrent and federal

---

[13] Leonard V. Harrison and Elizabeth Laine, *After Repeal*, pp. 11, 13.

and state functions overlap. In both areas of control administration should be flexible and readily adaptable.

SHALL WE REORGANIZE?

The Commissioner of Narcotics, during the appropriation hearings in December 1934, made the following interesting remarks:

> In the last two weeks we threw a net over the traffic throughout the entire United States, and caught in that net about 800 peddlers; criminals of all descriptions, bank robbers, public enemies, petty thieves, and stick-up men.

> One man who was arrested had a record of ninety arrests, in the city of New Orleans. I would like to put his record in these hearings. It is the most astonishing thing I have seen. We caught him selling drugs. That is a remarkable instance; a man with ninety arrests, for crimes ranging from misdemeanor to murder.[14]

The record referred to includes these charges, some of them repeated two or more times: petty larceny; assault and battery; wounding less than mayhem; assault, beating, and wounding; disturbing the peace; manslaughter; shooting with intent to kill; assault by willfully shooting at; reckless and drunken driving; operating automobile with mutilated license plates; assault and robbery; malicious mischief; grand larceny; assault with intent to rape; robbery; larceny from person; possession of stolen property; and hold-up and robbery of United States mail truck. "Dutch" Normandale's record of versatility and perseverance covered about fourteen years (1917-31), during which time he was sentenced to the Louisiana Training Institute for from three to five years. He was once given a fine of $50 or sixty days in the parish prison; and, on a later occasion, $25 or thirty days. Well along in his criminal career, he received a sentence of

[14] *Treasury Department Appropriation Bill for 1936*, Hearings, p. 201.

several years in the Louisiana State Penitentiary; and, about three and a half years later he was convicted on the mail robbery charge and sentenced to the federal prison at Atlanta for two years. Here, evidently, was a dangerous, persistent, and incurable criminal. He was frequently caught but rarely punished for his state offenses; but he was both caught and punished for robbing the mails and peddling narcotics, which are federal offenses.

As a rule, the unregistered trafficker in drugs is an underworld character and a factor in the general problem of criminality.[15] When narcotic agents pursue and apprehend him, they are, in a way, paralleling the work of the Bureau of Investigation. Though the Post Office inspectors sent "Dutch" Normandale to prison for a brief interval, the Bureau of Investigation apparently never had jurisdiction over him. This particular narcotics peddler may not be typical; but the illicit drug trade certainly figures to a considerable extent in the problem of general criminality. Moreover, narcotics-law enforcement calls for close co-operation with state and local authorities. Would it not be logical, then, to transfer narcotics enforcement activities to the Bureau of Investigation? Yes, from one point of view, but quite illogical from others.

Effective control of dangerous drugs requires much more than merely the arrest and punishment of "dope" peddlers. It requires more even than the prevention of smuggling. It calls for international co-operation for the

[15] "Out of the 13,000 prison population, drug violators constitute about 2,173, or about 15 per cent of the population. . . . Narcotic violators, we find, according to the records of the Department of Justice, are the worst offenders in the country. Sixty-four per cent have previous criminal records, including crimes of violence. They top the list of criminals in the country having previous records." Statement of H. J. Anslinger in hearings on *Treasury Department Appropriation Bill for 1938*, p. 180.

immediate purpose of preventing illegal shipments from foreign countries and with the aim eventually of keeping production of the raw materials themselves within the limits of the world's medicinal requirements. Federal control of narcotics, therefore, is based on both statutes and international agreements. These represent an attempt to solve a difficult and complex social problem, important in the promotion of the public health, the elimination of vice, and the reduction of criminality. Since neither opium nor cocaine is produced in the United States, the limitations of the quantity in this country to our medicinal requirements makes necessary a calculation of what our medicinal requirements are and renders essential a strict regulation of imports and the prevention of smuggling. Within the country, promotion activities, the education of the public, and the regulation of professions and businesses are all essential. More particularly, administration of narcotic control involves action by permanent international agencies, continuous co-operation with foreign governments, co-operation between the federal government and the states, federal promotion of state legislation, federal regulation through licensing and registration, education, taxation, inspection, detection, apprehension, and prosecution.

In its international aspects, narcotics control brings in the Department of State, and the Public Health Service, the Bureau of Narcotics, the Bureau of Customs, the Coast Guard, and other units of the Treasury Department. In its domestic aspects, narcotics control involves the taxation and regulation of those engaged in the narcotics trade; the prevention of diversion from legitimate to illegitimate channels; the detection, apprehension, and prosecution of illicit dealers; the maintenance of institutions for the treatment of addicts; and the carrying on of educational and other preventive activities. Domestic control, accordingly, brings in, not only the Bureau of Narcotics, but also the Bureau of Internal Revenue and the Public Health Service of the Treasury Department, as well as other federal agencies. Still other agencies which obviously have duties in this connection include the Immigration and Naturalization Service, the United States attorneys, and other officials under the supervision of the Department of Justice.

The relations of the Bureau of Narcotics with the states are in some respects similar to those of the Bureau of Investigation; but they are in other respects significantly different. A large proportion of violators of the narcotic laws are in a special class and require specialized handling. In fact, to deal successfully with this special class of violators calls for much policy determination. It is not primarily a matter of applying the methods appropriate to general criminal-law enforcement. The assignment of educational and promotive functions of the Department of Justice would seem decidedly inappropriate; and would probably prove embarrassing to that Department. The regulatory functions involved in narcotics control would likewise be out of place in the Department of Justice.

It would of course be possible to transfer to the Department of Justice only the strictly law-enforcement functions of the Bureau. In large part, illicit traffic in narcotic drugs shows the same geographical distribution as crimes in general. Were such a transfer made, however, it is doubtful whether as a practical matter these functions could be performed any more efficiently than they are in the present set-up. Drug addiction, to be sure, is condemned on moral and health grounds by a large and apparently secure majority of the people. Public condemnation, in this connection, seems to be neither transitory nor sectionalized. It seems to have more numerical strength, permanence, and uniformity than the public disapproval of, let us say, lotteries or prostitution. But to assimilate narcotic enforcement to general crime control might make more difficult the maintenance of a proper balance between the various aspects of anti-narcotics administration. Moreover, international agreements require each power to maintain a separate administrative unit for narcotics control. The intention apparently was that the different control activities should be closely co-ordinated, and should not be subordinated to or confused with other administrative functions. The Bureau of Narcotics has also a large and respectable clientele among pharmaceutical manufacturers, physicians, and druggists, all of whom are subject to regulation and most of whom fully co-operate with the Bureau. This distinctively professional population group has strong and reasonable objection to being bracketed with the criminal element. On the whole, the present set-up seems to provide, as well as any that could be devised, the maximum integration and the necessary co-ordination, with the possibility of flexible adaptation to changes either in the problem or in public opinion.

It is generally agreed among students of law enforcement that vice, as distinguished from crime, should not be put within the jurisdiction of a regular police department or other general law-enforcement agency. When such an agency is made responsible for the suppression of vice, its responsibilities in this connection are likely either to be neglected or to become a corrupting influence. It is not certain that neglect or corruption has appeared or would appear, in the same form or measure, in a federal agency, as in a municipal police organization; but one may safely conjecture that the Bureau of Investigation will develop and function more satisfactorily if it is not burdened with the control of narcotics.

Stronger yet seem to be the arguments against a transfer of the Alcohol Tax Unit or its Enforcement Division to the Department of Justice. The primary function of the Unit is revenue collection; a secondary function is business regulation. Its enforcement work is strictly auxiliary. The Enforcement Division appears to have an inseparable working relationship with the remainder of the Unit; and the Unit itself is appropriately located in the Bureau of Internal Revenue. From the standpoint of taxation, a transfer of the Enforcement Division to the Department of Justice would be impracticable. Such a transfer would be equally inadvisable if the moral and health aspects of the liquor question, rather than the fiscal, were to be emphasized by the federal government. In the case of the Alcohol Tax Unit, co-operation appears to be closest with the Bureau of Customs, the Coast Guard, the Intelligence Unit of the Bureau of Internal Revenue, and the Federal Alcohol Administration. The relationship of the Alcohol Tax Unit with the states is quite different from that of the Bureau of Investigation.

Though the Federal Alcohol Administration lies outside the field of law enforcement, as the term is used in this study, one might question the necessity of continuing the Administration, either as a division of the Treasury Department or as an independent establishment. Economy and efficiency might be furthered by its abolition and the transfer of its functions to the Alcohol Tax Unit, the Federal Trade Commission, the Food and Drug Administration, and the Public Health Service.

CHAPTER XI

EFFICIENCY

The science of administration is about where medicine would be without pathology. Physical diseases were recognized and treated in the morning twilight of recorded history, when nothing to speak of was known about anatomy, physiology, and hygiene. The concept of positive health is a development of our own day; and the rules of hygienic living appear to have evolved largely from the gradually accumulated knowledge of the nature and causes of disease.

In political science, however, anatomy and physiology, the principles of hygiene, and the concept of positive health were early developments. Plato, though a first-hand observer of government, was mainly concerned in his *Republic* with sketching the anatomy and physiology of an ideal state. Through the ages, other philosophers followed with other utopias, attempts to imagine government as it ought to be, not to examine it in the light of its demonstrated imperfections. Since the date when administration began to be intensively studied, marked progress has been made toward mastering the details of its anatomy, physiology, and hygiene. We have been able to learn without much difficulty the essentials of structure, function, and operations. We early envisaged an ideal of administrative well-being; and this ideal we have been calling Efficiency. An administrative organization is considered efficient when it does the greatest amount of useful work at the least possible cost.

Efficiency, therefore, is an affirmative conception. Toward it, the modern student of administration adopts the attitude of the hygienist, rather than that of the pathologist; and too often he uses the term with much the same looseness as the average person speaks of health. Nevertheless, the student of administration feels fairly confident that he has found a number of conditions and factors that are favorable to administrative well-being. So he says to his patient: "I don't know exactly what ails you, if anything does; and I have no sure means of finding out. But, in any case, I can tell you how an administrative organization in your position, in your surroundings, and with your responsibilities ought to be constituted." The prescription may be anything from a change of departmental climate or a light reducing program to the amputation of a gouty bureau or the excision of a malignant duplication.

The hygienic or positive approach to problems of administrative organization is sound and beneficial, so far as it goes; but it lacks exactitude and falls far short of finality. The pathologic or negative approach, if it could be applied, might be more salutary; for inefficiency is not the opposite or the absence of efficiency, any more than disease is the opposite or the absence of health. There is no one general and unchanging condition which we can denominate inefficiency; but there are probably hundreds of different inefficiencies, just as there are hundreds of different diseases. Were we able to distinguish these various deviations from the optimum, we might be in a position to tag them with their characteristic symptoms, determine their individual causes, and ascertain the appropriate remedies. Are there any tests by which we can locate with certitude and measure with precision any inefficiency, if such there is, in the federal crime-control organization?

PURPOSES OF EFFICIENCY MEASUREMENT

Efforts to measure efficiency have three ends in view. The first is to determine whether, at any given time, an agency, or a subdivision or employee of it, is doing a satisfactory quantity or quality of work. It is possible for the directing officials of an agency who are in a position to observe daily the behavior of their employees to appraise operations with reasonable accuracy. To do so, these officials must, of course, be able administrators, competent to distinguish good work from bad, capable of setting practical and high standards, constantly alert, fully informed, and adequately resourceful. Not merely must they know the mechanics of effective and economical routine performance, but also, and above all, they must be intellectually and temperamentally equipped to judge and handle men and to create and maintain the necessary morale. If the chief of an agency and his principal assistants have been selected because of their qualifications and previous experience, if they have been on the job long enough to "take hold," if the salary scale of the employees under them is fair, if the entire force is under a genuine merit system, if appropriations are adequate, and if office space and equipment are satisfactory, we can feel reasonably certain that the agency, so far as its immediate tasks are concerned, is operating with relative efficiency.

Our certainty, however, can not go much further than the immediate tasks of a single agency, or than the operations within this agency that are susceptible of direct and continuous observation. Even though a government bureau is working smoothly and speedily, we still must seek further evidence of its ultimate results, its social effectiveness, and the soundness of its policies. Conceivably, a counterfeiting or smuggling gang may be as efficient, at any given time, as the law-enforcement agency that detects it. A gang of law-breakers can not be evaluated solely on the ground of its operating efficiency. The more efficient it is, the more pernicious.

The fingerprint collection in the Department of Justice at Washington is the largest in the world. Exacting standards of performance have been set for the Division of Identification. Its "searchers" are young, intelligent, keenly interested in their work. To appreciate the magnitude and liveliness of this organization one must actually see it functioning. It operates with the celerity of a modern printing press. The Division of Identification is an administrative precision machine. But does it really make more hits than misses? What is its batting average? In 1936, of each one hundred fingerprint cards received, more than fifty-three were identified by comparison with those already on file. The Division identified in that year 5,731 fugitives from justice; that is, persons who had actually committed crimes and were being sought by law-enforcement officers. In these cases, the Division was able to notify various police departments of the exact whereabouts of wanted criminals.

So far, so good; but is this as much as we can reasonably expect from the Division? Would it produce better results if the whole crime-control set-up of the national government were reorganized? Would the results be better if all of the separate federal identification files were consolidated? Such questions, of course, can be answered tentatively or approximately by falling back on our principles of hygiene, on considerations such as those discussed in previous chapters of this book. But the more searching inquiries can be answered conclusively only when we have devised tests and measurements that apply to more than a single agency and that go beyond immediate operations.

Accordingly, the second purpose of efficiency measurement is to make possible impartial statistical comparisons of separate agencies. A sound comparative method would assist substantially in appraising the administrative set-up. It would indicate the points in the law-enforcement organization where presidential or congressional investigation is called for; and, were inefficiency attributable to inadequate funds, the congressional appropriation committees could act with more enlightenment than at present. Agencies prone to become inflated with conceit might, to the good of all, be occasionally punctured; loose self-advertising propaganda would be discouraged; and a healthful rivalry among agencies might be engendered. Moreover, if the statistical basis for comparison could include state and local, as well as federal, agencies, we might be materially helped in making a decision whether centralization is preferable to decentralization, or whether we have reached the limits of desirable centralization.

The third purpose of measurement conceives efficiency in social terms and looks to the ultimate effects of administrative activity. This purpose is to determine with some conclusiveness whether our crime-control agencies are contributing as they should to the solution of the general problem of criminality. The taxpayer defrays the cost of administration. He also foots the crime bill. He is entitled to know whether the officials that he supports are ameliorating or aggravating the situation. Are they thoroughly effective, or only superficially so? Is it possible for him to be sure? Or must he remain in relative ignorance on this highly important point?

A sound method of appraisal will necessarily be statistical. Under an act of Congress, approved June 11, 1930, the Bureau of Investigation was charged with collecting and compiling crime statistics. The appropriation acts for each succeeding fiscal year have continued this function. The efforts of the International Association of Chiefs of Police had much to do with this development; and the Association's Committee on Uniform Crime Records acts in this connection in an advisory capacity to the Bureau of Investigation. Statistics are collected and compiled on a nation-wide basis. Manuals designed to be of aid in the maintenance and submission of data are furnished free; and bulletins containing the compilations made from the records received are published quarterly, along with some analyses and interpretations. Statistics are also compiled from fingerprint records of current arrests to show the percentage of previous records by offenses, the distribution of offenses between males and females, and the number and classes of offenses committed by different age groups and races. During 1936 there were 3,431 law-enforcement agencies throughout the country from which one or more monthly crime reports were received. Returns came in with some regularity from 2,318 cities, towns, and villages, representing a population of 65,639,430. Approximately 90.8 per cent of the cities throughout the country having a population in excess of 10,000 submit statistical reports regularly; and many of the smaller cities, towns, and villages, as well as about 1,100 sheriffs and state police departments, are in the reporting area.

The remainder of this chapter will be concerned in the main with observations on these and other statistics which are now compiled by the Department of Justice and which reflect either the problems and work of federal agencies or the problems and work, on a nation-wide basis, of state and local agencies. No attempt will be made to present an exhaustive review and criticism of these statistics or to construct in painstaking detail a better statistical system. The purpose is merely to show some of the more significant defects of our present tools and to suggest the general lines along which a more comprehensive and informative statistical apparatus might be developed. The problem of criminal statistics has long been under study. An adequate analysis of it would demand an examination of the state and local statistics that are now compiled by law-enforcement, judicial, prosecuting, penal, welfare, and other agencies throughout the country. We are aware that in some states, for example Massachusetts and New York, the importance of a comprehensive system of statistics is fully recognized and encouraging steps have been taken to establish an adequate centralized system. The complexities and difficulties that delay action are well known to informed students of the subject. To them, the present chapter will offer little that is not already familiar. But it seems that we all need to come, from time to time, to a fresh realization that crime statistics are of tremendous practical importance, that what we have now are lamentably insufficient, and that the obstacles in the way of an adequate national system are not insurmountable.

CASES

In order to compare work volume or accomplishment or both, we must find a unit of measurement applicable to all agencies. Theoretically, an appropriate unit would be an investigation or a case investigated. Not all of the federal agencies attempt to report the number of their investigations or cases. The Post Office Inspection Service reported 108,118 for the fiscal year 1935-36. The Bureau of Investigation received 46,587. The Investigative Unit of the Customs Agency Service had during the same period a total of 10,915 port examinations, drawback investigations, and investigations in foreign countries.[1] The Customs Patrol appears to have handled approximately 8,000 cases during the same fiscal period.

Cases and investigations, however, are of all sorts. Many of the federal cases, as we have seen, are noncriminal. Numerous postal cases, for example, relate to losses or damages which involve no violation of law. The Bureau of Investigation handles a considerable number of civil cases. Thousands of criminal matters are insignificant; and only a relatively small number are of major importance. A criminal case may take a few minutes or several months. The notorious "Count" Lustig counterfeiting case took literally years to terminate. On the Mattson kidnaping case, not yet closed at this writing,[2] the Bureau of Investigation has been concentrating scores of agents for several months. At the end of 1936, the average work load in the Bureau of Investigation was seventeen cases; in the Secret Service Division it was less than five; and the head of each agency considered that his men were much overloaded.

A patrolling force may or may not receive cases; but, whether it does or not, it goes out after them; and its efficiency should be gaged by the thoroughness of its patrolling, rather than by the number of its separate investigations. Indeed, if patrolling were a 100 per cent deterrent, there would be no cases at all. In Coast Guard operations, a "case" or investigation is practically meaningless. Its work, if measurable at all, must be expressed by an entirely different unit.

[1] There must have been, in addition, a considerable number of investigations on other matters.
[2] September 1, 1937.

Among the figures published in the reports of some state and municipal police departments are those of requests for assistance received and investigations made. *Uniform Crime Reports,* published by the Bureau of Investigation, is based on statistics of "offenses known to the police"; that is, those serious crimes or attempted crimes which come to the knowledge of the police through reports of police officers, of citizens, of prosecuting or court officials, or otherwise, not including those complaints which are shown on investigation to be groundless. These statistics have manifest deficiencies. Their accuracy may be questioned; and, even if the reports are uniformly complete and correct, they present only a partial picture of the crime situation.[3] Yet, they have value; and they represent by long odds the best that has thus far been achieved in the field of national crime statistics. No one would suggest their discontinuance. On the contrary, they should now be organized on a permanent basis and their content amplified.

Records of cases and investigations are doubtless needed by many law-enforcement agencies for purposes of internal operating control; but the figures compiled from such records seem of little if any value to outside students or to the public. It is probably out of the question to adopt and enforce among federal, state, and local agencies standardized definitions and classifications capable of producing comparable statistics of cases or investigations. In their present state, these figures are too misleading for publication. Our statistics as a whole would have more value if known criminal offenses were publicly reported by the federal agencies, rather than,

[3] "In publishing the data sent in by chiefs of police in different cities, the Federal Bureau of Investigation does not vouch for their accuracy. They are given out as current information which may throw some light on problems of crime and criminal-law enforcement." *Uniform Crime Reports,* Vol. VIII, No. 1, p. 2.

or in addition to, cases or investigations. We should then have at least one kind of material available for a comparison of federal with state and local agencies; and our meager knowledge of how much crime there is would be somewhat extended.

Two recommendations seem at this point to be justified: (1) that the sheriffs' offices, municipal police departments, and other local law-enforcement agencies should report known offenses to a state authority, probably the attorney general or state department of justice, which in turn should report to the federal Department of Justice; and (2) that known offenses should be reported to the Department of Justice, not only by the state, but also by the various federal crime-control agencies.

ARRESTS

A number of the federal agencies report arrests. During the fiscal year 1935-36, the Enforcement Division of the Alcohol Tax Unit arrested 30,913 persons; the Customs Agency Service made 1,746 arrests;[4] the Immigration Border Patrol apprehended 12,406 persons; the Post Office inspectors made 4,094 arrests for violations of postal laws; and the Secret Service Division arrested 3,153 persons. The Bureau of Investigation does not report the arrests which it makes; but, somewhat inconsistently, it compiles and publishes statistics, received from local police agencies, of offenses cleared by arrest and of persons charged (held for prosecution).[5]

Figures showing offenses cleared by arrest will differ from figures showing arrests. One arrest may clear a number of offenses, while an offense in which a num-

---

[4] Of which 759 were made by the customs agents and 987 by the Customs Patrol.

[5] For the latest compilation, see *Uniform Crime Reports*, Vol. VIII, No. 1.

ber of persons are implicated is only partially solved by
a single arrest. The figures in *Uniform Crime Reports*,
however, indicate the number of crimes for each of
which at least one of the offenders has been apprehended
and made available for prosecution. The figures include
also cases cleared in other ways, as by suicide, or incarceration for another offense. It is explained that the
figures relative to offenses cleared by arrest are conservative, because "there are instances in which the police clear
the crimes by arresting the guilty individuals but they
are unable to take credit for such clearances in their statistical reports due to the fact that it is not possible for
them to produce proof that the individuals arrested were
responsible for the crimes and because the persons arrested did not confess thereto, even though they had
been convicted of one or more other violations."[6]

Apparently, statistics of offenses cleared by arrest are
based largely on police opinion. Technically, no offense
can be cleared merely by arrest. A man is presumed to be
innocent until he is proved guilty; and he can be proved
guilty only by a plea or conviction in court. If the police
opinions embodied in these statistics are trustworthy, the
figures should represent only a small fraction of the total
arrests made; and, in that event, they would have little
quantitative meaning. As a matter of fact, the figures of
offenses cleared amount, apparently, to a quite considerable fraction of the arrests made. Perhaps as many as
90 per cent of the persons handed over to the prosecutor are covered in the tables of offenses cleared by arrest.
That the police reports in this respect are misleading is
suggested by the fact that in thirteen cities the police estimated in 1936 a total of 38,682 offenses cleared by arrest, while the total found guilty of the offenses charged

[6] The same, p. 23.

was reported as only 11,271 and the total found guilty of the offenses charged or of lesser offenses as only 14,790.[7]

Even if arrests were fully and accurately reported, they would still show different degrees of difficulty and of immediate importance. After the arrest and conviction of "Count" Lustig and his plate-maker William Watts, the amount of counterfeit money seized by the Secret Service sharply declined. These two were, at the moment, key men in this branch of criminality. During the years prior to their arrest, about 400 persons, it is said, were apprehended as passers of counterfeit notes made from plates prepared by Watts. If there were no makers of counterfeits, there could be no passers. Similarly, in the illicit drug trade, the smuggler, the illicit wholesaler, or the crooked registrant is, so far as enforcement results are concerned, more important than the peddler. In combating gangster crime, one "higher-up" may mean strategically more than a dozen hangers-on. Either a Dillinger or a "Pretty Boy" Floyd might, from the enforcement point of view, balance the scales against a thousand petty thieves. To be correctly evaluated, therefore, statistics of arrests should be weighted; but how?

But, perhaps, if we were to weight arrest figures intelligently, our method of weighting might be quite different from that of the newspaper headlines. We might attach more importance to one beginner in crime than to the ninety and nine spectacular gangsters. We should be seriously concerned with the juvenile delinquent or the adult first offender; because, when he is discovered, society has a chance to forestall the development of a criminal career. In dealing with disaster, the saving of one life is better than the recovery of a hundred bodies. For statistics of juvenile delinquents, however, and es-

[7] The same, p. 33.

pecially for those of readjusted juveniles, we must look
to the juvenile courts, the schools, and other child-wel-
fare agencies; and, unfortunately, the arrest of an adult
first-offender by the police gives no assurance that a
criminal career has been nipped in the bud. Nevertheless,
statistics of arrests gain much additional value when
classified by age, by the number of previous arrests, and
by previous offenses. Such data are now compiled from
fingerprint cards, representing a small fraction of arrests
for violations of state laws and municipal ordinances.
The figures for the first three months of 1937 show
that 18.3 per cent of these arrested persons were under
twenty-one years of age, and 35.3 per cent under twenty-
five years of age.

Arrests are not all of guilty persons. Many individuals
are arrested on suspicion and soon afterward released,
frequently with no charges filed against them. Raids,
drives, and drag-nets catch bystanders along with participants.

Moreover, the significance of arrests varies with the
policy of the enforcement agency. A comparatively small
number of apprehensions may indicate inactivity or negligence. On the other hand, it may reflect a conservative
policy, a practice of thoroughly investigating a case before making an arrest, or a desire to protect the innocent.
A relatively large number of arrests may be an evidence
of vigorous enforcement. But, contrariwise, it may be due
to carelessness, excessive zeal, or disregard for individual rights.

Statistics of offenses cleared by arrest, when they are
reported by police agencies, would seem to have little
if any usefulness. On the other hand, arrest figures,
despite their shortcomings, have value; and, without
them, no complete system of criminal justice statistics

can be constructed. At the present time, statistics of arrests are frequently, if not usually, included in the annual reports of state and municipal police departments.

The Bureau of Investigation publishes in *Uniform Crime Reports* figures showing the number of persons charged (held for prosecution) and the number released (not held for prosecution). The two figures combined should show the total number of arrested persons.[8] This number for the calendar year 1936 was, for the cities reporting, 3,784,892, of whom about 500,000 were released without being held for prosecution. From these figures, it may be estimated that the total number arrested by state and local agencies in the entire country was over 15,000,000 of whom perhaps more than a half were held for prosecution. Most of these arrests were for minor infractions of the law, such as violations of the traffic regulations, disorderly conduct, drunkenness, and vagrancy. For the crimes which are considered more serious, there may have been throughout the country more than 800,000 arrests, and as many as 700,000 held for prosecution.[9]

It goes without saying that such statistics should be classified by causes of arrest; and "on suspicion" should be one of the classifications.[10] They should also be broken down into other essential classifications. These figures should be reported by state and local agencies to an

---

[8] Provided the number released refers to those released by the police. If it refers only to those released by the prosecutor, we have no enumeration of those persons who are arrested and released by the police without the official intervention of the prosecutor.

[9] Murder; manslaughter by negligence; robbery; aggravated assault; burglary; larceny; automobile theft; embezzlement and fraud; buying, receiving, or possessing stolen property; forgery and counterfeiting; rape; violations of the narcotic drug laws; and carrying weapons.

[10] This classification is now used in *Uniform Crime Reports* in connection with statistics of persons charged (held for prosecution).

appropriate state department; and by all federal agencies to the Department of Justice at Washington.[11]

The compiled statistics of arrests could, of course, be reported directly to the central state authority by the various constables, town marshals, sheriffs, and chiefs of police. With reference to local arrests, however, it might be desirable to have the reports made by the county or district prosecutors; and such provision would seem particularly desirable so long as we have in each prosecutor's jurisdiction a multiplicity of separate agencies having powers of arrest. The state law should require each state or local agency of apprehension to report every arrest within twenty-four hours to the appropriate prosecuting official. Every release from custody should be similarly reported. This would involve sending to the prosecutor a duplicate of the original record of arrest and of the subsequent record of release.

The suggested procedure would serve more than one useful purpose. The prosecutor would be kept currently informed of persons held by the sheriff or by the police, and would be able, if he had the desire, to keep in touch with and at any time analyze the local enforcement situation. Prolonged detention of individuals on suspicion, without benefit of counsel and without the official knowledge of the prosecutor or the magistrate, would be less likely. When the police chose to hold a suspected person *incommunicado* or employ the "third degree" the prosecutor would definitely share responsibility. The law would enter the proceedings, as it should, with reasonable promptness after the beginning of detention.

The chief advantage of charging the prosecutor with the reporting of arrest statistics is that it would make

[11] Figures of arrests should, of course, be supplemented by figures showing number of persons brought to the courts otherwise than by arrest.

one man responsible for the statistical work in each county or district; and, from this point on in the statistical system, the state authority, so far as statistics are concerned, would deal with a manageable number of local officials.

PROSECUTIONS

The Department of Justice produces figures compiled from the reports of United States attorneys which

DISTRIBUTION OF CASES TERMINATED IN UNITED STATES DISTRICT COURTS, 1936[a]

Reporting Agency	Number of Defendants	Percentage Distribution
Department of Agriculture	1,279	2.4
Department of Interior	1,612	3.0
Department of Justice[b]	5,335	10.0
Department of Labor[c]	3,656	6.8
Post Office Department[d]	2,765	5.2
Treasury Department:		
Alcohol Tax Unit	23,238	43.5
Customs Bureau	724	1.4
Internal Revenue Bureau[e]	1,284	2.4
Narcotics Bureau	2,509	4.7
Secret Service Division	2,679	5.0
Other	476	0.9
Total Treasury	30,910	57.9
Other federal agencies and departments	477	0.9
Total all federal agencies	46,034	86.2
State agencies	410	0.8
Local police agencies	2,837	5.3
Private individuals	1,345	2.5
Total all non-federal agencies	4,592	8.6
Not reported	2,775	5.2
Grand total	53,401	100.0

[a] These figures do not represent the number of prosecutions *started* during the fiscal year, but those *terminated*.
[b] Bureau of Investigation.
[c] Immigration and Naturalization Service.
[d] Post Office Inspection Service.
[e] Other than the Alcohol Tax Unit.

show the number of defendants whose criminal cases were terminated in United States courts during specified periods, distributing the defendants among law-enforcement agencies and giving for each agency the total number and percentage of defendants, the number and percentage found guilty, and the number and percentage whose cases were otherwise terminated. These figures provide one possible basis for a comparison of federal law-enforcement agencies.

The table on page 250 shows the number of defendants, distributed among reporting agencies, whose cases were terminated during the fiscal year 1935-36.

During the fiscal year ended June 30, 1936 the total number of criminal defendants whose cases were terminated in the United States district courts was 53,401. Of these, 46,034 or 86.2 per cent were brought by federal agencies, and 30,910 or 57.9 per cent by Treasury agencies. The Alcohol Tax Unit led with 23,238 defendants or 43.5 per cent of the total number. The Bureau of Investigation was second with 5,335 or 10.0 per cent; the Immigration and Naturalization Service followed with 3,656 or 6.8 per cent; the Post Office inspectors produced 2,765 or 5.2 per cent; the Secret Service was a close fifth with 2,679 or 5.0 per cent; and the Bureau of Narcotics was not far behind with 2,509 or 4.7 per cent.

The table on page 252 shows the ratio for certain agencies between the number of arrests reported for 1935-36 and the number of defendants whose cases were terminated during the same year.[12]

[12] It might be more accurate to compare the arrests of one year with the court terminations during the following year; for, on the average, a considerable lag occurs between arrest and indictment and between indictment and the close of the trial. The interval elapsing between the first and final steps varies in different cases. On the whole, the percentages

Why should the ratio of defendants to arrests be so high for the Secret Service and so low for the Immigration and Naturalization Service? The difference between the two agencies in this respect is apparently explained by the differences in the offenses dealt with and in the nature of their enforcement operations. The Department of Labor has quasi-judicial powers with respect to

RATIO OF FEDERAL ARRESTS TO PROSECUTIONS, 1936

Reporting Agency	Number of Arrests	Number of Cases Terminated	Cases Terminated as a Percentage of Arrests
Alcohol Tax Unit.............	30,913	23,238	75.1
Customs Bureau.............	1,746	724	41.5
Immigration and Naturalization Service...................	12,406	3,656	29.5
Post Office Inspection Service..	4,094	2,765	67.6
Secret Service Division........	3,153	2,679	84.9
Narcotics Bureau	5,859[a]	2,509	42.8

[a] These are the "reported violations." There may have been more or fewer arrests.

deportation. If a deportable alien is arrested, he is not, as such, indicted, prosecuted, and tried in a court; but, nevertheless, he is disposed of. A total of 9,195 aliens were deported in 1936. If the number of those arrested and later deported were subtracted from the total of arrests (12,406), and the result then compared with the number of court defendants, it would appear that most of the apprehension activity of the Immigration and Naturalization Service represented productive, rather than unproductive, effort. The Secret Service is necessarily conservative in the making of arrests. It does not throw out drag-nets for counterfeiters. It rarely arrests on suspicion. It must first make sure of the evidence

given probably express with a fair degree of approximation the statistical differences which would ordinarily appear in the functioning of these six agencies.

and of its ability to connect the counterfeiting apparatus or the counterfeited money with the person arrested. If it makes arrests too freely or prematurely, it runs the risk of losing the evidence necessary for prosecution and conviction. Naturally, among the persons apprehended, a relatively high percentage will be indicted and prosecuted.

Even where the percentage of indictments and prosecutions is really low, this fact by itself does not prove that the agency concerned is wasting its efforts and appropriations. As we have previously seen, the Bureau of Narcotics deals in part with a peculiar class of violators; and the effectiveness of the Bureau's operations with respect to this class can hardly be measured by the number of prosecutions.

Enough has been said to demonstrate that we shall make little headway by attempting to test and compare federal agencies by ratios of indictments or prosecutions to arrests. Nor could we get very far by comparing the number of prosecutions with the enforcement personnel. Even could we segregate the enforcement personnel on a comparable basis, we should find that prosecutions, like cases and arrests, relate to crimes of different nature and varying degrees of gravity. We should also be failing to give due weight to patrolling and to other deterrent activities. Finally, with respect both to arrests and prosecutions, it is impossible on the basis of present figures to apportion credits and debits in those instances where two or more agencies act jointly or co-operatively. The Coast Guard, the Bureau of Narcotics, and the Immigration and Naturalization Service are attempting to keep some sort of record of joint cases or of assistance rendered by other agencies. However desirable it might be, it would be decidedly difficult to formulate and apply to all agencies a uniform method of giving credit. The Department of Justice, in the statistics which it compiles, appears to have made little effort to do so, probably for good reasons.

Nevertheless, if statistics of arrests, of indictments, and prosecutions were classified, intelligibly presented, and properly interpreted, they would have value in relation one to the other. We do not appear to have any statistics on a nation-wide scale published by the federal government which purport to show the number of persons prosecuted in the state courts and the number dismissed without trial.

Such figures should be included in any complete and sound system of governmental crime statistics. They are essential to the understanding and evaluation, not only of policing, but also of prosecuting and judicial agencies. They are essential also as checks on the prosecutor, who has become a most powerful figure in our system of dispensing justice. In his discretion he may, as he sees fit, refuse to prosecute. When he does so, he is required in some states to put his reasons on file and in some he must ask permission of the court. But in practice, said the Wickersham Commission in 1931, "with the crowded dockets of the modern city, these checks have been applied perfunctorily and are achieving little or nothing. . . . In practice in most of our large cities [the discretionary authority of the prosecutor] is a mode of disposing of criminal causes without trial and without review on grounds nowhere recorded and quite unascertainable."[13]

Figures showing the number of persons disposed of by the prosecutor without trial should be reported to

[13] National Commission on Law Observance and Enforcement, *Report on Prosecution*, p. 19.

the appropriate state agency. They may be thus reported by the prosecutor himself; but preferably by the clerk of the court wherever such cases are recorded by the court.

CONVICTIONS

We are now prepared to note the manner in which the federal defendants enumerated in the table on page

DISPOSITION OF FEDERAL CRIMINAL CASES TERMINATED IN FISCAL YEAR 1935–36[a]

Department of Origin	Number of Defendants	Found Guilty as Charged		Found Guilty as to Part		Found Not Guilty		Other Dispositions	
		Number	Per Cent	Number	Per Cent	Number	Per Cent	Number	Per Cent
Department of Agriculture.	1,279	879	68.7	68	5.3	88	6.9	244	19.1
Department of Interior....	1,612	1,201	74.5	93	5.8	74	4.6	244	15.1
Department of Justice.....	5,335	3,574	67.0	293	5.5	253	4.7	1,215	22.8
Department of Labor......	3,656	3,391	92.8	126	3.4	25	0.7	114	3.1
Post Office Department...	2,765	2,001	72.4	167	6.0	103	3.7	494	17.9
Treasury Department:									
Alcohol Tax Unit......	23,238	15,359	66.1	3,233	13.9	1,121	4.8	3,525	15.2
Customs Bureau.......	724	455	62.8	63	8.7	25	3.5	181	25.0
Internal Revenue Bureau	1,284	765	59.6	184	14.3	59	4.6	276	21.5
Narcotics Bureau......	2,509	1,654	65.9	419	16.7	69	2.8	367	14.6
Secret Service Division.	2,679	1,947	72.7	253	9.5	119	4.4	360	13.4
Other................	476	284	59.7	41	8.6	15	3.1	136	28.6
Total Treasury......	30,910	20,464	66.2	4,193	13.6	1,408	4.5	4,845	15.7
Other federal agencies and departments..........	477	263	55.1	21	4.4	37	7.8	156	32.7
Total all federal agencies..............	46,034	31,773	69.0	4,961	10.8	1,988	4.3	7,312	15.9
State agencies...........	410	325	79.3	23	5.6	8	1.9	54	13.2
Local police agencies......	2,837	1,682	59.3	317	11.2	152	5.3	686	24.2
Private individuals.......	1,345	919	68.3	40	3.0	67	5.0	319	23.7
Total all non-federal agencies..........	4,592	2,926	63.7	380	8.3	227	4.9	1,059	23.1
Not reported...........	2,775	1,534	55.3	137	4.9	202	7.3	902	32.5
Grand total........	53,401	36,233	67.8	5,478	10.3	2,417	4.5	9,273	17.4

[a] Based on figures complied by the Department of Justice from reports made by the United States district attorneys.

250 were disposed of. The table on page 255 again distributes the defendants by agencies and shows for each agency the number and percentage found guilty as charged, found guilty as to part, found not guilty, and otherwise disposed of in the United States district courts during the fiscal year 1935-36.

Out of the grand total of 53,401 defendants, 36,233 or 67.8 per cent were found guilty as charged and 5,478 or 10.3 per cent found guilty as to part. Acquittals and other dispositions accounted for the balance. The Department of Labor is credited with the highest percentage found guilty as charged (92.8) and also the highest percentage found guilty either as charged or as to part (96.2). It had the lowest percentage of acquittals and the lowest percentage of other dispositions. The other agencies which have been discussed in this book ranked as follows, with reference to those found guilty as charged or as to part:

Narcotics Bureau	82.6
Secret Service Division	82.2
Alcohol Tax Unit	80.0
Post Office Inspection Service	78.4
Internal Revenue Bureau	73.9
Department of Justice	72.5
Customs Bureau	71.5

Had we ranked the agencies according to percentages found guilty as charged, the Secret Service Division would have led, with the Post Office inspectors second and the Bureau of Investigation third. The ranking according to percentage found not guilty was as follows:

Narcotics Bureau	2.8
Customs Bureau	3.5
Post Office Inspection Service	3.7
Secret Service Division	4.4

Internal Revenue Bureau 4.6
Department of Justice 4.7
Alcohol Tax Unit 4.8

It is believed that any ranking of agencies based on dispositions in the United States district courts in 1936 would place the Secret Service Division and the Post Office inspectors ahead of the Bureau of Investigation. It is worth noting, therefore, that in 1936, at least, a higher proportion of convictions was obtained in cases where apprehension and prosecution were located in separate departments than in those where the two functions were combined in the Department of Justice. May not this situation offer an interesting commentary on the current movement in the states to combine policing and prosecution in the same department?[14]

Moreover, we find the law-enforcement agencies themselves issuing, without explanation or interpretation, figures which do not check with those reported by the United States district attorneys. Thus, in the Bureau of Investigation section of the Attorney General's annual report for the fiscal year 1936, we find this statement: "During the fiscal year 1936 a total of 3,905 convictions was secured in cases investigated by the Federal Bureau of Investigation."[15] The district attorneys reported a total of 3,867 found guilty as charged or as to part. Evidently, the Bureau of Investigation and the district attorneys are using different methods of crediting cases. Still other discrepancies are left unexplained. For example, the Bureau of Investigation states that 117 persons were convicted in the federal courts in 1935-36 under the federal bank-robbery statute and only three

[14] This question will again be referred to in the next and concluding chapter.
[15] P. 131.

persons were acquitted.[16] In the same official report, the
Attorney General's statistics show only 114 defendants
tried for national bank robbery, only 53 convicted, and
no less than 31 acquitted.[17] Again, in his testimony before the House Appropriations Committee in January
1937, the Director of the Bureau of Investigation stated
that "the percentage of convictions obtained by the Bureau in cases which we investigated was 94.35."[18] Although this figure apparently represents the percentage
of defendants who were not acquitted after trial, in order to obtain it the cases which were otherwise disposed
of must be treated as if convictions had been obtained.
As we have seen, the percentage actually convicted
was 72.5.

The Assistant to the Commissioner of Immigration
and Naturalization testified in February 1937 that
convictions of immigration law violators had totaled
3,535 (the Department of Justice reports 3,517), that
acquittals had numbered 17 (25 according to the Department of Justice), and that dismissals were 197 (the
Department of Justice reports 114 "other dispositions").
The Secret Service Division was more modest. It reported to the House Appropriations Committee 1,633
convictions, though credited by the Department of Justice with 2,200.

Assuming that the figures reported by the district
attorneys to the Department of Justice are correct, do

---

[16] *Annual Report of the Attorney General*, 1936, p. 130.

[17] The same, p. 172.

[18] 75 Cong. 1 sess., *Department of Justice Appropriation Bill for 1938*,
Hearings before H. Committee on Appropriations, p. 92. On Nov. 16,
1936 the same official stated that "the Federal Bureau of Investigation
. . . is proud of its latest record which shows that only three out of
every hundred men walk free from the court-room once this organization
has assembled its evidence and placed that evidence before a judge and
jury. In other words, it averages 97 per cent of convictions." Address
before the United States Conference of Mayors, Nov. 16, 1936.

they demonstrate that one federal investigative agency is more efficient than another? Not at all. Naturally, the investigative agency is largely responsible for the collection of evidence, and in practice it frequently assists in the actual work of prosecution. The following statement, supplied by the Customs Agency Service, is offered as an illustration of such participation:

Criminal cases and civil suits for the recovery of penalties must, of course, be prosecuted by the United States attorneys. These cases are referred by the customs agents to the United States attorneys nominally and formally through the collectors of customs for the districts in which the offenses occurred. It is the practice of customs agents to have the case prepared practically in form for trial, and owing to the fact that the United States attorneys are many times not intimately familiar with customs law, it is the custom for the customs agent handling the case actively to assist the prosecuting attorney during trial. In some complex customs cases, it is left to the customs agent by the United States attorney to do a considerable portion of the legal research preparatory to trial, whereupon the United States attorney handles the case in court on briefs prepared by him from data secured from the customs agent.

It is the usual practice of customs agents before presenting a criminal or civil case to the United States attorney, to have interviewed and taken depositions from each witness; to have prepared all evidentiary documents and exhibits; and to have furnished a narrative brief giving in condensed form and in proper sequence the facts to be shown from the testimony of each witness. It is seldom necessary for the United States attorney himself to interview the witnesses before trial.

Nevertheless, the district attorneys directly, and the investigative agencies more remotely, share with the judge and jury responsibility for the outcome of trials. It is quite conceivable that the prosecuting officers are more effective in certain classes of cases than in others.

It is easier to obtain convictions in some categories of crime than in others. If the policy of an agency is conservative, it will arrest and prosecute only where it is reasonably certain of conviction. On the other hand, if the agency is in the spot-light of popular attention, if it is under public pressure to "do something," and if, in addition, the agency is ambitious and aggressive, it may "take chances" and frequently fail to obtain convictions. In certain categories of crime, the defendants, on the average, are not as able as in other categories to retain the best legal assistance.

Furthermore, the penalties imposed by law have something to do with the likelihood of convictions, especially in jury trials.

Convictions themselves are not all of the same kind or degree. The convicted defendant may be put to death, imprisoned for from thirty days to life, or fined from a nominal sum to several thousand dollars. A sentence may be suspended or the person sentenced may be placed on probation. Of the kidnapers convicted in 1936, imprisonment only was the sentence given to 76.2 per cent of the defendants; 74.4 per cent of immigration act violators received imprisonment only; and the same sentence was given to 69 per cent of those violating the national Motor Vehicle Theft Act. On the other hand, only 20.6 per cent of Internal Revenue Act violators were given imprisonment only; while 45.7 per cent were placed on probation or suspended sentence.[19] Of convicted counterfeiters and forgers, only 30.2 per cent were sentenced to imprisonment only and 32 per cent received probation or suspended sentence.

A light sentence may be as appropriate as a heavy one; but, when we are attempting to appraise the ef-

---

[19] Certain of those placed on probation or suspended sentence were also sentenced to imprisonment, fine, or both. These figures are derived from *Annual Report of the Attorney General*, 1936, p. 176.

fectiveness of an apprehending agency, we must consider the probability that, by and large, the weight of the penalty reflects roughly the difficulty of the case. We might consider, too, the fact that all of the kidnaping cases that went to trial were tried by jury; and in other cases brought by the Bureau of Investigation the percentage of jury trials was high.

Even if the difficulties already suggested were non-existent, there would still be a serious obstacle in the way of apportioning credit for convictions. In a considerable number of cases attributed to federal agencies, a part—and in some cases a substantial part—of the work of investigation, apprehension, and collection of evidence is performed by other law-enforcement agencies, federal, state, and local. For example, of the 3,905 convictions reported to have been obtained by the Bureau of Investigation in the fiscal year 1936, 1,570 or 40.2 per cent were under the national Motor Vehicle Theft Act; and it would seem that in many such cases substantial assistance must have been rendered by state and local law-enforcement officers.

Beginning in 1936, figures of convictions in certain localities have been published in *Uniform Crime Reports*. It would seem that such information should be reported by the clerks of court, not by police agencies. It may be noted, in passing, that in thirteen cities with a total population of 9,369,010, the percentage of convictions[20] in certain of the more serious classes of crime[21] was 63.6. The corresponding figure for all federal agencies was 79.8. This comparison might be interpreted as decidedly unfavorable to municipal police agencies. On the

[20] Those found guilty of the offense charged or of a lesser offense.
[21] Criminal homicide, rape, robbery, aggravated assault, burglary, larceny, and automobile theft.

other hand, the Pennsylvania State Police reported for 1934 a percentage of conviction (based on cases disposed of) of 77.9. The percentage reported by the Michigan State Police for the same year was 71.3; and that claimed by the New York State Police was 93.0. On the whole, however, the indications are that the "mortality" in state courts is considerably greater than in the federal courts; but it is not possible to say to what extent the police agencies are responsible for the unfavorable showing.

OTHER MEASUREMENTS

Most of the federal crime-control agencies, like the state and local forces, conduct activities which can not be expressed in terms of cases and which are not reflected in investigations, arrests, prosecutions, and convictions. Most of them have responsible employees who are not directly and continuously occupied with criminal investigative work. Each federal agency, therefore, presents figures calculated to illuminate from various angles the volume and efficiency of its work and the nature and importance of its accomplishments.

Thus, the Bureau of Investigation reports the number of identification cards received, the number of fugitives identified, the number of examinations made in the technical laboratory, and other similar data. The Coast Guard enumerates the lives saved and persons rescued, persons on board vessels assisted, persons in distress cared for, vessels boarded and papers examined, vessels seized, reported, or warned for violations of law, fines and penalties incurred by vessels reported, regattas and marine parades patrolled, instances of miscellaneous assistance, derelicts and other obstructions to navigation removed or destroyed, value of derelicts and other obstructions recovered, value of vessels assisted (including cargo), and persons examined for certificates as life-boatmen. With respect to its aircraft, the Coast Guard reports the number of miles cruised, area searched in square miles, time of flights in hours, vessels and planes identified, requests for aircraft to engage in search, persons and vessels assisted, emergency medical cases transported, smuggling vessels located, suspicious planes sighted, smugglers' landing fields located, and stills located and reported. The Customs Bureau, in reporting its law-enforcement activities, points to the number and value of seizures, and the amount of fines and penalties collected. The Enforcement Division of the Alcohol Tax Unit reports the number and aggregate mash capacity of the still seized, the quantity of mash seized and destroyed, gallons of spirits seized, number of automobiles and trucks seized, and the appraised value of all seizures. The Secret Service Division calls attention to the number of counterfeit note issues discovered, the face value of counterfeit notes captured, and the number captured or seized of metal plates, negatives, dies, molds, and miscellaneous paraphernalia. The activities and accomplishments of the Immigration Border Patrol are represented by a tabulation which shows miles patrolled by motor, train, horse, boat, aircraft, and afoot; the number of conveyances examined—freight trains, passenger trains, automobiles, buses, boats, and other; persons questioned; seizures of automobiles (number), other conveyances (number), liquor (quarts), and miscellaneous (value); the estimated value of all seizures; and the different agencies to which apprehended persons and seized property were delivered.

Similarly, state and municipal forces enumerate such items as miles patrolled, automobiles recovered, value of property recovered, fines collected, inspections made, pistol permits issued, criminal records compiled, criminal index cards filed, traffic warning letters issued, buildings inspected, persons resuscitated, disorderly crowds dispersed, and other like matters.

As most of the agencies are able to produce such figures for a period of years, they are in a position to illustrate quantitatively the increase or decrease of their operative activity. These and similar statistics are of undoubted value to the directing officers of an agency, and probably serve a useful purpose in the annual appropriation hearings. As measures of efficiency, however, they are only of casual interest; and as means of comparing one agency with another they are practically worthless. Statistics of this nature can be piled up and broken down *ad infinitum;* and the agency with the most impressive array of figures is not necessarily the best organized or the best administered.

THE ULTIMATE TEST

In any event, figures such as we have previously discussed can not be expected to tell the whole story. The ultimate objective of criminal-law enforcement is not, or at least should not be, the catching and punishment of persons and the confiscation of property. We shall know that we have a sound policy, an appropriate organization, and effective administration only when we are satisfied that crime is being reduced. Is any crime-control agency really making progress toward a solution of its special problems? Are all of the agencies together solving the basic problem of criminality?

In order to obtain the appropriations which they consider necessary, a law-enforcement agency, like any other administrative service, finds itself between the horns of a dilemma. On the one hand, it must reveal tangible accomplishments; on the other, it must show its inadequacy. It must report progress, but not too much; for, if it demonstrates that its problems are disappearing, it will be arguing in effect for a cut in its appropriations. Government bureaus rarely do that.[22]

The Director of the Bureau of Investigation expressed the opinion in 1936 that the kidnaping menace had been largely eliminated and that the activities of his Bureau had contributed to that happy result. Similarly, he pointed out, bank robberies had gradually declined since the passage of the national Bank-Robbery Act on May 18, 1934. According to figures supplied to the Bureau by the American Bankers' Association, there was an average of sixteen robberies per month of national banks and member banks of the Federal Reserve System during the five years preceding the passage of the act. Since the Bureau of Investigation has had jurisdiction over those robberies, the average has steadily decreased. From May 18, 1934 until the end of that year, there was an average of 11.8 bank robberies per month. During the year 1935, the average dropped to 6.4 robberies per month; and, during the year 1936 until May 18, there had been an average of 4.6 robberies of national banks and member banks of the Federal Reserve System each month.

The nation-wide development of fingerprinting criminals since the organization of the Identification Division of the Federal Bureau of Investigation in 1924 has also had, the Director of the Bureau believes, a prohibitive

---

[22] In fairness to the agencies under discussion, it should be pointed out that, of those that stress their present inadequacy, some do so, not because crime is increasing, but because new laws have imposed additional duties on their personnel. Moreover, the growth of the country's population or changes in economic conditions may account for an additional volume of work.

effect upon further criminal activities of individuals who have once been fingerprinted; since, in his opinion, they have come to realize that, while they can cross the continent and change their names a dozen times, they cannot prevent the revelation of their true identities through their fingerprints.

The Director testified recently that his personnel in Washington performed in 1936 a total of 110,576 hours of overtime work; and, during the five months from July 1 to December 1, 1936, employees in the field worked 224,144 hours overtime. "The average work load today is 17 cases per man, when he ought to be carrying not more than 10." Of 15,580 cases pending on January 1, 1937, 6,689 were unassigned. The Bureau has asked for eighty-one additional special agents.[23]

According to the Chief of the Secret Service, it is the policy of his organization "to make counterfeiting impossible, as far as may be, rather than to permit such activities to develop to sensational proportions. It is only by such a policy that the prevailing confidence in our currency can be preserved."[24] The several types of criminality within the jurisdiction of the Secret Service have not been eliminated. The number of persons arrested by the Secret Service in 1934 was three times greater than in 1924; and the amount of counterfeit money confiscated was five times as great in 1934 as in 1924. The amount seized in 1935 represented a further substantial increase; but in 1936 the figure fell below that of 1934. The Chief of the Secret Service expressed the opinion in January 1937 that the counterfeiting situation was about the same, or had been about the same, for the "last few months.

[23] *Department of Justice Appropriation Bill for 1938*, Hearings, pp. 56-98.
[24] Excerpt from memorandum submitted to The Brookings Institution.

For several years previous to that the counterfeiting situation was becoming aggravated, and the violations had increased to a considerable extent, but during the last few months they have been about stationary.

"There is another portion of our work, however, which is increasing to a great extent, and that includes the investigations we are required to make with reference to checks. We find that more and more checks are being stolen and forged. . . ."

Secret Service operatives had five cases per man in 1936, considered by the Chief of the Service "an exceedingly heavy load." The work of the Secret Service was three or four months behind, over 2,000 check cases were pending, and the force was working from 12,000 to 16,000 hours overtime each month.[25]

In some narrow categories of crime, it is possible that the activities of the Post Office inspectors are having a demonstrably preventive effect. It is more likely, however, that tangible preventive efforts by Post Office inspectors will usually take the form of making crime difficult rather than of eliminating the criminal urge. The so-called postal crimes or crimes against the mails may be reduced, and undoubtedly have been, by providing protective practices and devices. The importance of such safeguards in the prevention of crime may be inferred from the following quotation:

Almost continuously since the close of the late war the security of the mails against the attacks of bandits has occupied the serious attention of the Department. So far as practicable improvements have been made in the routing of the mails, the scheduling of employees, the distribution of firearms, and otherwise, with a view to making the attacks of bandits as difficult

---

[25] *Treasury Department Appropriation Bill for 1938*, Hearings, pp. 551-73.

or as dangerous as possible. Notwithstanding these efforts some 200 robberies occur each year.

During the past summer a thorough study of various phases of this subject was made by experienced inspectors and particular attention was given to the practicability of using metal containers or other devices in the transfer of registered mail between post offices, stations, or depots. The conclusion has been reached that no system of devices and practices can be found which would render registered mail reasonably invulnerable to attack while in transit, except at such cost as would be prohibitive.

It is the conclusion of inspectors, with which the Department fully agrees, that while all reasonable precautions should be taken to guard against the attacks of bandits, one of the best possible preventives of crimes of violence against the mails is the fear of consequences.

It is no secret that at innumerable points throughout the United States large values in registered mail are transported daily under conditions which would make it relatively easy for bandits to secure them. Since the cost of protecting such values adequately while in transit appears to be prohibitive, it is obvious that common prudence requires that the number of inspectors be sufficient to give to robbery cases, when they do occur, such full and unrelenting attention that the criminal world shall know that it is not safe to commit assault upon mail custodians.[26]

During the appropriation hearings in December 1936, the Chief Inspector of the Post Office Department stated that "desperate efforts" had been made "to cope with the increase in the volume of work." He explained that it would "take forty-eight men a full year to reduce the arrearage to the point where it stood in 1933," making no allowance for the fact that inspectors were working overtime and had failed to take 8,709 days of annual leave. Obscene mail had been "increasing tremendously" and it "would keep twenty-five men busy for a year

[26] 74 Cong. 2 sess., *Post Office Department Appropriation Bill for 1937*, Hearings before H. Committee on Appropriations, pp. 128-29.

cleaning it up." The inspectors had 2,761 mail-order fraud cases on hand, compared with 1,772 a year before. "The number of major postal robberies is much less than it was formerly"; but in 1936 there were about 250,000 losses in the mail.[27]

The smuggling of alcohol and alcoholic liquors, "which was resumed in April 1934 and which reached a peak in May 1935, representing an annual revenue loss of about $10,000,000 in internal revenue and about $25,000,000 in customs duties, has been terminated (June 1936) as the result of a vigorous campaign by the co-ordinated law-enforcement agencies of the Treasury Department."[28] The Treasury's campaign against alcohol smugglers appeared at the end of the fiscal year 1936 to have been conspicuously successful. It was reported by the Department that on that date, for the first time in sixteen years, not one foreign smuggling craft was off the Atlantic coast of the United States. The success of the campaign was due to more than one factor; but the effort to co-ordinate the field enforcement agencies of the Treasury doubtless contributed to the result. It is probable also that operations against other forms of smuggling and tax evasion have been more effective since the Treasury Department in 1934 organized the co-ordination of its agencies on a more formal and definite basis.

With reference to the illicit traffic in alcoholic beverages, Harrison and Laine remark:

The Alcohol Tax Unit, Coast Guard and Customs Service have been competently directed. Enough good work has been

---

[27] *Post Office Department Appropriation Bill for 1938*, Hearings, pp. 110-57.

[28] 75 Cong. 1 sess., *Treasury Department Appropriation Bill for 1938*, Hearings before H. Committee on Appropriations, p. 607.

done to give encouragement to Treasury officials in their in-
cessant war on the bootlegger, but they are still confronted with
a colossal task. . . .

. . . .

Treasury officials took pride in the increased number of
seizures and arrests and concluded that the bootlegger was
"definitely on the way out." Is it not equally logical to conclude
from these figures that the bootlegger was on the way back, his
business having been sufficiently remunerative in the past and
promising for the future to enable him to make replacements of
seized stills so fast that, month after month, the enforcement
officers found more and more to do?

. . . .

We do not wish to detract from the credit due to law-
enforcement officers for their successes in combating the bootlegger. The seizure of 16,680 stills, and conviction of 18,521
persons by the federal authorities during a single year is a good
showing. But these huge figures give little encouragement for
the belief that we are making satisfactory headway in the prevention of criminality associated with liquor. The bootlegger
is too firmly entrenched. Two and one-half years after repeal
he is found to maintain one-half or more of the business he
enjoyed during prohibition.[29]

Certain signs point to a reduction of the illicit traffic
in those narcotic drugs which are subjects of federal law.
Though the prices of these drugs on the illicit market
appear to have been about the same in 1936 as in 1935,
there was more adulteration and increased pressure on
legitimate stocks. With reference to drug addiction, the
Commissioner of Narcotics told the House Committee on
Appropriations in December 1936 that, in his opinion,
addiction was not increasing. On the contrary, "in many
of the states there is a marked decrease in drug addiction,
particularly in California, Pennsylvania, and some of the
Rocky Mountain states. In other places it is holding its
own." According to the Commissioner "the marihuana

[29] *After Repeal*, pp. 205, 207, 210.

problem seems to be jumping up"; and the practice of race-horse doping is "still going on in diminishing volume."[30]

The statistics presented in *Uniform Crime Reports* reveal decreases, during the six-year period 1931-36, in all types of crime reported, with the exception of rape, aggravated assault, and larceny.[31] The Bureau of Investigation, as we have previously noted, dates the decrease in bank robberies from the extension of federal jurisdiction on May 18, 1934. At about the time the new federal anti-crime statutes were being enacted, however, Michigan's Commissioner of Public Safety was reporting that that state had built "through its state police and the unity of its law-enforcement agencies, a virtual immunity to operations of organized gangs."[32]

The Director of the Bureau of Investigation referred in March 1936 to the "armed forces of crime which number more than 3 million active participants."[33] Three months later he stated that "the criminal standing army of America" numbered 500,000, " a whole half-million of armed thugs, murderers, thieves, firebugs, assassins, robbers, and hold-up men."[34] About six months afterward he gave the total criminal population as 3,500,000 and the number of crimes as 1,500,000.[35] Five months

[30] *Treasury Department Appropriation Bill for 1938*, Hearings, pp. 180-206.
[31] Vol. VII, No. 4, pp. 131-35. It can not be certain, however, that the decreases shown were actual.
[32] *Annual Report of the Department of Public Safety*, State of Michigan, Jan. 1, 1934 to Jan. 1, 1935, p. 9.
[33] Address before the *New York Herald Tribune* Round Table Forum, Mar. 11, 1936.
[34] Radio address under auspices of the Hi-Y Clubs of America, June 22, 1936.
[35] Addresses before the Third National Convention of the Holy Name Societies, Sept. 19, 1936, and before the Chicago Boys' Clubs Dinner, Nov. 9, 1936.

later he stated that 4,300,000 persons were engaged *by day and by night* in the commission of felonies and estimated that 1,333,526 major felonies were committed in the United States during the year 1936.[36] In these estimates he refers only to major infractions and disregards "the millions of petty crimes which often are not even reported, the pilfering of possessions from an automobile, the theft by a servant of a few dollars, the filching of supplies from commercial houses, the stealing of trinkets from the desks of office employees."[37] What is the basis of his estimates of the criminal population? Presumably, convictions and records of arrests. In an address about a year ago, he stated that "the files of the Bureau of Investigation show that there are actually 3 million convicted criminals. Beyond this there are enough more with police records to demonstrate that an average of one out of every twenty-five persons in the United States of America has at least had his brush with law-enforcement agencies and is inclined toward criminality."[38] In the same address he declared that "there are today in America 150,000 murderers roaming at large"; but it appears from *Uniform Crime Reports* that in 987 cities with a total population of 35,450,666, the police were cognizant of only 3,582 cases of criminal homicide, and, of these, 2,936 or 81.9 per cent had, according to the police, been cleared by arrest.

[36] Italics have been inserted. Address before the Annual Dinner of the American Newspaper Publishers Association, Apr. 22, 1937. For the method of reaching these estimates, see *Uniform Crime Reports*, Vol. VIII, No. 1, p. 20.
[37] Addresses before the Chicago Boys' Club Dinner, Nov. 9, 1936 and the Third National Convention of the Holy Name Societies, Sept. 19, 1936.
[38] Address before the Daughters of the American Revolution, Apr. 23, 1936.

These public statements have been referred to, not in crticism of the official making them, but to show that we have not yet reached the point of clearly assessing our problem. We are not yet able to give it even approximate quantitative or qualitative measurement. We are still in the realm of guesswork. Knowledge is the condition precedent of long-run efficiency.

SUMMARY AND CONCLUSIONS

We started this chapter by pointing out the absence of pathologic method in the study of administration, and by asking whether there are any dependable tests or measurements to locate whatever inefficiency there may be in the crime-control organization. The measurement of efficiency has three purposes: to control operations, to compare separate agencies, and to show ultimate social results. We have taken up one by one the units of measurement that are most frequently employed in statistical presentations: cases or investigations, arrests, prosecutions, and convictions.

On certain specific points, we have already reached conclusions; for example, that statistics of known offenses, now reported directly to the Bureau of Investigation, should be transmitted by local agencies to a state agency, which in turn should report to the federal Department of Justice; that these statistics should be made more comprehensive by requiring the various federal crime-control agencies to report to the Department of Justice the offenses known to them; that classified figures of arrests should be included; that arrests as made should first be reported locally to the prosecutor, who should report periodically to the state agency; and that statistics of indictments, prosecutions, convictions, acquittals, and other court dispositions should be included. Such a statistical system would show the situation at each stage of the process of criminal justice. But apparently we must establish, not one system, but two parallel systems, each capable of interpreting the other; one to show the number and disposition of classified offenses and the other to show the number and disposition of classified offenders.

Since crime statistics should be used to locate areas of efficiency and inefficiency and to evaluate agencies and set-ups, it would seem that the functions of collection, compilation, and dissemination should not be assigned to one of the several crime-control units. In the state, they should be viewed as an essential and mandatory part of the duties of the supreme court, of the judicial council, or of the attorney general or state department of justice. In the federal government, they should be assigned to a subdivision of the Department of Justice other than the Bureau of Investigation.

At present, we are unable to tell whether crime is increasing or decreasing, except in a few categories and there only roughly. The fact seems to be that we do not know with any exactness how much crime we are suffering from; and a statistical system based wholly on reports from public agencies will not suffice to remove our ignorance. If we are to make any progress toward sound reorganization, toward intelligent policy, and toward an effective application of social resources to the solution of the problem, we must have statistics that go nearer to the roots of the problem. The situation points to one of the most perplexing problems in statistical administration that has ever confronted public agencies. It is a problem that must be given appropriate emphasis in the reorganization of federal functions, in the rebalancing of federal-state relations, and in the general planning of future national policy.

CHAPTER XII

THE FUTURE

In our vision of tomorrow's civilization, the background—the America of the last half century—appears a vast loom on which the weavers of destiny have been toiling with lightning-fast fingers, working the warp and woof into an infinitely complicated pattern. A variegated fabric has taken shape, apparently lacking in artistry but miraculously possessed of life. When we scrutinize a minute section of it, we see for a moment some hopeful indications of wise mastery; but only for a fleeting moment. Then the fabric spreads and thickens; the old fibres thrust forward in new directions and strange threads appear; the form and colors change; and we must start again to understand what we are looking at. One thing seems sure: the whole is knitted together. Pull out a single thread and unravelling begins. No part is independent of other parts.

Social, economic, and psychologic forces are acting and interacting in American life. No group, class, region, or unit acts alone or can stand alone. Government tries both to obey and to command. The servant of trends, which it only half understands, it strives nevertheless to guide and control.

Even forty years ago, America was still the promised land and Americans were the chosen people. Now, we have grown acutely sensitive to social maladjustment and social waste; and we are the more sensitive because we realize that when a wrong affects one it affects all. Hence our consciousness of erosion, floods, poverty, disease, and crime. Hence our interest in planning, programming, co-ordination, and reorganization. But history teaches us that, while we should distrust trends, we must plan modestly and reorganize cautiously. Wisdom is not monopolized by the present. Sometimes, the better part of present wisdom is to check the tendencies of current planning and return to that which the past thought wise.

CO-ORDINATION OF FEDERAL AGENCIES

It is true that federal law-enforcement agencies have "just growed"; and the result is a sizable number of fairly well differentiated species. Nine healthy specimens have paraded for our inspection. There would, of course, be many more, had we not somewhat arbitrarily excluded those that have taken root in the State, War, Navy, Interior, Agriculture, and Commerce Departments and in the independent establishments. But the nine which we have selected have been enough to pose the problem and to clarify—perhaps decide—the issues.

All of these agencies are engaged, directly or indirectly, principally or incidentally, in the war against crime, in the protection of the lives and property of the people. It is quite logical to argue that crime control is both fundamental and essential, and that it is, accordingly, one of the major functions of the federal government. Its objective is social security; but, since that term has already been misappropriated by the supporters of pensions, insurance, and so forth, let us say that the aim of criminal-law enforcement is public safety. Anyway, we seem to have one major function and one important objective. Furthermore, it may be argued, we have one technique—the investigative, detective, or police technique. Thus, if one adopts certain broad preconceptions, it is easy to become disturbed over the multiplicity of separate federal forces, the scattering of powers and duties, and the apparent diffusion and confusion of responsibility. One may guess that in such an "unplanned" set-up, there must be much overlapping of jurisdictions, duplication, lost motion, jealousy, and conflict. In previous chapters, we have run across some of these symptoms of an organization problem; and we can readily admit that, in the face of well-equipped, active, and ruthless criminality, any avoidable disunity is a serious mistake. The obvious remedy for disunity is consolidation, the establishment of a single federal police agency, a practical application of our national motto, "E Pluribus Unum."

Other plausible arguments may be advanced for a drastic consolidation. Consolidation would obviate the possibility of jealousy and of competition for appropriations. Combination of field offices might result in some economies. A larger personnel would make possible greater flexibility in operations and, in an emergency, a prompter and more numerous concentration of men. A single powerful agency could bring to bear on all violations of law the wide knowledge of criminality which has been accumulated by and is now segregated in the various agencies. Each of the agencies has urgent and non-urgent, major and minor, cases. The flow of some cases is fairly constant and predictable; but others constitute emergencies which can not be prepared for in advance and can not be postponed. It may be assumed that, if all cases were sluiced into one channel, the total flow would become relatively constant. Therefore, it may be assumed, appropriations and operations would be better planned, and division of work and specialization more intelligently provided for.

Crime, as we have seen, is an integrated problem.

Law-breaking is fluid. It goes in the direction of the largest profits. Crime frequently pays; and it tends to flourish in the legal categories and the geographical areas where enforcement is weak. Concentration of law enforcement in one field of crime may appear to be successful; but the result may be merely to drive criminals out of that field into another. When bootlegging becomes precarious, counterfeiting increases. When it is unsafe to rob national banks, then state banks, payroll messengers, jewelry stores, and commercial strongboxes are victimized. When opium becomes difficult to get, those disposed to use drugs turn to marihuana. Thus, it may be argued, one federal agency should be equipped to deal with the criminal in all of his aspects; and only with such an agency could we hope to attain the maximum of balance and adaptability.

The Bureau of Investigation would, it may be assumed, provide the nucleus of the consolidated agency; but, of the total personnel of the agencies which have been examined in this study, the Bureau has less than 10 per cent. From the point of view of personnel, expenditures, capital investment, and complexity of technical operations, the Coast Guard is much larger; but our maritime police simply do not fit into a department dominated by lawyers.

A unification of federal crime-control agencies may, by destroying their separateness, eliminate overlapping *among* them; but no reorganization of their functions can remove, or even greatly reduce, the total amount of overlapping. Centralization of investigative work will in certain cases increase overlapping. One example will suffice. Investigative duties pertaining to certain Veterans' Administration matters have been assigned to the Bureau of Investigation and the Secret Service. This arrangement is an economical one; but it obviously creates overlapping between the Veterans' Administration on the one hand and the Bureau of Investigation and the Secret Service on the other. Such overlapping could have been avoided only by setting up in the Veterans' Administration another investigative unit similar to the Bureau of Investigation or the Secret Service. In this case, overlapping was the lesser of two evils. As a matter of fact, in most instances overlapping is not an evil in itself. It merely presents, here and there, possible hazards.

Most agencies reveal a mixture of internal and auxiliary with general law-enforcement functions. Auxiliary and internal law enforcement may be as essential as general law enforcement. The collection of revenues, the execution of the immigration laws, and the operation of the postal system are functions not to be lightly regarded. Many of the agencies engaged in auxiliary and internal enforcement are closely articulated with the departments or bureaus where they are now located and inextricably involved in operations which can not be viewed as of secondary importance. The transfer of such agencies to a different department would divide responsibility for the conduct of various federal services, would create more overlappings and occasions for jealousy and friction than now exist, and would necessitate the establishment of complicated and expensive coordinating mechanisms.

The law-enforcement structure has been built up in a practical, experimental way; but, if it shows defects, theory alone must not be permitted to dictate its reconstruction.

Occasionally, one can find in an administrative organization two agencies with similar functions, each having pronounced peaks and slacks of work, and the peaks of one occurring during the slack periods of the other. In such a case, economy will usually result from consolidation, for a substantially uniform load will be substituted for seasonal or cyclical variations. To a slight extent, the work of most federal law-enforcement agencies is seasonal. This is true, for example, of some activities of the Coast Guard, such as ice or fish patrolling. The work of the Customs Patrol is seasonal in so far as it relates to agricultural products and wool and to travel across the borders. The tasks of the Immigration Border Patrol vary to some extent with the seasons on both the Canadian and Florida borders. The work of the Bureau of Investigation, the Secret Service, and the Post Office inspectors fluctuates; but the fluctuations are not to any important degree seasonal, periodic, or predictable. Viewing the law-enforcement field as a whole, one is struck by the absence of peaks and slacks. Such variations as occur are pretty well taken care of within each agency as it is at present organized.

With reference to the federal set-up, the discussion in preceding chapters has led to three recommendations: (1) that certain functions of the Secret Service Division be transferred to the Bureau of Investigation; (2) that certain functions of the Post Office inspectors be transferred to the same Bureau; and, (3) that studies be made of the field organizations of the Bureau of Customs and the Immigration and Naturalization Service to determine the practicability of local consolidations or local interchanges of personnel and work. These recommendations do not contemplate any reduction in the number of separate federal crime-control agencies. Within the Treasury organization, however, the present movement is toward closer co-ordination and perhaps eventual consolidation. This tendency seems to be sound. Closer co-ordination is also needed between agencies located in different departments; for, though the law-enforcement work of an agency may be wholly auxiliary or internal, it possesses, if it maintains a substantial field force, the capacity to assist at times in general crime control. Adequate means should be at hand for the efficient utilization of this capacity.

It is possible that sufficient co-ordination may be brought about in an entirely informal manner. We have found among federal law-enforcement agencies indications of much co-operation and a general recognition of the need of co-operation. We have seen that certain jurisdictional difficulties have been met by inter-agency understandings. The extent to which co-operation and co-ordination have been developed is a measure of the extent to which the dangers inherent in overlapping have been avoided. Nevertheless, jealousies and antagonisms persist. Just as operating efficiency must be built on a foundation of morale, so the way to inter-agency co-ordination must be paved with cordial personal relations. It might be that if the heads of the federal law-enforcement agencies were to meet at luncheon once a week, the desired personal relationships would quite naturally be established. All are men of ability and character; and they form that kind of group in which mutual respect and mutual liking normally appear and grow. One would expect the President to instruct them to get together frequently for informal discussions of their common problems.

If this plan can not be initiated or does not work out satisfactorily it may be necessary to set up by executive order a more formal co-ordinating committee, representative of the agencies concerned, or a single law-enforcement co-ordinator, preferably in the Bureau of the

Budget. Neither the co-ordinating committee nor the co-ordinator should, it is believed, have anything but advisory powers. In any event, administrative policies with respect to publicity, propaganda, and the public giving of credit to other agencies should be re-examined, their proper limits fixed, and uniform regulations imposed.

A continuing contribution would be made to co-ordination and co-operation if certain aspects of post-entry training were centralized. Certain subjects are more or less common to the training courses of all law-enforcement agencies; for example, the law of evidence, the law of searches, seizures, and arrests, relations with prosecuting officers, ascertainment and evaluation of clues, handwriting, use of small arms, and first-aid. The bringing together in one place of all law-enforcement recruits for at least a portion of their training would not only serve the ends of economy but would have the effect of getting the new law-enforcement agents acquainted with one another and thus furthering co-operation and co-ordination in their subsequent operations. The Director of the Bureau of Investigation has said that the National Police Academy, to which picked men from state and local police forces are admitted, creates the material for later co-operation between federal agents on the one hand and state or local officers on the other. Would not enrollment in the same school favor co-operation also among federal operatives in different departments? If centralized training in certain subjects is feasible, the logical place for it would seem to be the Department of Justice.

It is barely possible that something may be gained by further consolidation of identification material and identification work. It is not clear whether at present unnecessary duplication exists; but the subject may repay detailed study.

With regard to the federal set-up, then, the principal aims should be to concentrate general criminal-law enforcement in the Bureau of Investigation, to leave internal and auxiliary enforcement functions in the appropriate departments and bureaus, and to establish and maintain co-ordination among all agencies which are or may be concerned in any way or at any time with general crime control. Reorganization of federal units, however, will clear up only one aspect of the problem. What shall we do about the division of powers and the overlapping of functions between the federal government and the states? About the multiplicity of local police authorities?

FEDERAL-STATE-LOCAL RELATIONSHIPS

Current controversies over the expansion of federal activities are generally concerned with economic and social policies in the fields of business regulation, labor, agriculture, and public welfare. The centralization in the field of criminal-law enforcement, which has been going on with accelerating speed in recent years, appears to have received general approval.

In the first place, how far have we gone on the path toward national policing? The Census of 1930 found that the detectives, marshals, constables, sheriffs, and policemen in the United States numbered 169,240. In 1936, the federal law-enforcement agencies which have been examined in preceding chapters had a total personnel of about 17,000. Of these, about 10,000 belonged to the Coast Guard, a maritime agency. Federal enforcement officers operating on land constituted probably no more than 4 per cent of the total police personnel of the country. New York City has a police establishment three times as large as the federal land force.

The total expenditures in the fiscal year 1935-36 of

these federal agencies operating on land amounted to approximately 21 million dollars.[1] This amount is probably less than 10 per cent of the total cost of policing in the United States. New York City alone spent about three times as much on its police department.

The number of arrests is not reported by all federal agencies; but, from the data at hand, it appears that they may have made between 75,000 and 100,000 arrests during the last fiscal year. Either figure is insignificant compared with the estimated number of arrests made by state and local agencies. The arrests made by seven state police forces considerably exceed those made by all federal agencies;[2] and the state forces do only a small fraction of the apprehension work in their respective jurisdictions. The New York City Police Department alone made 732,233 arrests in 1935.

During the fiscal year 1936, the United States district courts terminated the cases of 46,034 criminal defendants brought to the courts by federal agencies. About three-fourths as many criminal cases were handled during the same period by the Municipal Court of Boston alone. It is estimated that the courts of Ohio tried in 1931 no less than 520,600 criminal cases, not including 130,270 known traffic bureau cases.[3] The municipal and district courts of Massachusetts handled 202,350 criminal prosecutions in 1932.[4]

Judged by such concrete criteria as are available, we

[1] This figure represents the total amount expended on all activities. The amount expended on criminal-law enforcement was considerably less.

[2] Massachusetts (1933), 13,749; Michigan (1933), 11,241; New Jersey (1932), 27,450; West Virginia (1931), 14,241; Oregon (1933), 9,416; New York (1934), 50,459; Pennsylvania (1932), 14,358; total, 140,914.

[3] Ruth Reticker and Leon C. Marshall, *Expenditures of Public Money for the Administration of Justice in Ohio*, 1930, p. 37.

[4] *Annual Report of the Commissioner of Correction*, p. 126.

do not appear to have gone very far toward centralizing criminal-law enforcement in the federal government. On the other hand, the Bureau of Investigation, which reflects fairly clearly the expansion of federal criminal jurisdiction, is a rapidly growing agency. Its expenditures rose from $1,972,820 in the fiscal year 1931-32 to $5,097,057 in the fiscal year 1935-36, an increase of 158.4 per cent. Our problem obviously has to do with a trend rather than a situation, with planning for the future rather than repairing damage already done. Apparently, the belief still generally persists that the federal government is capable of discharging whatever responsibility is placed upon it. If it fails, it is then proposed, as in the prohibition era, to increase its manpower or stiffen its penalties; or, through subsidies, to subject state and local police departments to federal control. If, when, and as these things are done, it may be expected that the sense of state responsibility will progressively become more blurred, thus increasing the tendency toward centralization on a national scale.

It may readily be admitted that such effects can not be proved in advance. It is also quite possible that the example set by federal enforcement agencies, up to this time, may have strengthened rather than weakened state and local administration. The Director of the Bureau of Investigation recently expressed the opinion that national training of key men in state and local agencies "removes the argument for the establishment of a national police."[5] According to Attorney General Cummings, it is not the purpose of the federal government,

. . . to usurp the functions of the state and local police units. It is not the desire to extend activities in violation either of constitutional limitations or the customs of our people. The motive

[5] See pp. 112-13.

is to attempt to meet a need which long has existed; and to assist, complement, and serve the law-enforcing agencies of America.[6]

But how can we be assured that the future will be cast in the mould of present purposes?

During the appropriation hearings in December 1934, the Commissioner of Narcotics explained that, if an attempt were made by the federal government to control marihuana, "You would have to put a tax on corn plasters and medicines containing it." But, he added,

. . . the way to control that drug, as I told the chiefs of police at this crime conference, is to go back home and have a city ordinance enacted.[7] We get requests from chiefs of police all over the country, after raiding criminal hideouts and finding marihuana, asking us what to do about it. We tell them, "Your city council can enact an ordinance overnight to make unlawful cultivation, possession, and sale."

Down in Florida they had a horrible tragedy. A young boy who used the drug killed his whole family. Public opinion was aroused. They passed a uniform narcotic drug act. . . . The state has the power. They have been making headway in Florida and California against the marihuana peddler.[8]

The Commissioner went on to explain that marihuana could not be controlled by the federal government through the interstate commerce clause, since there is practically no interstate commerce in the drug. Stating that he would not recommend federal regulation of this substance, he was asked if his opposition "was due to the fact that it would take a larger force to enforce it." He replied:

Oh, no, sir; not that. It is a question of having the states say, "All right, Uncle Sam is doing it."

[6] *Proceedings of the Attorney General's Conference on Crime*, December 10-13, 1934, p. 458.

[7] The same, pp. 354-55.

[8] 74 Cong. 1 sess., *Treasury Department Appropriation Bill for 1936*, Hearings before H. Committee on Appropriations, p. 210.

I am putting a marihuana provision, included in the proposed uniform state narcotic drug law before every legislature next month, to enact. If the states will go along with that, then the federal government ought to step in and co-ordinate the work, but until the states become conscious of their own problem I think it is a mistake for the federal government to take on the whole job.[9]

Two years later, the Commissioner testified:

The states have certainly gone to work on this law. We have now only the District of Columbia, Tennessee, and South Carolina that do not have marihuana legislation.[10]

Nevertheless, a bill was drafted in the Treasury Department and introduced in the 1937 session of Congress to suppress the marihuana evil through the federal taxing power. If it passes, Uncle Sam once more will be "doing it."

The tendency is now, as we have seen, to define the jurisdictions of federal law-enforcement agencies largely through applications of the interstate commerce, taxing, and postal clauses of the Constitution. With reference to general crimes, which make up increasingly the jurisdiction of the Bureau of Investigation, reliance is chiefly on the interstate commerce clause. The result is a multiplying of concurrent jurisdictions and of overlapping operations. Is this result in the long-run desirable?

State and local administration, it would seem, can be strengthened, without extending federal jurisdiction, by centralizing law enforcement *within* the states through the creation of state police departments and allocating to such departments the criminal-law enforcement functions of the counties and municipalities, except possibly a few of the most populous ones. If this were done, we

[9] The same, p. 211.
[10] 75 Cong. 1 sess., *Treasury Department Appropriation Bill for 1938,* Hearings before H. Committee on Appropriations, p. 184.

should have perhaps a hundred police forces, instead of tens of thousands; co-ordination among the states would be enormously facilitated; and the police organization of each state would be simplified, lifted out of its various dark pockets, and brought fully into the spotlight, enabling an easier appraisal by state and national opinion of its efficiency and adequacy. According to available evidence, merely the establishment of a state police brings a substantial improvement in law enforcement, perhaps a greater improvement than has resulted from any expansion of federal activities.

In the absence of intra-state centralization, federal law-enforcement agencies have felt compelled to deal directly with the local subdivisions of the states. The present system of federal criminal statistics, for example, is based on information which, for the most part, is contributed by municipal police chiefs directly to the Federal Bureau of Investigation. It is true that a method of statistical reporting through state agencies could have been worked out only after long delay; but it is possible that the delay might have been justified. Indeed, it is probable that, even now, if we are to have an adequate national system of crime statistics, it must be a composite of state systems. The establishment of various contacts directly between federal and local agencies tends to freeze into permanence our extremely decentralized system; and, when the program of state integration becomes more or less eclipsed, the only available alternative to disintegration naturally appears to be federalization. Having found what we think is a quick and easy short-cut, we abandon the slower, and apparently more devious routes. But the long way around may be in the end the shortest way home.

Much emphasis has been placed, and rightly placed,

on the interstate, regional, or national character of modern crime. Because notorious gangsters frequently operate without regard to state boundaries, we are disposed to think that all crimes are now of the same nature. In the absence of pertinent statistics, one is tempted to draw conclusions from the cases that receive most public attention; and these cases are usually those where the perpetrators are not promptly caught, where they repeat their crimes in different localities, and where pursuit necessarily covers much territory. If one may hazard a guess, it would be that a majority of criminal cases are strictly local, from the commission of the crime to the apprehension of the criminal, and that a considerably larger majority are purely state affairs. If this guess is correct, the prior need with respect to the bulk of criminal-law enforcement work is for administrative improvement by and within each state.

The first basic criticism of the present trend toward centralization, therefore, is that it skips the logical next step in administrative development. It tends to short-circuit the possibility of remedial action through state integration.

Another occasion for pause is suggested by the current and impending expansion of federal functions in other directions. Suppose, for example, that industry should be brought comprehensively under federal control, let us say through a system of federal incorporation, chartering, or licensing. Recall that the robbery of a national bank has long been a federal offense and that lately the robbery of any bank insured with the Federal Deposit Insurance Corporation has been placed within federal jurisdiction. Recall that offenses against property constitute the heart and bulk of the crime problem. Assuming federal control of business, would it not appear logical and necessary to give to federal agencies jurisdiction over robberies of federally incorporated, chartered, or licensed businesses? And why should not federal jurisdiction extend to all crimes committed against such businesses? And by such businesses? And also to violations of law in connection with labor disputes? If and when federal jurisdiction is so extended, we shall be approaching with seven-league boots a complete nationalization of criminal-law enforcement.

It may be plausibly argued that a national police force could be democratically controlled and would be used only for the purposes of democracy. The makers of the Constitution were fearful of large standing armies; and they were disposed to put their trust in a decentralized militia. They had had little, if any, experience with strong police forces under executive control. But, at the present time, the police in the United States outnumber the soldiers of the regular army. A second criticism of the modern trend, therefore, might well be that it has failed thus far to include a rational appraisal of the relation of policing to democracy.

We have taken note in previous chapters of the large rôle that prevention must play in the solution of the crime problem. We have noted, too, the irreconcilability of the prevention and enforcement philosophies. An effective policy of crime control demands that the two philosophies shall be kept in balance. One should not be permitted to run away with the other, for brutality lies at one extreme and sentimentalism at the other. A balancing in one policy of two antagonistic points of view appears to be feasible in the long run only when the same governmental unit is responsible for the formulation of policy and the organization of administration. Programs of crime prevention must be locally applied; for the problem of prevention varies decidedly from one community to another and the agencies which must be co-ordinated for prevention purposes vary with respect to set-ups, relationships with one another, and relative influence. In the field of crime prevention, federal agencies can assist and promote; but it is difficult to see how they can direct and control. In the field of enforcement, which is, in any event, more spectacular than prevention, federal direction and control already appear to be producing an imbalance in popular thinking, public policy, and administrative aim. The scales seem to be dipping toward the extreme police philosophy.

Our third criticism of the current trend, therefore, is that it fails, and apparently must fail, to adapt itself to an enlightened and coherent crime-reduction program. Federal enforcement activities which are not reconciled with state and local preventive effort may be simply sowing the seeds of ultimate disorganization.

A sound national policy should rest on a practicable and efficient division of responsibilities between the federal government and the states. Such a policy would seek to avoid overlapping and, what is worse, duplication. It would attempt to differentiate five classes of law-enforcement activities: (1) those that pertain to the internal administration of federal departments and establishments; (2) those strictly auxiliary to other federal administrative functions; (3) those directed at general crimes or other evils of an interstate nature; (4) those concerned with intra-state crimes or intra-state conditions affecting health and morals; and (5) those necessary for the co-ordination of the states and the promotion of better state administration. Federal legislation has by no means ignored the existence of such a classification. The chief difficulties at present have to do with the third, fourth, and fifth classes of activities. We have not thus far been able, if we have been willing, to draw a sharp distinction between crimes and other evils that are inter-state and those that are intra-state; and we have not yet established a program, based on sound policy, for the co-ordination and promotion of state activities.

A STATE DEPARTMENT OF JUSTICE

In state reorganization movements, much has been said about the desirability of creating in each state a "real department of justice," modeled after the federal department, an organization combining and co-ordinating the functions of policing, prosecution, and liaison with the courts. Unfortunately, state attorney generals are too frequently lawyers and little else, with no outstanding administrative ability or capacity for leadership in criminal-law enforcement. More unfortunately, they are, as a rule, elective officers, who are, naturally, "in politics." To be sure, though the Attorney General of the United States is appointed, he is not always an outstanding administrator and he is by no means removed from "politics." Nevertheless, some attorney generals, notably Bonaparte, Wickersham, Stone, and Cummings, have shown exceptional and constructive concern for the development of the Bureau of Investigation.

It may be advantageous to have the federal police force joined in one department with the prosecutors; but the federal prosecutors—the district attorneys—are appointed by the President and are not either technically or actually directly responsible to the Attorney General. The district attorneys, moreover, are "in politics." According to the figures produced by the Department of Justice, some agencies outside the Department appear to be more successful in obtaining convictions than is the

Bureau of Investigation. Prison, parole, and probation administration is located in the federal Department of Justice; but, in the states, the trend, which is probably sound, is toward an independent correctional system or its inclusion in a department of public welfare. So far as its general crime-control and service functions are concerned, the Bureau of Investigation has a very loose connection with other agencies of the Department of Justice; in practice, it operates almost independently of departmental direction; it seems to be at variance, on matters of parole policy, with its associate, the Bureau of Prisons; and it is probably no better co-ordinated with the district attorneys than are the customs agents or Post Office inspectors. On the whole, the federal Department of Justice is far from a perfect model for the states to copy. The Bureau of Investigation might have done as well—or better—if it had been, from 1924 on, an independent establishment directly under the President. But a proposal for such a change now would be uncalled for; and, if the Bureau is to be in any executive department, the Department of Justice is the preferable location.

RESEARCH AND PROMOTION

We commonly assume that federal agencies, because they are federal, must be vastly superior to state and local agencies. That federal law-enforcement administration is really more efficient, considering all circumstances and making all due allowances, has often been asserted or taken for granted but never factually proved. To be sure, the ratio of convictions to prosecutions seems to be considerably higher in federal than in state courts; but the difference may be due, not to the police, but to the judges, the prosecutors, the law, or other factors.

Evidently, the Federal Bureau of Investigation is much more generously supported financially than is the average state or local police force. The 1937 budget provided salaries for the special agents from $2,960 to $5,911. In the New York state police, a trooper starts at $900 and the base salary of a captain is $3,400.[11] In other state police forces, the base salaries, as a rule, are probably lower.

The salaries of local policemen throughout the country are on the average less than those of state police and are far below those of the federal "G-man." For example, the average salary of Indiana policemen in 1932 was about $1,600; and the figure is probably not much, if at all, higher at the present time. It is believed, though it can not be shown statistically, that the ratio of overhead to operating costs is greater in the Bureau of Investigation than in most state and local organizations. Moreover, the federal agency apparently spends more than do state and local units for clerical assistance, and for the purchase and maintenance of equipment and material; and few state or local forces have quarters as spacious and luxurious as those now occupied by the Bureau of Investigation.

You can get efficiency anywhere, up to a point, if you are willing and able to pay for it. Beyond the point where money ceases to talk, the state and local agencies are now handicapped by two sets of conditions: (1) lack of unity and co-ordination, due to the multiplicity of separate and overlapping jurisdictions; and (2) defects and deficiencies in internal organization and administration, particularly personnel administration.

The Federal Bureau of Investigation is doing much, as we have seen, to co-ordinate and supplement the oper-

[11] These are 1935 figures.

ations of state and local agencies. What is it doing to remove the defects and deficiencies in their internal organization, administration, and personnel? If the Bureau is engaged in promotional activities, what are its
objectives? Precisely what is it promoting?

Certain other federal agencies, such as the Department of Agriculture, the Social Security Board, the Public Health Service, the Children's Bureau, the Bureau
of Narcotics, and the Office of Education, are actively
promoting, within their respective fields, what they consider to be the improvement of legislation, organization,
and administration in the states. Sometimes the promotive effort is confined to propaganda, speeches, conferences, dissemination of information, argument, persua-
sion. Sometimes such activities are reinforced by authority to grant or withhold financial aid. Within the
states, certain state departments are also busily promoting, and also in many cases dispensing subsidies. State
departments do not, at least openly, presume to promote
better federal organization and administration; but they
tutor the counties. Doubtless, county agencies, likewise,
are paternally disposed toward townships and villages.
Generally speaking, each level of government views the
next lower level as fertile soil for missionary work. Each
is engaged in picking motes from the children's and
grandchildren's eyes without much attention to the beam
in its own.

During the first nine or ten months of 1936, officials
of the Bureau of Investigation appeared at about
seventy-four conventions of law-enforcement officers.
Most of these conventions included sheriffs and municipal police officers. One included prosecuting attorneys.
Two were meetings of coroners; two or three, of identification officials; and one or two, of justices of the peace.

In this list of conventions, forty of the forty-eight states were represented, as well as the provinces of Quebec and Ontario in Canada. Before a number of these conventions the Director of the Bureau spoke. He addressed, in addition, such organizations as the International Association of Chiefs of Police, the Kiwanis International, the Hi-Y Clubs of America, the Boys' Clubs of America, the Daughters of the American Revolution, the Holy Name Societies of New York City, and the United States Conference of Mayors. Some of these addresses were broadcast; several were mimeographed and disseminated by mail. They hammer home in picturesque phraseology, with frequent use of invectives, the magnitude and gravity of the crime problem. They stress the need of co-operation in combating crime. They denounce "rotten politics" and condemn state parole systems. On the whole, they are informative and arousing; but comparatively little appears to have been said regarding positive measures for the improvement of the organization and administration of state and local policing.

By advertising the activities of a federal agency until it becomes a symbol of efficiency in general criminal-law enforcement, we may be repeating the follies of the Eighteenth Amendment; and perhaps this time we shall not come so quickly to an acute realization of our error— if we have made one. It is not proposed here to criticise the legitimacy and usefulness of such professional and civic contacts. The question is, whether federal promotive effort in this field, if it is to be continued, should not be re-examined with respect to policy, content, and aim.

It is quite possible that certain promotive activities might be incompatible with the primary functions of the Bureau. For reasons already sufficiently explained, a police, detective, or investigative agency can not assume effective leadership in a crime-prevention program. If it promotes at all, it can do so efficiently only within its own special field. Even within this field, it might be inadvisable for the Bureau to promote, directly and actively, the reorganization of state and local enforcement agencies and the improvement of their personnel and procedures. A thorough and honest "sizing-up" of a local police department might prejudice co-operation between that department and the federal agency; and the gains from such a promotive policy might be more than offset by the losses. The present improvised policy of the Bureau is to give first place to its own operating effectiveness and to co-ordination of and co-operation with other agencies. It assumes no responsibility for the deficiencies of other agencies, federal, state, or local. This may be the safest position to take; and, without further mandate from Congress, it is probably the only one that can be taken.

The Bureau has also prepared and distributed several special publications, dealing with such subjects as identification, classification of fingerprints, admissibility of ballistics evidence, and police training. The Bureau conducts on a small scale research of two types. It collects, compiles, and interprets crime statistics and it experiments with instruments and methods of crime detection.[12]

A sound program of promotion must be based on research, but not on the narrow types of research at present conducted by the Bureau of Investigation. Promotion, in the broad sense, is the means of getting a plan adopted and keeping the plan in effective operation. Pro-

[12] Research in law enforcement is also done by the research unit of the General Counsel's Office of the Treasury Department. See *Treasury Department Appropriation Bill for 1938*, Hearings, pp. 78-79.

motion is the *modus operandi* of governmental leadership, of stimulated and controlled progress. Promotion
without a policy is an engine without a fly-wheel or a
safety-valve; and a policy without research is a truck
that appears to be loaded, but isn't. Researchless policy
is merely dressed-up guessing.

The proper functions of the Bureau of Investigation
seem to be: investigation, detection, apprehension, and
identification, co-ordination of the operations of state
and local police forces, research and training in police
techniques, and the rendering of services, within the
scope of these functions, to other agencies, federal, state,
and local. Apparently, the Bureau is not an appropriate
agency for broad research, fundamental policy formulation, and long-range promotion. These should be the
responsibilities of a separate administrative unit, probably of a division of research in the Department of Justice, outside both the Bureau of Investigation and the
Bureau of Prisons. The Wickersham Commission seems
to have thought that the collection of crime statistics
should be assigned to the Bureau of the Census. Perhaps
it should be, if it were entirely a matter of enumeration.
But crime statistics such as those now published are ob-
tainable only from law-enforcement agencies and they
are useful chiefly to those agencies. If these statistics are
revised and expanded, as suggested in the preceding
chapter, they will still be reported by law-enforcement,
prosecuting, and judicial authorities; and they can best
be collected and interpreted first by state agencies and
later by a federal agency in the same field.

An immediate need exists for research with two broad
purposes: (1) to fix the limits of federal participation in
general crime control; and (2) to accelerate the reorganization of crime-control agencies within the several

states. When these two aims are realized, we shall have made measurable progress toward a stabilized nation-wide crime-control administration. We shall no longer be drifting with a trend; we shall have a policy. But before we can have productive research, we must organize a nation-wide and nationally centered statistical system. Let us note one more specific illustration of how statistics may contribute to planning and reorganization. The Director of the Bureau of Investigation, during the hearings on his 1938 appropriations, remarked:

> Another important feature of the crime statistics data is the number of police and the ratio of the number of police in the community to crime in that community. . . .
> . . . Where you have a smaller ratio of police to the population, you have a larger volume of crime. Where you have a larger number of police per thousand of population, the crime rate is reduced. . . .[13]

If this correlation is not accidental or deceptive, might it not be possible to establish other correlations; say, between the crime ratio and the type of police organization, the tenure of office of the chief of police, or the training of the personnel? Why, one may ask, do some cities have 2.3 policemen per 1,000 inhabitants while others have 0.9 of a policeman? To what extent and in what areas is inadequate policing due to lack of taxable wealth? In many rural districts, it certainly is. Does the existence of a state police department equalize police protection throughout a state? Are crime rates lower in states that have state police forces? Do the facts indicate the need of federal financial aid? If such aid were granted by the federal government and administered by the Department of Justice, would the Department be then in a better tactical position to promote a nation-wide reorganiza-

---

[13] The same, p. 71.

tion, and, if it should be willing, stop the trend toward federalization?

Eventually, if we are really to plan our campaign against crime, we must ask the question whether an increase or decrease in crime should be attributed to enforcement, protection, deterrence, or prevention. Crime is due to a variety of causative factors and can be reduced only through a mobilization of the total resources of society. Enforcement is only one resource. It is possible that efficient law enforcement may substantially reduce or even eliminate certain types of crime, just as the enforcement of health regulations has almost, if not completely, eliminated certain diseases. In the case of other types of crime, however, probably the best that efficient law enforcement can ever do is to reduce certain offenses to a minimal rate. That there is somewhere a fixed minimum, or at least a point of diminishing returns, is suggested by the fact, just mentioned, that, in certain areas and with respect to certain offenses, violations are known to decrease when the enforcement personnel is increased. The taxable resources of the community, however, set a limit to increases of governmental personnel. The minimal rate, if it ever can be statistically fixed, should provide a standard by which law-enforcement agencies may measure their ultimate efficiency.

The planning, establishment, and operation of a nation-wide system of crime and crime-control statistics will require patient and concerted action by the country's leading administrators and statisticians. Fortunately, a good start has already been made both nationally and locally. To finish the job may well be set as the first goal of the promotive efforts of the Department of Justice; and to obtain permanent reporting of adequate and comparable statistics from each state may require something more than persuasive or alarmist propaganda. Certainly, a uniform draft law on the subject will have to be offered to each state legislature. If and when the act is passed, substantially uniform regulations should be issued to insure its full execution. To hasten the enactment and safeguard the execution of the law, one thinks at once of federal financial aid. This obvious device is now frequently and glibly prescribed as a panacea for all sorts of national, state, and local ills. It may be that some other method may be found to accelerate state action. If not, the Congress might justifiably stop for a period the expansion of federal crime-control agencies and, in lieu of appropriating directly to them, authorize the payment of a part of the cost of those state statistical systems which are established along the lines of the uniform law and administered in accordance with standards fixed by the federal Department of Justice.

Thus, in the end we find that we must return to fundamentals before we can safely chart our future course. The heart of the problem is not in the set-up of federal agencies or in the distribution of functions among them. The problem in general is static and concrete only in relatively minor details. In the main, it is constituted of dynamic and imponderable factors; and a reorganization inspired by sincerity and courage must take such factors into account and find ways to control them. Such a reorganization can not be satisfied with superficial rearrangements, spectacular activity, or immediate results. It will demand a broad understanding of facts; a studied appreciation and utilization of emotional currents, ideas, and philosophies; and a comprehensive reappraisal and revision of public policy.

INDEX

Inter-agency service, 88-89
Interior, Department of, 36, 38-
39, 159, 219
Internal Revenue, Bureau of, 23,
30-31, 69-72, 82, 116, 205-
13, 217. *See also* Intelligence
Unit
Interstate Commerce Commission,
20, 99, 170
Interstate compacts, 47-48
Interstate co-operation, 47-48
Investigation, Federal Bureau of,
25, 37, 38, 41, 73-79, 86, 87-
114, 226
conflicts, 104-06
co-operation and co-ordination,
100-03, 139
crime statistics, 240
expert service, 94-96
identification work, 89-94
inter-agency services, 88-89
internal and auxiliary activities,
107-09
jurisdiction, 77-78, 98-99
Law Enforcement Bulletin, 97,
107
National Police Academy, 112-
13
overlapping, 97-100, 138, 152
reorganization, 113-14, 201-04
set-ups, 109-11
state-local relations, 106-07,
113-14
training, 111-13
Investigations,
civil, 24-25
personnel, 25-26

Jurisdiction,
federal, 43-45, 50-53
state, 45-48
Justice, Federal Department of, 14-
15, 20, 25, 31, 74-79, 108.
See also Investigation, Federal
Bureau of

Kidnaping, 51-52, 56, 59, 79, 265

Labor, attitude of, 5

Law enforcement,
auxiliary, 30-34, 37, 107-09
general, 28-30, 37
internal, 35-37, 107-09
See also Crime control
Life saving, 23, 66-67, 154-55
Life-Saving Service, 66-67, 168
Lighthouses, Bureau of, 66, 168,
169, 174
Lindberg Law, 51
Loans and Currency Division, 122,
127
Local agencies, 8

Mail tracings, 37, 139
Marine Inspection and Navigation,
Bureau of, 20, 151, 158
Marshals, United States, 25, 74-75
Military Intelligence Unit, 103
Mint, 116, 117, 126
Morals, 22-23, 223-29
Motor Vehicle Theft Act, national,
51, 78, 103

Narcotics, Bureau of, 23, 41, 79-
83
co-operation and co-ordination,
100-01, 139, 157, 172, 184,
185, 210, 217-20
expert service, 96
functions, 213-15
identification work, 93
overlapping, 138
reorganization, 124-25, 229-34
set-ups, 215-16
state relations, 215
training, 172, 216-17
Narcotics control, 23, 56, 79-83,
153, 217-29, 270-71
National Park Service, 20, 39-40,
98
Naval Intelligence Section, 103
Navy Department, 38, 99, 155,
159, 168-69

Offenses. *See* Crimes
Operations, statistics of, 262-64
Overlapping, 26-27, 53-59, 97-
100, 115-17, 278-79

Planning, 60-62